LOAVES AND FISHES

SOCIETY
OF BIBLICAL
LITERATURE

DISSERTATION SERIES

William Baird, Editor

Number 54

LOAVES AND FISHES
The Function of the Feeding Stories
in the Gospel of Mark

by
Robert M. Fowler

Robert M. Fowler

LOAVES AND FISHES
The Function of the Feeding Stories in the Gospel of Mark

Scholars Press

Distributed by
Scholars Press
101 Salem St.
P.O. Box 2268
Chico, California 95927

LOAVES AND FISHES
The Function of the
Feeding Stories in the Gospel of Mark

Robert M. Fowler

Ph.D., 1978
University of Chicago

Supervisor:
David L. Bartlett

© 1981
Society of Biblical Literature

Library of Congress Cataloging in Publication Data

Fowler, Robert M.
    Loaves and fishes.

    (Dissertation series / Society of Biblical Litera-
ture ; no. 54) (ISSN 0145-2770)
    Bibliography: p.
    1. Bible. N. T. Mark VI, 30–44–Criticism, inter-
pretation, etc. 2. Bible. N.T. Mark VIII, 1–10–
Criticism, interpretation, etc. 3. Feeding of the
five thousand (Miracle) I. Title. II. Series: Dissertation series (Society of Biblical Literature)
BS2585.2.F68   226'.706   81-2749
ISBN 0-89130-486-X (pbk.)   AACR2

Printed in the United States of America
1 2 3 4 5 6
Edwards Brothers, Inc.
Ann Arbor, Michigan 48106

TABLE OF CONTENTS

The central thesis of this dissertation, namely, the
Markan composition of the Feeding of the Five Thousand
(Mark 6:30-44), was first presented in a seminar paper written
for Norman Perrin's New Testament Seminar in the Winter
quarter of 1976. With his warm encouragement, I continued to
work on the thesis as the topic of my dissertation. I regret
deeply that he did not live to oversee the writing of this
dissertation, which I now dedicate to his memory.

When one loses a revered mentor, one seldom finds so able
a substitute as David L. Bartlett; to him I owe a profound
debt of gratitude for his generous availability, astute advice,
and penetrating criticism. I am grateful to Dean Joseph M.
Kitagawa who negotiated the arrangement whereby I was able to
work with Mr. Bartlett; Dean of Students Larry L. Greenfield
also helped in many ways to keep the trauma and confusion of
my degree program to a manageable minimum. I also wish to
thank my dissertation readers, Jay A. Wilcoxen and Anthony
C. Yu, for their helpful comments. In my years at the Divinity
School I have been fortunate to have had a close association
with my fellow students, especially those in the Bible field.
Together we have enjoyed what has often amounted to a perpetual
seminar discussion; the quality of this dissertation has no
doubt been enhanced by the questions and criticisms of my
peers. Finally, I wish to express my gratitude to my wife,
Susie, who has "endured all things" (1 Cor. 13:7).

Except where noted, I have followed the Greek text of
The Greek New Testament, ed. Kurt Aland et al., 3rd ed. (New
York: United Bible Societies, 1975). Most of the English
translations of biblical texts are based on the Revised
Standard Version with my own modifications added. The
abbreviations used are those listed in the "Instructions for
Contributors," *Journal of Biblical Literature* 95 (1976):331-46.

CHAPTER I

THE FEEDING STORIES IN THE GOSPEL OF MARK:

DOUBLETS AND PRE-MARKAN CYCLES

Interpreters of the gospel of Mark have long been intrigued by the presence in the gospel of two very similar stories, the Feeding of the Five Thousand in Mark 6:30-44 and the Feeding of the Four Thousand in Mark 8:1-10. The extensive similarities between the two stories, which include a number of verbal agreements, have led most scholars to regard the pair as a "doublet," two variants of a single story. For many years now the scholarly consensus has been that Mark found two accounts of the same story in his *Vorlage* and included both versions in his gospel, perhaps not even realizing that he was telling the same story twice. It is usually argued that the similarities in the two stories indicate that they are variants of the same story, while the differences between the two, especially with regard to the numbers (of loaves, people, baskets), demonstrate precisely the kind of variation in detail that one expects to find in stories that are the products of oral tradition.

The possibility that we have a doublet in Mark is not limited to the two feeding stories. Virtually every interpreter of the gospel has observed material clustered around the feeding stories that is also similar in form or content. As an example, one may observe that each feeding story is followed by an account of a lake crossing (6:45-56, 8:10), a controversy with Pharisees (7:1-23, 8:11-12), a story dealing with "bread" or "leaven" (7:24-30, 8:13-21), and a healing story (7:31-37, 8:22-26), stories that appear to constitute two parallel cycles of stories in Mark 6-8. Many have argued that these two whole sections of the gospel, Mark 6:30-7:37 and 8:1-26, are themselves a doublet: different versions of the same cycle of stories found by Mark in his sources and placed side by side in the gospel. Exegetes have also attempted to uncover other pre-Markan cycles or catenae containing one or both of the feeding stories; some of these attempts involve

Mark 6-8, others Mark 4-6, and still others Mark 4-8. Inasmuch
as the scholarly discussion of the feeding stories in Mark is
dominated by the attention given to the problem of the doublet,
whether a doublet of individual stories or a doublet of story
cycles, we will conduct a detailed analysis of a representative
sampling of such discussions below.

Besides the doublet problem associated with the feeding
stories, the study of the feeding stories provides an extremely
significant test case for theories regarding the interrelationship of the four canonical gospels. As is noted in
every New Testament Introduction, the Feeding of the Five
Thousand is the one miracle story found in all four gospels.
When one assumes the Two-Source hypothesis, one is led to
conclude that Matthew and Luke each borrow the story found in
Mark. Interestingly, Matthew preserves both the Feeding of the
Five Thousand (Matt. 14:13-21) and the Feeding of the Four
Thousand (Matt. 15:32-39), as well as all of the other
material clustered around these stories in Mark, while Luke
relates only the Feeding of the Five Thousand (Luke 9:10-17),
having chosen to depart from the Markan story-line immediately
after the first feeding story and resuming his use of Mark
only with the Caesarea Philippi episode, thus omitting Mark
6:45-8:26.

Perhaps a far more interesting question is the relationship
of the stories found in Mark and John. If one accepts the
prevailing scholarly opinion that John wrote his gospel without
knowledge of the Synoptic gospels, then one must conclude that
John derives his version of the story (John 6:1-15) from an
independent source similar to the source commonly thought to
lie behind Mark's account. Moreover, since the Feeding of the
Five Thousand is followed in John, as it is in Mark, by the
Walking on the Water (John 6:16-21; cf. Mark 6:45-52), one may
argue that the connection between the feeding story and the
water-walking episode was a primitive connection in the
tradition which later found its way independently into the
gospels of Mark and John. This judgment is confirmed in the
minds of some by the observation that the two stories in John

bear some features that seem to reveal a more primitive stage
of the tradition than in Mark.[1] In our own work we will not be
concerned immediately to explore the relationship between
Mark's feeding stories and those found in the other gospels;
our interest lies largely with the stories in Mark. However,
we will keep in mind these other stories as we study Mark, for
any new conclusions we may come to with regard to the feeding
stories in Mark may vitally affect how we view the origin and
significance of the other gospel feeding stories. This would be
particularly true were we to challenge the current consensus
that the content and shape of the feeding stories in Mark owe
more to their pre-gospel origin in early Christian communities
than to the editing or rewriting of the evangelist. Were we to
claim, for example, that Markan composition plays a far greater
role in the shaping of the feeding stories than previously
suspected, then we might be inclined to see if perhaps the
evangelist John borrowed from the material composed by the
evangelist Mark, instead of so quickly relegating the origin
of the stories in both Mark and John to the all too hazy mists
of pre-gospel tradition.

We will return to this question later, but now we need to
turn our attention to several significant attempts to uncover
cycles of pre-Markan tradition underlying the present text of
Mark 6-8.

The Parallelism Between Mark 6:30-7:37 and 8:1-26:
Luke H. Jenkins and Vincent Taylor

Perhaps the most common hypothesis regarding pre-Markan
sources in chapters 6-8 is the suggestion that 6:30-7:37 and
8:1-26 are variants of the same cycle of stories. This
suggestion has been defended, or at least given serious
discussion, by generations of New Testament scholars until it
has obtained the status of a redoubtable piece of scholarly
lore. Almost any commentary on Mark that one picks up contains
a chart displaying a concise synoptic comparison of the two
cycles,[2] although detailed discussions of this hypothesis are
relatively rare. One such discussion is found in the article by
Luke H. Jenkins, "A Marcan Doublet," published in 1942.[3]

Jenkins outlines the material as follows:
1. Desert Feeding (6:31-44/8:1-9a)
2. Voyage Across Lake (6:45-52/8:9b-10a)
3. Arrival (6:53-56/8:10b)
4. Conflict with Authorities (7:1-23/8:11-12)
5. Avoiding Realm of Antipas (7:24-30/8:13-21)
6. Healing East of Lake (7:31-37/8:22-26)[4]

Jenkins begins his exposition of this "sustained doublet" by
pointing out the extensive verbal agreements between the two
feeding stories by means of a detailed synoptic comparison;[5]
it is easy to see why one might want to call these stories a
doublet. Once past the feeding stories, though, Jenkins is
forced to rely on more subtle and ingenious argumentation in
order to maximize the similarities in the two cycles and
minimize the differences. He is hampered by no longer being
able to point to extensive verbal agreements (except perhaps
in 6); so he must search out other elements common to both
cycles. When verbal parallels do arise but do *not* face each
other in the chart (e.g., 6:51-52/8:17-18), he asserts that a
"misplacement" has occurred. If a salient feature in one
cycle has no corresponding feature in the other cycle, it may
either be explained away as a minor peculiarity or it may be
ignored altogether.[6] Jenkins's methodology is sufficiently
flexible to meet any exigency, and that is precisely the
problem. If one is caught up in the rush to find parallels
among these stories, and if one does not read his article
carefully, then one may fail to perceive that the criteria
for establishing "parallels" are modified to suit the evidence.
Having begun with the feeding stories as he has, one assumes
that to have a doublet means that one has two stories that
"can be confidently asserted to be the same":[7] the plot,
characters, and even much of the vocabulary are the same. Once
past the two feeding stories, however, the criteria for
observing a doublet varies from story to story: 2 and 3 are
doublets because they both involve a boat voyage; 4 is a
doublet because Pharisees are mentioned in both versions of the
doublet; 5 displays two attempts to avoid the territory of

Herod Antipas (although Herod is mentioned in only one of the
two versions); 6 contains a shared healing technique: use of
spittle. In other words, the point of contact between matched
elements is variously a repeated motif, overlapping sets of
characters, a common geographical locale, and the recurrence of
a particular healing technique. Anywhere else in the biblical
literature these observations would scarcely be regarded as
evidence for doublets, but since these stories are found
within the vicinity of the feeding stories, one is inclined to
read into these stories the kind of agreements that one so
easily perceives in the feeding stories. On the other hand, it
would be wrong to deny altogether that there are common threads
running through the pattern of Mark 6-8. That much at least
we can accept wholeheartedly. Nevertheless, the evidence in
support of the claim that Mark 6:30-7:37 and 8:1-26 represent
a "sustained doublet" is scant and unpersuasive.

With regard to this supposed parallelism between Mark
6:30-7:37 and 8:1-26, Vincent Taylor could well be referring to
Jenkins's article when he notes, perhaps with tongue in cheek,
that "the agreement is striking, especially when it is described
in its simplest terms."[8] Avoiding the tendency to use
harmonizing and thereby prejudicial labels for the corresponding
portions of the two cycles, Taylor attempts to make his chart
of the two cycles more descriptive:

A	B
1. The Return of the Twelve and the Departure to a Lonely Place (6:30-34)	1. -------
2. The Feeding of the Five Thousand (6:35-44)	2. The Feeding of the Four Thousand (8:1-10)
3. The Crossing, the Storm, and the statement that the disciples did not understand concerning the loaves because their heart was blinded (6:45-52)	3. ⎫ The Crossing and Landing at Dalmanutha [8:10]
4. The Landing at Gennesaret including a summary statement regarding the healing ministry (6:53-56)	4. ⎭

5. The Controversy with the Pharisees about Defilement, inserted as an introduction to the journey into the region of Tyre (7:1-23)

5. The Controversy with the Pharisees about Signs (8:11-13)

6. The journey into the region of Tyre and the story of the Syro-Phoenician Woman (The Children's Bread) (7:24-30)

6. The Recrossing of the Lake (to Bethsaida) and the story of the failure to understand the mystery of the loaves and the leaven of the Pharisees (8:14-21)

7. The journey continued and the Healing of the Deaf Mute (7:31-37)

7. The Healing of the Blind Man (8:22-26)

It is Taylor's opinion that A2-4 and B2-4 do indeed form a doublet.[9] Sections A5-7 and B5-7 are more problematic, however, inasmuch as the controversies (A5 and B5) and the healings (A7 and B7) are "quite different," and A6 and B6 have nothing in common except their references to bread.[10] Unlike 6:35-56 and 8:1-10, therefore, Mark 7:1-37 and 8:11-26 do not stand as a doublet. The stories in these sections are to be taken as accounts of separate incidents. Moreover, Mark 7:1-23 is a secondary addition to its context; it "is loosely connected with its present context and was probably compiled independently."[11] Therefore, having perceived that A2-4 and B2-4 are variants of the same narrative and that 7:1-23 has been introduced secondarily into its present context, Taylor feels able to untangle what at first seemed to be two cycles and to reconstruct tentatively "the original order of events": 6:30-56, 8:11-22a, 7:24-37, 8:22b-26 (A1-4, B5-6, A6-7, B7).[12]

There are several problems with Taylor's treatment of Mark 6:30-8:26, not the least of which is his persistent proclivity to find an authentic chronology of historical events behind the stories in the text. More important for now, though, is his judgment that 6:35-56 and 8:1-10 form a doublet. First, we note that he somewhat casually neglects Mark 6:30-34 (his A1), the almost universally recognized *Sammelbericht* with which the Feeding of the Five Thousand is introduced. The neglect of these verses in Taylor's discussion is a tacit admission that they do not belong with either feeding story, and this in spite of the fact that he believes 6:30-34 is based on traditional material.[13] On the other hand, when he reconstructs "the original order of events," 6:30-34 is included as if it belonged to the original version of the feeding story. Is 6:30-34 to be regarded as part of the feeding story or not?

A similar difficulty manifests itself in the material immediately following the feeding story in both cycles. Taylor never adequately explains how 6:45-56, a section which includes a boat crossing, a storm, Jesus' walking on the water, a statement of the disciples' incomprehension, the arrival at Gennesaret, the gathering of a crowd, and a summary statement of Jesus' healing activity, is to be regarded as a legitimate match for 8:10, the blunt declaration of a boat trip to Dalmanutha. One must surely conclude that the doublet which Taylor, to his credit, has reduced from A1-7/B1-7 to A2-4/B2-4 must be further reduced to A2/B2; i.e., the two feeding stories themselves. These stories, and these alone, stand as a doublet in light of Taylor's analysis.[14] Once again, having begun with what Jenkins calls a "sustained doublet," we have retreated from this position until only the two feeding stories remain. With this brief review of the discussions of Jenkins and Taylor we may safely lay to rest the hypothesis of variant cycles in Mark 6:30-7:37 and 8:1-26. Even though we must reject this hypothesis, we must admit that it is inspired by the valid perception of parallelism in this material, primarily with the feeding stories but also with other material in Mark 6-8.[15] That one receives intuitions of repetition or duality when reading Mark 6-8 cannot be denied. However, the explanation that two variant cycles of stories lie behind Mark 6:30-8:26 is inadequate. Consequently, we may turn to other significant efforts to uncover sources lying behind the early chapters of Mark.

A Pre-Markan Complex in Mark 3-6: Leander Keck

Another effort to recover a pre-Markan cycle is the widely quoted article by Leander Keck, "Mark 3:7-12 and Mark's Christology."[16] Keck begins by challenging the common notion that the *Sammelbericht* in 3:7-12 begins a new section in Mark; rather, he claims that it is the conclusion of the first major section of the gospel.[17] Moreover, it is not entirely a Markan composition as is so often thought, but a Markan expansion of a traditional summary account. He arrives at this conclusion by

beginning at the end of the unit and working towards the
beginning. First, 3:11-12 may be "peeled away" as a Markan
addition since it demonstrates the "messianic secret." Now, if
vv. 11-12 are Markan, then Mark's use of προσέπιπτον in v. 11
must have been inspired by the presence of ἐπιπίπτειν (v. 10)
in his source. Similarly, Mark must have borrowed the
πλῆθος πολύ of v. 8 from the traditional πολὺ πλῆθος of v. 7b.
Thus, v. 8, with all of its geographical references, along with
the references in v. 7bc to Galilee and Judea, is a Markan
addition to the tradition along with vv. 11-12. This leaves
one with an "Urtext" of 3:7ab, 9-10, the pre-Markan, traditional
summary.

This Urtext has two salient features: the mention of the
boat and the notion of touching Jesus. With regard to the
former, the stories in Mark that use the boat begin in 4:35-41
(after a possible editorial use of the boat motif in 4:1)
and continue in 5:1-20, 6:31-52, and finally 6:53-56, another
summary quite similar to the Urtext in Mark 3:7-12. Other
"boat material" is found in 8:1-21, but this is largely
redactional, Keck claims, especially vv. 14-21. For the most
part, the boat material in Mark lies in and between the two
summaries in 3:7-12 and 6:53-56. Similarly with the motif of
touching Jesus, the motif is found in these two summaries and
in a story within a story found between them: the story about the
hemorrhaging woman who seeks to touch Jesus (5:24b-34), which
was intercalated at a pre-Markan stage into the story about
Jairus' daughter (5:21-24a, 35-43). This "double cluster" of
stories in Mark 3-6, one utilizing the motif of the boat and
the other the motif of touching Jesus, has a common set of
boundary markers in the form of two similar summary statements,
which apparently stood at the beginning and end of the pre-
Markan complex which we find scattered now in Mark 3:7-12,
4:35-5:43, 6:31-52, and 6:53-56.

As corroborating evidence for the discovery of this complex
of stories, Keck offers the observation that the stories
consistently show no evidence of the trappings of Judaism;
there is no debate or controversy with Jewish figures in them,

no mention of the Kingdom of God or of forgiveness of sins.
On the other hand, Jesus is consistently portrayed as a
Hellenistic wonder-worker, a θεῖος ἀνήρ:

> The implication of these observations is clear: Mark
> contains two streams of miracle material: one closely
> related to the Palestinian scene and the message of
> Jesus in its native setting; the other relatively
> unrelated to Jesus' message (except, of course, in
> the thought of Mark). The former stands under the
> rubric, "the strong man" (3:37); the latter
> under the stamp of the hellenistic θεῖος ἀνήρ whose
> divine power is manifested on earth.[18]

Mark takes up these stories dominated by a θεῖος ἀνήρ
perspective in order to bring them under the sway of his own
cross-centered theology, thereby counter-balancing and
correcting a theological stance that he cannot fully accept.[19]
In the process, the evangelist has broken up the complex,
mixing its components with other material, thus constructing
the present text.

A number of significant criticisms may be directed at
Keck's work. First, Keck begins by arguing that 3:7-12 functions
in the gospel as the conclusion of the first major section
(1:16-3:12); it serves as "a good summary of what has been
said so far" and it "does not introduce anything."[20] This is an
unusual claim for Keck to make, since virtually every exegete
points to the prospective function of this unit; i.e., it
introduces motifs into the story that are developed only later.[21]
Besides, it is unnecessary to argue, as he does, that a unit
which concludes one section of the gospel cannot introduce the
next section. Norman Perrin has observed that this section, as
well as others in the gospel, has a transitional function--it
provides a retrospective view of what has preceded and a
prospective view of the events to follow.[22] It is also surprising
that Keck suggests that 3:7-12 is strictly a concluding unit
since he proceeds to argue that this unit is in fact the
introductory unit in the pre-Markan complex. Apparently he is
arguing that the unit has one function in the pre-Markan
complex and another in the gospel itself, but he has not made
himself clear on this point. Indeed, Keck himself points out
how the boat motif and the touching-Jesus motif are introduced

in 3:7-12 and are later "echoed" in the conclusion of the
complex (6:53-56). Mark 3:7-12 may not lead directly into
3:13ff., but it certainly has the prospective function of
introducing major motifs for future development.

Second, we cannot allow to go unchallenged Keck's
attempt to find a traditional core of material behind the
present text of 3:7-12. It is generally agreed that 3:7-12 is
wholly a Markan composition,[23] and he has been unable to
place that supposition in doubt. His separation of tradition
and redaction begins strongly enough with the observation that
vv. 11-12 display the favorite Markan theme of the Messianic
Secret, although one might question why he begins at the end
of the unit rather than at the beginning. In the very next
step, however, he errs by inferring that a Markan use of
προσπίπτω in v. 11 is inspired by the traditional use of
ἐπιπίπτω (a *hapax legomenon* in Mark) in v. 10. Quite the
contrary, the repeated usage of cognates is a typical example of
Markan repetition or *duality*, as Frans Neirynck calls it.[24] As
Neirynck's careful study has demonstrated, duality in Mark
("repetitions, pleonasms and duplications") is so pervasive
and so characteristic of the gospel that distinctions between
various pre-Markan sources, or between tradition and redaction,
based solely on repetitions or duplications, must be questioned.
Mark is so fond of double expressions that both halves of these
expressions may be properly attributed to him.[25] With regard to
the cognate verbs in 3:10-11, instead of finding tradition and
redaction here, we are inclined to see a typically Markan
double expression. The same holds true for πολὺ πλῆθος of v. 7
and πλῆθος πολὺ of v. 8. Such repetition is utterly
characteristic of Mark.[26] In light of Neirynck's work, it would
be unwise to continue to assign one of these phrases to Mark
and one to his source--they are both from the hand of the author,
serving to frame the geographical references in v. 8.[27]

With these observations, we realize that Keck's attempt
to separate tradition from redaction has not succeeded. It is
unnecessary, but would be quite possible, to point out
additional indications of Markan composition in 3:7-12 that

confirm the conclusion that Mark is entirely responsible for the composition of this unit.[28]

Third, although Keck argues for the traditional origin of the entire reconstructed complex, he only endeavors to show the traditional origin of 3:7-12. The rest of the complex is regarded as traditional simply on the basis of its coherence with this introductory unit. In making so sweeping a claim, he declines to discuss the possibility of Markan redaction in all of these other pericopes.[29] This becomes particularly crucial in the case of the final summary statement in 6:53-56, which is itself generally regarded as a Markan composition.[30] Keck does not even attempt to demonstrate that this unit is traditional; he merely implies that it is so by analogy to 3:7-12. Having rejected his claims with regard to the tradition behind 3:7-12, we are scarcely able to accept unsupported assertions regarding other, similar units.

Fourth, although all of the material in Mark involving the motif of touching Jesus is included in Keck's reconstructed complex, not all of the "boat material" lies within the complex. Indeed, the boat material lying outside of the complex (4:1, 8:1-21) is specifically recognized by Keck as bearing the marks of Markan redaction. If this other boat material is Markan, how does one demonstrate that the boat material within the complex is traditional? In Keck's work, we must conclude, the distinction between traditional and redactional use of the boat motif has apparently been made by an arbitrary, subjective process--no clear, persuasive criterion is offered for making this distinction.

Fifth, the mention of the boat material found in 8:1-21 brings us back to the feeding stories which have a rather insignificant role in Keck's complex, although the Feeding of the Five Thousand is a part of the complex. But *why* is it included in the complex? Granted, the boat appears in the introduction of the feeding story (6:30-34), but it has no role whatsoever in the story itself; neither is the motif of touching Jesus present. How does this particular story fit into the traditional complex that is supposedly unified by the motifs of the boat and touching Jesus?

The second feeding story receives even less attention. In his haste to uncover the complex of tradition found between 3:7-12 and 6:53-56, Keck fails to consider the connections between those particular stories and stories outside of the complex. Hence any possible connections between the two feeding stories, connections which might subvert his argument for the existence of the complex, are ignored. He does offer two brief, enigmatic allusions to Mark's use in chapter 8 of the "parallel cycle of the feeding and the lake stories for his own ends."[31] Exactly what this cycle is parallel to, what its origin is, or what the extent of Mark's modification of the cycle is, Keck does not say. If there is some connection between the two feeding stories, and that would seem to be undeniable, then the neat isolation of the pre-Markan complex as he has seen it begins to break down.

Sixth, with regard to the non-Jewish θεῖος ἀνήρ orientation of the complex, the criticisms offered by Snoy are cogent. First, although it is true that the stories isolated in the complex show no conflict with Judaism and no mention of the Kingdom of God or of forgiveness of sins, there are other stories in Mark where these traits are equally lacking: 1:40-45, 8:22-26, 9:14-29, 10:46-52. The absence of these traits in the stories that Keck has isolated does not adequately distinguish the stories as a pre-Markan cycle of stories.[32] Secondly, the distinction between Hellenistic and Jewish miracle traditions is offered gratuitously and is not demonstrated. As Snoy has observed: "En effet, les mêmes notions religieuses en matière de miracles étaient répandues dans les provinces orientales de l'empire romain, et la distinction tentée par Keck entre deux catégories de miracles ne tient pas."[33]

Keck's essay has brought to the fore the methodological problems in the attempt to recover pre-Markan cycles of tradition. Keck gives scant attention to the question of valid criteria for discovering cycles of pre-gospel tradition. When a criterion is used, e.g., following a motif as it is used in stories and summary accounts, it is not used rigorously and

consistently. As we have noted above, Keck pursues the boat
motif only as long as he finds it within the material with
which he is concerned; he offers no clear reason for deciding
that certain instances of the boat motif lie within the cycle
and others lie outside of the cycle. If attempts to reconstruct
pre-gospel cycles are to succeed then we must have a
methodology that is more clearly defined and rigorously applied
than the one we see here.

"Vormarkinische Wundergeschichtensammlung" in Mark 3-6: Rudolf Pesch

A pre-Markan cycle of miracle stories very similar to
Keck's has been proposed by Rudolf Pesch in the first volume
of his commentary on the gospel.[34] Pesch's cycle, however, has
a carefully organized chiastic shape with a *Schachtelung*
(intercalation) lying at the center of the cycle (D: 5:21-43):

A.   Summarium (3,7-12)

B.   Stillung des Seesturm (4,35-41)

C.   Heilung des Gerasener Besessenen (5,1-20)

D.   Heilung der Blutflüssigen und Auferweckung des
     Tochter des Jairus (5,21-43)

C^1. Speisung der Fünftausend (6,32-44)

B^1. Seewandel (6,45-51)

A^1. Summarium (6,53-56)[35]

Contrary to Keck, Pesch categorically denies the θεῖος ἀνήρ
flavor of these stories, emphasizing instead the Old Testament
background they presuppose. Nevertheless, most of the criticisms
we directed towards Keck's cycle apply, *mutatis mutandis*, to
Pesch's cycle. Especially important to note is the absence of
a clearly stated and rigorously applied methodology for
reconstructing pre-Markan collections of tradition. This
methodological question has been sharply addressed by Frans
Neirynck in his review of Pesch's commentary.[36]

Neirynck observes a radical shift in Pesch's thinking, as
seen by a comparison of Pesch's earlier *Naherwartungen. Tradition
und Redaktion in Mk 13*[37] with the recent volume of his
commentary. In the more recent volume Pesch is far less willing
to acknowledge occurrences of Markan redaction in the gospel. To
cite just one example, Pesch no longer regards intercalation

(*Schachtelung*) as a Markan compositional technique; he now
argues that this operation has been carried out at the pre-
gospel stage of the tradition by a pre-Markan redactor.[38]
Examples of Markan redaction pointed out by Pesch in the
course of the commentary on Mark 1-8 are so few, in fact,
that Neirynck is able to collect the references and print out
the texts on a two page chart,[39] and many of these only
involve the addition of εὐθύς or πάλιν to the traditional
material.[40] According to Pesch, Mark adheres closely to
his sources, modifying them only slightly. He performs
"konservative Redaktion": "Der Redaktor Markus ist kein
Inventor, sondern Bearbeiter von Tradition, er verhält sich
kaum literarisch produktiv, sondern 'unliterarisch'
konservativ."[41] The emphasis on "konservative Redaktion"
is almost the hallmark of the commentary.[42]

As with Keck's cycle, the boat motif is a major unifying
feature of Pesch's cycle, occurring in the *Sammelberichte* at
the beginning and end of the cycle and linking the internal
units together. Pesch argues that what we have here is a
series of stories tied together redactionally at a pre-Markan
stage by the imagery of the *Seefahrt*.[43] The same question
arises here as it did with Keck's cycle: how is one to
distinguish between the admittedly *Markan* redactional use of
the boat motif[44] and the *pre-Markan* redactional use of the
motif? Neirynck has raised this issue most perceptively in
his review:

On concédera volontiers à Pesch le caractère rédactionnel
des versets en question, mais comment peut-il prouver
que la rédaction se situe à un niveau antérieur à Marc?
Il ne suffit pas d'y trouver le vocabulaire propre
d'un itinéraire en bateau . . . . Puisque Pesch attribue
le même motif dans 8,10.13 à la rédaction marcienne . . . ,
on est en droit de lui demander sur quoi il se base pour
conclure autrement dans 3,7-6,56. Il écrit à propos de
4,35-36: 'Die Rekonstruktion einer vormarkinischen
Sammlung von Wundergeschichten erübrigt also die Annahme
eines mk-redaktionellen Eingriffs in VV 35-36, wofür die
sprachliche Fassung des Textes auch keine Anhaltspunkte
bietet . . . .' Une telle phrase peut être retournée:
'Die Annahme eines mk-redaktionellen Eingriffs erübrigt
die Rekonstruktion einer vormarkinischen Sammlung in
VV 35-36, wofür die sprachliche Fassung des Textes auch
keine Anhaltspunkte bietet.' Il suffit de remplacer dans

le commentaire sur 4,35-36 *vormarkinisch-* par *markinisch-redaktionell*, car il ne contient aucune indication spécifique d'une origine prémarcienne.[45]

As with Keck, the methodology employed by Pesch is formulated imprecisely and applied inadequately. If one operates with the presupposition, as Pesch does, that Mark is a faithful preserver of tradition, then the temptation arises to explain the text so as to justify the presupposition of faithful preservation of tradition. Are certain words in the proposed cycle *hapax legomena* in the gospel? Then they must demonstrate the difference between the vocabulary of the cycle and that of the gospel. Do certain other words recur again and again both in the cycle and in the gospel? Then we have here evidence of the integral, homogeneous nature of the whole of pre-Markan tradition.[46] Neirynck recognizes clearly the danger of such 'mixed bag' tradition and the need for greater methodological precision:

> La tradition prémarcienne lui sert de fourre-tout: la 'Variabilität der Ausdrucksweisen' s'explique par la diversité des traditions, et s'il y a homogénéité stylistique dans l'évangile, c'est parce que la tradition prémarcienne 'schon ähnlich stilisiert war.' Pour faire avancer la discussion, nous aurons besoin de plus de précision.[47]

Such absolute flexibility, always bending to account for all of the evidence on the basis of one's own presuppositions and thereby allowing no other hypothesis even to be considered, is ultimately a fatal ambivalence.

"Vormarkinische Sammlung" in Mark 4-6:
Heinz-Wolfgang Kuhn

We will examine one last example of an argument for a pre-Markan collection of miracle stories found in chapters 4-6, this being the section of Heinz-Wolfgang Kuhn's *Habilitationsschrift* which addresses "Das Problem einer vormarkinischen Sammlung in Mk 4,35-6,52."[48] Earlier in this monograph Kuhn considers the possibility of a parallel between Mark 6:33-7:37 and 8:1-26, which he rightly, in our opinion, rejects.[49] The differences between these two sections simply cannot be minimized, but more importantly for Kuhn, when one raises the question of the *Sitz im Leben* of these supposed parallels then one reaches an impasse--no clear, single *Sitz im Leben* for these variegated complexes seems to be in view. It is better, Kuhn suggests, to conclude that Mark has brought together here a variety of individual stories, of which only the feeding stories, possibly with a sea journey attached, and the healing stories, may be variant accounts.[50]

Although he has rejected a pre-Markan parallel between 6:33-7:37 and 8:1-26, Kuhn is more favorable to the suggestion that a miracle collection underlies Mark 4:35-5:43 and perhaps also 6:32-52. As one might expect from his critique of the familiar double-cycle theory, the form critical question of *Sitz im Leben* is raised here and proves to be the decisive factor in Kuhn's assessment of the material. Indeed, it is fair to say that Kuhn's methodology in the entire book is form criticism, but rather than applying form criticism to individual pericopes he attempts to shift the form critical focus to large units; i.e., pre-gospel collections of tradition. Whether this methodology can be successful in uncovering pre-gospel collections of material now embedded in the gospel is a matter of serious doubt, as we shall point out below.

Kuhn begins his discussion of the collection behind Mark 4-6 by repeating the common suggestion that the four miracle stories in Mark 4:35-5:43 were already connected at a pre-Markan stage.[51] To these four stories Kuhn adds two more: the feeding story and the water-walking episode in Mark 6:32-52. What induces Kuhn to decide on these six stories is the form critical observation that these stories share a common genre, the *Novelle* or Tale, and consequently share a common *Sitz im Leben*, the primitive Christian mission.[52] In particular, these stories bear the imprint of the kind of θεῖος ἀνήρ ideology typified by the *Überapostel* who plagued Paul, as evidenced in 2 Corinthians.[53] It is the presence of these common traits, shared by all six stories, that prompts Kuhn to propose that these stories were connected in a pre-Markan collection.

Although the form critical observations are of primary importance for Kuhn, he does offer one *redaktionsgeschichtlich* observation that he believes strengthens the *formgeschichtlich*

argument. This involves a description of the editorially
formulated structure of the gospel in chapters 3-6.[54] These
chapters are framed, as we know by now, by the two summary
accounts in 3:7-12 and 6:53-56. Lying between these are two
major sections, one involving Jesus' teaching activity
(4:1-34) and one his wonder-working (4:35-5:43). Preceding
Mark 4:1-34 (in 3:13-35) and following Mark 4:35-5:43 (in
6:1-31) are corresponding sections, especially inserted by
Mark, each containing a scene wherein Jesus is misunderstood
among his own people (3:20-35, 6:1-6) and one in which he
chooses or commissions his disciples (3:13-19, 6:7-31[55]).
Were it not for a minor problem one would have a nicely
chiastic structure created by Mark out of the sources lying
before him:

> 3:7-12 Summary
>> 3:13-19 Jesus and his disciples
>>> 3:20-35 Jesus and his family
>>>> 4:1-34 Jesus as Teacher
>>>> 4:35-5:43 Jesus as Wonder-Worker
>>> 6:1-6 Jesus and his compatriots
>> 6:7-31 Jesus and his disciples
> 6:53-56 Summary

The problem is, of course, that 6:32-52 must also be taken
into account. But Mark 6:32-52 contains the last two stories
of the supposed six story collection and therein lies Kuhn's
solution to the problem. One should not be surprised that Mark
relates only four of the six stories in succession; relating
all six stories consecutively would create an unwieldy mass
("ein 'erratischer Block'") of homogeneous material in the
gospel. Instead, Mark holds two of the stories in abeyance,
eventually using them after 6:7-31, even though placing them
there spoils the neat symmetry that he has worked so hard to
create--Mark will go to such lengths to find a place for and
thus preserve these two stories.[56]

To his credit, Kuhn advances his proposal quite tentatively;
it is "nicht sicher."[57] Neither is it persuasive. The problem

is, once again, that the methodology used is unequal to the
task.[58] Determining the genre and *Sitz im Leben* of a group of
stories does not appear to be a sufficiently precise tool to
warrant claims for or against their pre-Markan origin. When
one adopts the broad and often nebulous categories of '*Novelle*'
and 'ϑεῖος ἀνήρ,' what are the criteria for isolating a smaller,
pre-Markan group of such stories within these wider boundaries?[59]
Dibelius, for example, points out at least four other *Novellen*
in Mark: 1:40-45, 7:32-37, 8:22-26, and 9:14-29.[60] On what
basis are these excluded from the collection? Kuhn argues that
they are clearly "less miraculous"[61] than the stories in Mark
4-6, but this is an extremely subjective judgment and open to
debate. The same question applies to the stories portraying
Jesus as a ϑεῖος ἀνήρ: on what basis are other stories which
are not thought to be in the collection, but (it could be
argued) displaying the same ϑεῖος ἀνήρ model, excluded from
the collection? It is not immediately clear, for example, that
Jesus is any less of a ϑεῖος ἀνήρ in 7:32-37, 8:22-26, and
9:14-29 than he is in 4:35-6:52.[62]

Since we have strayed momentarily outside of the borders
of Kuhn's pre-Markan collection, let us stay here awhile and
take this opportunity to reestablish contact with Mark 8:1-10,
the feeding story that is outside of the cycles proposed by
Keck, Pesch, and Kuhn. These interpreters each admit some kind
of parallelism between the two feeding stories, but their
respective proposals, all very similar in substance, do not
lead them to consider this parallelism to any great extent.
But as long as the question of the relationship between the
two feeding stories remains unresolved, as we believe it is,
any hypothetical pre-Markan cycle(s) containing one or both
of them is cast into the shadow of doubt created by this
unanswered question. Since Kuhn follows Dibelius so closely,
it is especially interesting to see what Dibelius does with
8:1-10. Dibelius, following Wendling,[63] regards 8:1-10 as a
lackluster, stunted copy of the Feeding of the Five Thousand.
It is so nondescript that Dibelius merely offers the negative
judgment that it is neither a *Paradigm* nor a *Novelle*: it is not

placed in any of Dibelius's categories.[64] So we have here the
rather unusual situation of two stories, one a copy of the
other (Wendling), but not of the same genre. This judgment
could easily lead one, as it perhaps has with Kuhn, to ignore
the patent points of contact between the two accounts. For
our part, at least, we will continue to hold the two stories
together in a tension until we are satisfied that the tension
has been relieved by an adequate treatment of the doublet
problem. More specifically, it will not suffice to deny, as
Keck, Pesch, and Kuhn have done, a complete correspondence
between 6:30-7:37 and 8:1-26, acknowledge nevertheless the
parallel feeding stories, and proceed to look elsewhere (e.g.,
Mark 4-6) for a pre-Markan cycle. There is an intersection in
the data examined in the attempts to find pre-Markan cycles
behind Mark 4-6 and 6-8. The cycles found in Mark 4-6 overlap
with those of Mark 6-8, so one cannot legitimately pursue
either enterprise in isolation from the other. The pivotal
passage is 6:30-52, the Feeding of the Five Thousand and the
Walking on the Water--all the theories considered thus far
involve these verses. But whenever 6:30-44 is considered so
also must 8:1-10 be considered; to deny this maxim, we believe,
is to deny the truism that the two feeding stories function
as a matched pair in the gospel.

To return to Kuhn's thesis, even if one were to grant to
him that he has isolated a cycle of *Novellen* which portrays
Jesus as a θεῖος ἀνήρ, the question still remains: was this
cycle constructed before Mark or by Mark himself? What evidence
is there to preclude the possibility that Mark himself found
individual stories of similar cast and gathered them together for
the first time? Or the possibility that he found dissimilar
stories and brought them together, reshaping them and endowing
them with a common character? Or indeed the audacious
possibility that Mark created one or more of the stories *in toto*,
perhaps using other stories as models? With these questions we
move from the forum of form criticism to that of redaction
criticism, thus shifting the focus from the study of the
traditional material used by the evangelist to the study of the

evangelist's particular and characteristic use of that
material. The bulk of Kuhn's work lies in the former area; he
makes only a tentative excursion into the latter realm. As we
have noted, though, a form critical argument for a pre-Markan
cycle is alone inadequate. If it is to be regarded as valid, it
must have additional, redaction critical confirmation that the
connections between the stories lack the characteristics of
Markan literary style and thus have a claim to be traditional
material. The connection of the stories in Mark, especially
those in 4:35-5:43, is actually the crux of Kuhn's (and the
others') thesis, not the common genre or *Sitz im Leben*. It is
with regard to the connections between stories that the thesis
either stands or falls. Kuhn's attention to this crucial material
is totally insufficient; his only attempt to provide redaction
critical support for his thesis is the ungainly argument that
Mark separates 6:32-52 from the other stories to avoid
presenting "ein 'erratischer Block'" of homogeneous material,
even though the evangelist must thereby destroy the balance of
a pattern he has created. This argument is pure supposition;
the primary supposition of a pre-gospel miracle collection is
supported by a supposition of a disrupted pattern in Mark 3-6.
All the while the crucial seams and connections binding together
both the stories of the collection and the Markan pattern
into which the stories are placed remain unexamined.[65]

Pre-Markan Miracle Catenae in Mark 4-8: Paul J. Achtemeier

One of the more ambitious attempts to recover pre-Markan
cycles of miracle stories is the effort by Paul J. Achtemeier to
reconstruct parallel catenae of miracle stories underlying the
text of Mark 4-8. The first of Achtemeier's two articles, "Toward
the Isolation of Pre-Markan Miracle Catenae,"[66] is devoted to the
reconstruction of the catenae from the present text of Mark;
the second article, "The Origin and Function of the Pre-Marcan
Miracle Catenae,"[67] addresses the question of the original
Sitz im Leben of the catenae and discusses the changes in the
catenae wrought by Mark in the process of incorporating them
into the gospel. Each catena begins with a sea miracle, ends

with a feeding miracle, and contains three healing miracles, for a total of five stories in each catena:

Catena I	Catena II
Stilling of the Storm (4:35-41)	Jesus Walks on the Sea (6:45-51)
The Gerasene Demoniac (5:1-20)	The Blind Man of Bethsaida (8:22-26)
The Woman with a Hemorrhage (5:25-34)	The Syrophoenician Woman (7:24b-30)
Jairus' Daughter (5:21-23, 35-43)	The Deaf-Mute (7:32-37)
Feeding of the 5,000 (6:34-44, 53)	Feeding of the 4,000 (8:1-10)[68]

In the first article, Achtemeier analyzes Mark 4-8 and attempts to distinguish between those sections that have been heavily influenced by Markan redaction and those that have been less influenced. He finds traces of Mark's hand mostly in sections concerning Jesus' "teaching activity"--6:1-33 and 7:1-23--although other sections, like 6:54-56 and 8:11-21, are also Markan. Having eliminated these Markan constructions, he is left with the ten miracle stories from which he draws the two catenae. Unlike the other suggestions for pre-Markan miracle cycles that we have examined, this reconstruction requires some rearrangement of the stories--Mark has not left them in their original order.

The major shift introduced by the evangelist in the first catena was to remove the story of the woman with the hemorrhage (5:25-34) from its place following the Gerasene demoniac (5:1-20) and to insert it within the story of Jairus' daughter (5:21-23, 35-43), a typically Markan use of the technique of intercalation.[69] Moreover, Achtemeier suggests that 5:21ab, which coheres so well with the preceding story of the demoniac, was the original introduction to the story of the woman and that 5:21c was attached to it by Mark to provide an entry into the story of Jairus' daughter which then follows.

The major restoration of original order made by Achtemeier in the second catena is the removal of the healing of the blind man (8:22-26) from its position as the tenth and last miracle story in Mark 4-8 and its repositioning after the walking on the water (6:45-51). The clue that induces Achtemeier to suggest this shift is the mention of the city Bethsaida in both stories. At the beginning of the sea miracle in 6:45-52 the disciples set out for Bethsaida; they arrive, however, not in Bethsaida but in Gennesaret (6:53). For the solution to this puzzling inconsistency Achtemeier relies upon the work of T. Snoy on Mark 6:45-52.[70] Snoy argues that the mention of Bethsaida in 6:45 is a part of the traditional account of the sea miracle which Mark has preserved. Mark 6:53, though, with its mention of Gennesaret, is the original ending to the Feeding of the Five Thousand; it was detached from the feeding story so that Mark could append the sea miracle directly to the feeding story. So the two place names in 6:45, 53 were derived from two separate stories and were made to appear contradictory when the two pieces of tradition were first joined by Mark.[71] Since a departure for Bethsaida is mentioned in 6:45 but no arrival in that city is explicitly mentioned, Achtemeier suggests that the story that originally followed 6:45-51 is now located in 8:22-26, a story which begins with the statement: "And they came to Bethsaida." We should also take special care to note that Snoy's claim that the feeding story and the sea story were first joined by the evangelist and were not already joined in pre-Markan tradition, a claim which contravenes what is probably the scholarly consensus regarding the connection of the stories, allows Achtemeier to do what has not been done in the other cycle theories we have discussed, and that is to disengage these two stories and to place them in different cycles. In the other theories we have examined the intimate connection between these stories has been allowed to stand as a pre-Markan connection. In light of Snoy's work, however, Achtemeier is able to separate these stories, placing the first in the first catena and the second in the second catena.

In the second article, in which Achtemeier discusses the original *Sitz im Leben* of the miracle catenae, we encounter once again that theological characterization of Jesus with which we have become quite familiar in our survey of proposals for

pre-Markan miracle cycles: the θεῖος ἀνήρ. By making full use
of the fact that each catena ends with a feeding story that is
often thought to have eucharistic overtones, he ventures so
far as to suggest a very specialized type of presentation of
Jesus as θεῖος ἀνήρ, that of a "eucharistic liturgy."[72] As in
other discussions of the θεῖος ἀνήρ concept in Mark, comparisons
to the opponents of Paul in 2 Corinthians are drawn and, as in
other discussions, the claim is made that Mark adopts the
θεῖος ἀνήρ material only to bring it under the domination of
his own, radically different, cross-centered theology.[73]

Having offered this brief summary of Achtemeier's articles,
we may now offer some criticisms of his work. Perhaps the
fundamental problem with this attempt to reconstruct pre-Markan
sources is the hasty and superficial manner in which tradition
and redaction are separated. On the redaction side of the ledger,
large sections of non-miracle material (Mark 6:1-33, 7:1-23)
are too quickly laid aside as Markan compositions concerned
with Jesus' "teaching activity,"[74] although this is clearly a
woefully inadequate description because of the variety of
material found in these sections. On the tradition side of the
ledger, the miracle stories are just as quickly pronounced
free of the signs of Markan editorial activity. Sweeping
proclamations like the one pronounced over Mark 5:1-20 are
typical: "Whatever the origin of this story may have been,
there are no clear indications of Markan editorial work in the
story as we now have it."[75] One would expect that such a
categorical denial of Markan redaction in a pericope would
be supported by a detailed, rigorous investigation of the
language of the text to check for the signs of Markan redaction,
but it is precisely this kind of rigorous attention to the
language of the miracle stories that is lacking in Achtemeier's
work.[76]

As in other attempts to reconstruct pre-Markan miracle
cycles, the crux of the matter lies with the connections
between the miracle stories. Were the stories connected before
Mark or were they connected for the first time by Mark himself?
Too often Achtemeier assumes a priori that if a connecting

verse performs its function well, successfully tying two
stories together in a smooth, unobtrusive manner, then it
must be pre-Markan. Regarding 5:21 he writes: "The introductory
vs. 21 is so closely bound up with the preceding story and flows
so well from it that it seems to be part of a narrative in
which these stories followed one another prior to their use by
Mark."[77] As this argument is presently formulated, there is
simply no justification for this conclusion. To be sure, the
conclusion may in fact be true, but it would have to be
demonstrated by a careful examination of the language of
5:21 to be credible. This Achtemeier has not done.[78] On the
other hand, if such an examination of the connecting verses in
the miracle stories demonstrates that they were often introduced
by Mark, as Snoy and Van Cangh claim, then the thesis of pre-
Markan miracle catenae begins to disintegrate rapidly. Mark
5:21 is only one example; similar examples elsewhere in the
catenae are numerous.[79]

Another problem endemic to cycle theories that manifests
itself in Achtemeier's work is the problem of the parallelism
or duality of the twin catenae. It is clear that Achtemeier
somehow regards the catenae as parallel to each other--but
just exactly how they are parallel, how this came about, or
what significance the parallelism has is never explained.
Thus the doublet problem remains as perplexing as ever.
Obviously, one may point to the striking agreements between the
two sea stories (4:35-41, 6:45-51) and thereby strengthen one's
claim to have discovered parallel catenae. On the other hand,
the kind of agreements found in these stories are nonexistent
in the middle three healing stories of each cycle, so one
hears little said about parallelism when these stories are
discussed. "Healing story" itself as a label is purposely
vague in order to encompass such diverse stories as an
exorcism, a resuscitation of a dead child, and a healing of a
blind man with spittle. The only thing any of these middle
stories have in common is the position they share in the chart;
if one limits the use of the term doublet to those stories that
display some kind of agreement with regard to their content or

vocabulary, then only the sea stories and feeding stories, of all the stories placed in corresponding positions in the two catenae, may be called doublets. The perceptive reader will note, however, that Achtemeier has included both halves of another possible doublet (7:32-37, 8:22-26) within the same catena, totally ignoring the extensive verbal parallels between them, parallels which are eagerly pointed out by those who argue for parallel cycles in 6:30-7:37 and 8:1-26. The latter argument for parallel cycles in Mark 6-8 observes the agreements in the feeding stories and in the two healings in 7:32-37 and 8:22-26; it does not deal with the agreements found in the two sea stories. Achtemeier's thesis of parallel catenae in Mark 4-8 keeps in view the agreements between the sea stories and feeding stories; it ignores the agreements in the two healing stories. Would it not be possible to treat all three candidates for the term doublet with equal seriousness? Of course, in so doing one may not be able to unearth anything quite as orderly and aesthetically pleasing as two parallel miracle catenae lying beneath the surface of the present text, but one may find that such reconstructions are not necessary for a valid, sensitive appreciation of the text.

This comment brings to light a danger faced by all who attempt to reconstruct Mark's *Vorlage*: the temptation to interpret the reconstructed *Vorlage* instead of the gospel of Mark. Of course, no one ever does this consciously; Achtemeier, for example, would claim that his fundamental objective is the elucidation of the gospel of Mark, but it is clear that he believes this can only be done in Mark 4-8 by observing how Mark has modified the catenae. Consequently, hiding in Achtemeier's work is the implicit principle that the miracle catenae are preeminent over the text of Mark. One can only understand Mark 4-8 properly if one has previously reconstructed the catenae, perceived their original *Sitz im Leben*, and observed how Mark modifies the catenae and corrects the theological errors in them. It is not inaccurate to say that the text upon which the hermeneutical process is centered is the dual text of the catenae; Mark 4-8, in contrast, is merely the product of mechanical copying and editing.

When we stop to think about it, it is amazing to consider that the observation of duality or parallelism in Mark 4-8 has invariably prompted exegetes to attribute this phenomenon to pre-Markan sources--very few exegetes in this century have claimed that the author of the gospel had anything to do with it.[80] One of the major reasons for this may be found in the triumph of form criticism in modern critical biblical scholarship, and the emphasis it has placed on the units of oral tradition behind the gospels and the development and preservation of that tradition in the early Christian communities. Seen from this perspective, the gospels are essentially community products, not the compositions of individuals. This understanding of how the gospels came into being has been modified extensively by the development of redaction criticism (or, as some prefer, composition criticism), which attributes a far greater role to the individuals who molded the gospels into their present shape. Indeed, many interpreters of the gospels, particularly those who have been introduced to the work of literary critics outside the field of biblical studies, would prefer to characterize the evangelists as imaginative authors who give their compositions the stamp of their own individuality rather than merely as editors who are passive recipients and conservative custodians of tradition.[81]

Attempts to explain the parallelism in Mark 4-8 on the basis of cycles of pre-Markan tradition adopted and redacted by the evangelist have not succeeded. Such proposals often abound in ingenuity[82] but demonstrate a lack of clarity and rigor with regard to the methodology employed. In numerous cases connections between stories which are presumed to be pre-Markan are shown to be the work of the evangelist when a detailed study of their language is undertaken. It can no longer be assumed that the presence of an orderly and thoughtful arrangement of material in the gospels is an indication of well preserved pre-gospel tradition. To the contrary, one must acknowledge the autonomy of the authors of

the gospels and be willing to acknowledge, if necessary, the
skill and imagination with which they wrote. Attempts to solve
the doublet problem by appeals to parallel traditions have not
succeeded; perhaps it is time to reconsider the possibility
that such duality is the intentional handiwork of an author
and not the chance preservation of variant traditions.

Duality in Mark: Frans Neirynck and Emil Wendling

This same sentiment has been articulated by Frans
Neirynck, who has laid the foundation for such an undertaking
in a series of articles later reprinted in his book *Duality in
Mark: Contributions to the Study of the Markan Redaction*.[83]
Neirynck has conducted a review and reassessment of the role of
"repetitions, pleonasms and duplications" in Mark, phenomena
for which he prefers the broader and less prejudicial term
"duality." The treatment given the topic of duality in Mark
is careful and exhaustive; subsequent discussions of doublets
or other similar phenomena in Mark can ill afford to neglect it.

The first of the three articles published by Neirynck on
this topic, "Mark in Greek,"[84] is the Greek text of Mark in a
special typographical arrangement. In it the verses of the text
are given various spatial arrangements to emphasize the
natural structure of the text. Underlining is also used to call
attention to certain features of the text.[85]

The second article, "Duality in Mark,"[86] is an exhaustive
attempt to gather and categorize every possible instance of
duality in Mark. The categories employed range from examples on
a small scale, such as compound verbs followed by the same
preposition, to occurrences on a wider scale, like doublets or
"sandwich arrangements." Thirty categories in all are examined,
including virtually every type of duality ever suggested as a
Markan characteristic. The result is, as one would expect, a
considerable mass of undigested data; one cannot simply use the
lists as veritable tables of Markan stylistic traits.

The last of the three articles, "Duplicate Expressions in
the Gospel of Mark,"[87] provides one with a valuable
Forschungsbericht of the role of duality in Markan studies, a
preliminary study by Neirynck on one general category of duality

in Mark (the duplicate expression), and his tentative
conclusions about duality in Mark on the basis of this study.
As he makes clear in his thorough review of the literature, in
which he discusses much of the literature from the nineteenth
century, "the phenomenon of duality was never a neglected topic
in the exegesis of Mark." It is "one of the traditional topics
in the study of Mark."[88]

The area in which Markan duality has always been of great
importance is source criticism. The recognition of repetition or
duplication has often been regarded as a primary tool for
separating one stratum of tradition from another or for
distinguishing tradition from redaction. Already in the
nineteenth century the feeding stories were taken as evidence
for variant traditions,[89] but probably more importantly for
gospel studies in general, the battle over the priority of Mark
was in large part fought over the interpretation of pleonasms
and repetitions in Mark. Are the Markan pleonasms the result
of Mark's conflation of elements drawn from Matthew or Luke
(so the advocates of the Griesbach hypothesis), or were these
pleonasms first penned by Mark, for whatever reason, and later
shunned, each in his own way, by Matthew and Luke (so the
Markan priorists)? In either case, there is a tacit agreement
that duality is a common characteristic of Mark, even though
the interpretations of that characteristic differ decisively.

Typical of many source critical debates over the function
and significance of duality in Mark is the problem of the
incomplete or inaccurate description of the evidence at hand;
often one gathers only the evidence which supports one's
thesis. The virtue of Neirynck's work is that it tries to render
an exhaustive accounting of the evidence before undertaking
analysis and interpretation. His conclusions, therefore, though
based on preliminary studies, merit serious attention, and one
of those conclusions is that the common notion that duality in
Mark is to be regarded as an invitation to separate source
from source or tradition from redaction is no longer tenable.[90]

The preliminary study in which Neirynck engages concerns
those occurrences of duality that may be conveniently placed
under the rubric of duplicate expressions, or more specifically,

duplicate temporal and local statements, double questions,
antithetic parallelism, and the use of direct and indirect
speech. From category to category, his findings are consistent.
On the whole, Neirynck finds that there is very little actual
redundancy in Mark's use of duplicate expressions.[91] Invariably,
the second expression adds clarity or precision to the first;
they are not merely juxtaposed synonyms. Indeed, rather than
using the term duplicate expression, one may speak more
accurately of a single "progressive two-step expression."[92]
The two-step expression, Neirynck observes, is virtually
ubiquitous in Mark; it is with considerable justification that
he suggests it "be placed on the list of the characteristics of
Markan usage."[93]

As we have mentioned, the study of duplicate expressions
in Mark only begins the needed study of duality in Mark based
on the full accounting of the evidence provided by Neirynck.
One might well ask if this kind of two-step construction,
found so often in Mark at the level of phrases and sentences,
is found also at the level of larger units of material, perhaps
entire pericopes. The consideration of such possibilities is
promoted by Neirynck's tantalizing observation that the
language and style of the gospel are homogeneous--the kind of
composition one finds at the level of individual sentences
one also finds in larger units:

> . . .on the whole, the evidence is rather impressive,
> especially the fact that a kind of general tendency can
> be perceived in vocabulary and grammar, in individual
> sayings and in collections of sayings, in the construction
> of pericopes and larger sections; there is a sort of
> homogeneity in Mark, from the wording of sentences to the
> composition of the gospel. After the study of these
> data one has a strong impression of the unity of the
> gospel of Mark. It can be formulated as a methodological
> principle that the categories we distinguished hold
> together and that no pericope in Mark can be treated
> in isolation.[94]

With regard to our particular concerns in this study, there is
little comfort in these words for those who would explain the
repetition of Mark 4-8 on the basis of different sources
copied faithfully by Mark and still discernible in the gospel.
There is much encouragement afforded here, however, for those

who suspect that the evangelist deserves much of the credit for
the doublets and other repetitions in Mark 4-8. Could Mark have
intended a two-step progression in, for example, the two
feeding stories, a progression analogous to the two-step
progression he is fond of using in smaller units? If so, how
much of the material would he have composed himself in order to
achieve this end?

Before leaving Neirynck's work we should by all means refer
to the important role in the discussion of doublets in Mark
attributed by Neirynck to Emil Wendling, the author of *Ur-Marcus*
(1905) and *Die Entstehung des Marcus-Evangeliums* (1908):

> The book of Wendling on the *Ur-Marcus* hypothesis is
> especially important for our topic of duality in Mark.
> With it the study of the doublets entered definitively
> into the field of Markan exegesis, and since Wendling
> did not consider them as source or tradition doublets,
> his work still has some relevance for present-day
> redactional study. He criticized the double tradition
> complex advanced as the solution to the problem of
> the so-called "dublettenartigen Parallelismus" in Mk
> vi. 31-viii. 26, and it seems to me that far too
> long his critique has been neglected.[95]

Wendling's alternative to the thesis of a "dublettenartigen
Parallelismus" in 6:31-8:26 was the radical claim that Mark
6:45-8:26 is entirely the composition of the evangelist, thus
effectively attributing the creation of all the doublets in
Mark 4-8 to the evangelist himself.[96] Wendling's work is
characterized by careful attention to the unifying threads
running throughout the gospel, thereby demonstrating the
abundant contribution of the evangelist to the final text.
Many of his insights are still quite valid and merit the fair
reexamination which should now be possible due to the
development of redaction criticism in recent decades. In his
own day, Wendling's work, as Neirynck observes, "could not be
ignored";[97] he was taken seriously by the generation of scholars
that followed him. Nevertheless, studies like Wendling's, in
which the evangelist was conceded a major role in the creation
and organization of the gospel material, were destined to be
submerged beneath the rising tide of *Formgeschichte*, which, for
its part, emphasized the role of the Christian community as the

entity which created and shaped the gospel material. Eleven years after the publication of *Entstehung* Karl Schmidt responded to Wendling in the typical form critical manner:

> Die beiden Speisungsgeschichten sind sicherlich Dubletten. Aber im übrigen scheint es mir, dass man zu sehr mit dieser Dublettentheorie arbeitet. Die evangelische Überlieferung kennt in grösserer Reichhaltigkeit voneinander unabhängige Geschichten und Motive, die vielfach miteinander verwandt, aber doch nicht ohne weiteres voneinander abhängig sind.[98]

Contrary to Wendling's claim to have discovered an integral unit in 6:45-8:26 composed by the evangelist, the tendency of orthodox form criticism was to see in this section distinct, independent, traditional stories which were gathered (or found gathered), but not composed, by the evangelist. Only two stories are definitely a doublet, the feeding stories in Mark 6 and 8, but, curiously, it is usually Wendling's analysis of these two stories that is referred to by later critics as the standard discussion of the relationship of the feeding stories.

The analysis of the two feeding stories in *Entstehung* is in fact one of the few detailed examinations of the language of the two stories.[99] Wendling concludes that 8:1-10 is secondary to 6:32-44; the evangelist has used 6:32-44, a story from the M^2 stratum of Mark's *Vorlage*,[100] as a model for the composition of his own version in 8:1-10. Herein lies perhaps the most crucial presupposition with which he operates: the presence of 6:32-44 in Mark's *Vorlage*.[101] Having decided earlier that the Feeding of the Five Thousand belongs to the *Vorlage*, the discovery of direct verbal connections between that story and the Feeding of the Four Thousand can only lead to the conclusion that the evangelist is borrowing phrases from 6:32-44 as he constructs the second story. Mark 8:1-2, Wendling demonstrates, has a direct verbal connection with 6:34, 36 and is therefore an introduction composed by the evangelist out of components derived from the traditional story.[102] The verbal agreements are clear:

6:34 καὶ . . εἶδεν πολὺν ὄχλον   8:1 . .πολλοῦ ὄχλου ὄντος
καὶ ἐσπλαγχνίσθη ἐπ᾽ αὐτούς,
ὅτι ἦσαν ὡς πρόβατα
μὴ ἔχοντα ποιμένα.   καὶ μὴ ἐχόντων

36 . . ἀγοράσωσιν ἑαυτοῖς
τί φάγωσιν.   τί φάγωσιν. .
                      2 σπλαγχνίζομαι ἐπὶ τὸν
                      ὄχλον ὅτι . . . οὐχ
                      ἔχουσιν τί φάγωσιν.[103]

In addition, the situation portrayed in 8:1-2 clearly presupposes the first feeding story: πάλιν in 8:1 points directly
to the earlier account of a similar feeding.[104]

The evidence that there is a direct link between 6:34,
36 and 8:1-2 is impressive, and the conclusion that 8:1-2
is the secondary adaptation dictates the path to be taken in
Wendling's comparison of the remainder of the two stories.
Whenever there are points of contact found later in the
stories, the claim is made that the text of 8:1-10 is
secondary. However, if one were to examine each case
individually, one could just as easily claim in each separate
case that the direction of the dependence is precisely the
opposite of that suggested by Wendling. The presupposition of
the primacy of 6:32-44, supposedly confirmed by the secondary
nature of 8:1-2 in relation to 6:34, 36, is allowed to
determine too easily the direction of dependence between the
two stories. One must consider the possibility that, if one
started without the presupposition of the priority of 6:32-44,
one could conceivably argue that the direction of dependence is
the opposite direction: Mark 8:1-10 may be the traditional
story (with some Markan redaction), while 6:30-44 may be a
story created by Mark using the other story as a model. It
is precisely this possibility for which we will argue in this
study.

It was rather unfortunate that Wendling began his
comparison of the feeding stories as he did, by pointing out
the verbal agreements between 6:34, 36 and 8:1-2, because, as
we shall show below, the verses in *both* stories are redactional--
they were all composed by Mark. Consequently, it is meaningless
to speak of the priority of one or the other story on the basis
of these particular verses. In spite of that, it is here that
Wendling sets the course for his comparison of the stories by
his initial conclusion that 8:1-2 is dependent upon 6:34, 36.
The kind of study conducted by Wendling deserves to be repeated
but *without* his presupposition that 6:32-44 is in Mark's

Vorlage and *with* the insights into Mark's vocabulary and
style that have been gained in the seventy years since
Wendling.

The Feeding Stories in the Gospel
of Mark: A Thesis

It is this kind of detailed, careful examination of both
stories, using the accumulated knowledge of Mark's
vocabulary, grammar, thematic concerns, and compositional
techniques, that reveals a sharp distinction between the
stories. The presence of a striking number of *hapax legomena*
and the conspicuous absence of Markan vocabulary and literary
characteristics leads one to conclude that the bulk of Mark
8:1-10 was obtained by Mark from his *Vorlage*, although the
pericope does bear the signs of some Markan redaction,
especially at the beginning (8:1-2) and at the end (8:10). On
the other hand, the characteristics of the Markan hand are
present in 6:30-44 from beginning to end. Markan composition
has long been recognized in the introductory verses of the
Feeding of the Five Thousand and sometimes in the transitional
verses between the feeding story and the following sea miracle.
Markan composition is equally observable, we maintain, in the
intervening verses, especially since we may perceive the
evangelist abandoning the non-Markan vocabulary and syntax of
8:1-10 as he composes his own version of the story.

Therefore, this reassessment of the language of the feeding
stories leads to the conclusion that Mark 8:1-10 is essentially
a traditional story taken by Mark from his *Vorlage* and placed
in the gospel with a minimum of modification. The evangelist
used this story as a model for the composition of 6:30-44,
developing and expanding it into the story we know as the
Feeding of the Five Thousand. Since the evangelist was so
centrally involved in the production of this pair of stories,
we will have to devote special attention to the possible
reasons for this compositional activity. Why would he want
to retell the old story and place his own, newer version first
in the gospel? The answer to this important question lies in the
common observation that there appears to be a conflict between

Jesus and his disciples in these stories. Especially perplexing
for generations of interpreters has been the apparent ignorance
of the disciples in Mark 8:4 of how one is to "feed these men
with bread here in the desert" after having witnessed and
participated in a similar feeding of five thousand men just
two chapters earlier. Such ignorance, commentators have
insisted, is "psychologically impossible,"[105] which confirms
the supposition that the feeding stories are variants of the
same story repeated by Mark. One of the usual elements of the
story, it is argued, is the element of the disciples'
unawareness of what Jesus is about to do, so when variants of
the story are repeated, the statement of their ignorance is also
repeated and they are accidentally made to look incredibly
obtuse. Such argumentation evaporates, however, when one
realizes that the evangelist is well aware of the portrayal of
the disciples implied by the inclusion of two feeding stories in
the gospel. One sees this plainly in 8:19-21 where Jesus
himself recollects for the disciples the two feeding incidents
which he observes they have failed to understand. The failure
of the disciples to comprehend the feedings is something the
author intentionally works into his story, not an illusion
created by the fortuitous preservation of variant accounts.
As if Mark 8:19-21 were insufficient evidence, we are now
making the additional claim that Mark has composed one of the
feeding stories himself, thus removing whatever doubt there
might have been about his bearing full responsibility for the
significance, both explicit and implicit, of the twin stories.

Methodology

In this study the feeding stories will be examined in two
stages. The first stage will be a redaction critical analysis
of the language of the stories in an attempt to distinguish
between Markan and non-Markan composition. The second stage may
be called literary critical. Here we will examine the narrative
function of the feeding stories in Mark 6-8 and in the gospel
as a whole. As we shall see, the first stage leads smoothly into
the second, as our perception of the editorial work of the
evangelist reveals to us the importance of being able to lay

aside the concern for tradition/redaction distinctions in order
to appreciate the gospel as an integral whole.

Of fundamental importance in our redaction critical study
is the body of knowledge now available concerning Mark's
vocabulary, grammar, compositional techniques, and thematic
concerns. These insights are scattered throughout the literature
on Mark; however, there are a number of studies, e.g., those of
Stein, Snoy, Donahue, and Annen, in which the references to
the literature have been conveniently collected.[106] In the
older literature, the observations concerning Mark's
characteristic vocabulary and literary style made by Hawkins,
and by the commentators Swete, Lagrange, and Taylor, are still
quite valuable.[107] In addition, there have been significant
articles and monographs devoted solely to the Markan language
and style by Turner, Dobschütz, Zerwick, Bird, Kilpatrick, and
Doudna.[108] Among the remaining articles, monographs, and
commentaries which contain valuable insights into the language
and style of Mark we may point to the works of Schweizer,
Best, Rigaux, Lambrecht, Van Cangh, Neirynck, Kelber, and Kee
as especially helpful.[109] This listing is, of course, far
from exhaustive, but it provides a solid basis with which to
begin our work.

As we conduct our redaction critical study of the feeding
stories, we will encounter some of the same phenomena that
literary critics have dealt with in their study of non-
biblical literature. At the appropriate time we will refer to
their work for insights that might be applicable to our texts,
but not having seen yet where our own work will lead it would
be premature to allude to the work of these critics now. For
now it is sufficient to indicate in a more general way the
implications of a literary critical approach to the gospel of
Mark.[110]

In shifting from the familiar methodology of
Redaktionsgeschichte to a more general literary critical
approach to the text, one may be said to be simply adopting a
new vocabulary with which to discuss the text, to be sure a
vocabulary which embodies an attitude toward the text still

somewhat unfamiliar to contemporary biblical scholarship, which has become accustomed to the categories of historical criticism. For the most part this new vocabulary substitutes broader, more generic terms for the narrow, specific terms so commonly used in gospel studies. The problem with the customary vocabulary is its restrictive nature. By adopting this vocabulary, one commits oneself to the narrowly defined cluster of concepts implied by the familiar terms evangelist, gospel, theology, and community. Exchanging these specific and rather prejudicial terms for more generic ones may allow us to see the old text with new eyes.

First, we will speak of Mark as an *author* and not simply as an evangelist or redactor: the term author has neither the inherent theological flavor of the former nor the latter's connotation of mechanical, unimaginative copying and editing. Moreover it gives proper recognition to the person who created the gospel, the person who, regardless of the sources he might have used, bears the full burden of responsibility for the shape and structure of the final product.

Second, we may begin to speak of the gospel more generally as a *literary work*. This does not mean that it is a noble literary achievement when measured by a particular standard of literary aesthetics. We are merely saying that it is a piece of literature, in the sense that it is an intentional and finished construct, a story with plot, characters, complication, and denouement. As a piece of literature, the gospel has an integrity, a certain wholeness to it which should be acknowledged by those who interpret it. It is a fatal error to move from the standard axiom that the gospel tradition originally circulated as individual sayings and stories to the conclusion that the gospels are simply collected masses of individual pieces with no great coherence. The whole is more than the sum of its parts. The gospels do in fact display unity and coherence, but that can only be seen if one entertains the possibility of a holistic approach to them and avoids an overly fragmented, pericope-by-pericope reading of the texts. Only by approaching the gospels as literary works, i.e., as integral wholes, can we see how all the individual pieces fit together to make the whole.[111]

Third, we will seek the author's *meaning* or *message* before
beginning to concern ourselves with his theology. The meaning
of the text may indeed be heavily theological, but that is a
judgment that can fairly be made only after the total
configuration of the author's intended meaning is perceived.
If one decides before approaching the text that the discovery
of the theology of the writer is the goal to be obtained, then
theology is probably what one will find, whether it is there
or not. The temptation is to mold the evidence to fit one's
expectations: major and minor theological statements alike are
elevated to the heights of theological sublimity; profound
theological significance is found in the most trivial, non-
theological affirmations; all the while the elements of the
text which resist all efforts to be interpreted theologically
are purposely ignored because they are irrelevant to the matter
at hand. On the contrary, we must allow the author the freedom
to say what he wishes in the way he chooses; the imposition
of our own concerns upon his text is not improper in itself,
but we should at least be aware of what we are doing and wait
to do it until the author has had his chance to speak.

Finally, we will find it advantageous to speak of the
author's *readers* or his *audience* rather than referring constantly
to the unknown Christian community to which many believe the
gospel was first addressed. As in the above examples, the
broader term is preferable, for we do not in fact know who
the first readers of the gospel were, nor do we know who the
author was, when he wrote, or what the circumstances were. Even
if the first readers were Christians, it is impossible to tell
how familiar they were with the Jewish Scriptures, the stories
told about Jesus, the traditions of the Church concerning
community life and worship, or the establishment of the
leadership in the Church. Quite often the knowledge that a
scholar attributes to the first readers of Mark bears a
striking resemblance to the knowledge of Christian tradition
possessed by that scholar himself, a scholar who has before
him in his study a copy of the Septuagint, the corpus of the

Pauline letters, and the standard works of *Formgeschichte*.
It is a most instructive and valuable exercise, as we shall
see later, to attempt to read the gospel as one who knows
nothing of Christian tradition and history would read it.
In such a reading one is utterly dependent upon the
author to lead one every step of the way through the text.
This approach at first seems banal, but it is surprisingly
fruitful. When one begins to pay special attention to how
the author guides his reader through the text, how he drops
hints about the true nature of his characters, or how he
inserts his own subtle commentary on the turn of events, one
begins to perceive the stratagems devised by the author to
persuade, cajole, or dupe the reader. One begins to understand
how the author gets a reader to see in the story what he wants
him to see there. Such stratagems are not beyond the skill
of Mark, as one can see if one reads with the intent of being
self-conscious about how one reads. Of all the facets of
literary criticism implied by the terms author, literary work,
meaning, and reader, it will be attention to the role of the
reader of Mark that we will find most productive in this
study.

CHAPTER II

THE FEEDING OF THE FOUR THOUSAND AND THE

FEEDING OF THE FIVE THOUSAND

We will commence our analysis of the language of the two
feeding stories with an examination of the second story in Mark,
the Feeding of the Four Thousand (Mark 8:1-10). This is simply
a matter of expediency; our reasons for analyzing the stories
in reverse order will become more apparent as we proceed.
Nevertheless, it should be made clear that it is extremely
important, as we have noted, not to assume a priori that one
story is older than the other.[1] Even so, if we should discover
that one of the two stories is the antecedent of the other and
that the later story is dependent upon the earlier narrative,
then we must make use of that knowledge. It so happens that our
analysis of the feeding stories reveals that the Feeding of the
Four Thousand is indeed the earlier of the two stories and that
the Feeding of the Five Thousand is dependent upon it. The
demonstration and discussion of the evidence leading to this
conclusion will progress most smoothly if we are allowed to
begin with the narrative that our studies have revealed to be
the older narrative.[2]

Markan Redaction in Mark 8:1-10

Before embarking on our examination of the language of
8:1-10 we should make a few remarks on Markan and non-Markan
characteristics. The primary principle used to determine whether
a word or phrase is characteristic of Mark is its frequency
in the gospel. A word or phrase appearing frequently in a
variety of locations in the gospel has a good claim to be a
characteristic feature of the gospel and hence of its author's
literary style. On the other hand, a word or phrase that is
extremely rare or unusual in the gospel may well be a feature
preserved from a pre-Markan source. A judgment regarding the
frequency of a word or phrase in Mark is often a judgment of
its relative frequency in comparison with Matthew and Luke.
It has long been known that there are certain common expressions
and syntactical constructions in Mark that are regularly modified by Matthew and Luke. The redaction critic who wants to
examine a text for Markan characteristics has available an

43

abundance of literature in which the standard traits of Mark modified by Matthew and Luke are catalogued.[4] Although many of these observations were originally made in the midst of the debate over the interrelationship of the synoptic gospels, they prove to be valuable and effective tools in the effort to uncover the locations in the gospel where the author's composition is most prominent. Fortunately, there is wide scholarly agreement over the characteristics of Mark's composition; one finds little disharmony in the literature over what features should be labeled Markan.

When looking for typically Markan characteristics, we not only look for language that appears more frequently in Mark than in Matthew or Luke, but we also look for recurring words and phrases specifically in the places where we can safely expect to find signs of the redactor's hand: seams, insertions, and summaries. If the study of these redactional junctures reveals a recurrent vocabulary or phraseology, then we have good reason to add these features to the list of Markan characteristics. Furthermore, words and phrases that are commonly used to express well-known Markan themes, such as the Messianic Secret or the misunderstanding of the disciples, also have a strong claim to be distinctively Markan features. More important than each of these individual criteria, however, is the fact that in actual practice these phenomena tend to coalesce and reinforce one another--words occurring frequently in Mark often occur most frequently in seams, insertions, and summaries, which in turn is exactly where Mark often imposes his thematic concerns upon the material. When we discover an impressive convergence or conjunction of Markan characteristics we are reassured that we are indeed in touch with the author's composition.

A similar situation exists with regard to language that is uncharacteristic of Mark, either because it is rare or because it is unusual. Words and phrases that occur rarely in the gospel are almost uncharacteristic by definition. Most striking, of course, are the occurrences of *hapax legomena*, words that appear only once in a work. The *hapax legomena* in Mark may often originate from Mark's sources, but this is not always so,

because many are simply required by the context in which they
appear and are probably chosen by the author himself. Perhaps
more interesting than rare words and phrases are those that
are unusual as well as rare. We may define an unusual word or
expression as one that is not only rare but also one for which
an alternative word or expression exists that is greatly
preferred by the author. For example, the verb ἐρωτάω appears
only three times in Mark while the compound verb ἐπερωτάω
appears twenty-five times. The former verb is both rare and
unusual in Mark--the author clearly prefers the compounded
form of the verb. Just as in the case of Markan characteristics,
here too we emphasize that isolated instances of non-Markan
language should not be given undue attention. However, if there
is a conjunction in a particular passage of several traits
that are rare or unusual, then one may have the basis for a
claim that this material was derived by the evangelist from
his *Vorlage*. When surveying either Markan or non-Markan
characteristics we seek not scattered, isolated instances but an
unmistakable convergence of evidence.

The body of knowledge now available regarding the Markan
literary style may be put to good use in an attempt to
distinguish Markan redaction from pre-Markan tradition in the
feeding stories. When beginning such an attempt we do well to
recognize the extreme difficulty of such an undertaking.
Redaction criticism is far easier to use in the case of Matthew
and Luke where the interpreter actually possesses at least part
of their *Vorlage*: the gospel of Mark. The scholarly penchant
for the hypothetical pre-Markan story cycles examined in
Chapter 1 is a symptom of the yearning to have available the
materials with which Mark worked, just as we possess, or can
reconstruct in the case of Q, some of the material used by
Matthew and Luke to compose their gospels. Unfortunately,
these pre-Markan sources often turn out to be mirages,
disappearing when one examines them more closely. The more
successful redaction critical work on Mark is far more modest
in the scope of its activity, often limiting its attention to
the "seams, insertions, and summaries" of Mark,[5] those components
of the gospel universally acknowledged to be the work of the

evangelist. Of course, the signs of Markan composition--his
favorite vocabulary, syntactical tendencies, compositional
techniques, and recurring themes--are not restricted to
seams, insertions, and summaries. They are found scattered
in greater or lesser concentration throughout the gospel, a
sign that the author did not reproduce his sources without
modification but rewrote his sources considerably. This
point has been stated forcefully by Stein, Van Cangh, and
Annen:

> Mark has made our task more complicated, however,
> because he has "markanized" the traditions, both oral
> and written, which were available to him. He has done this
> by retelling the traditions in his own words and in his
> own style.

> Il est évident, in effet, que le donné traditionnel tout
> entier a été retravaillé par Marc et porte l'empreinte
> de son style propre.

> Die Untersuchung der Formulierung allein ist deswegen
> nicht genügend, weil Mk auch übernommene Traditionen
> z.T. umformuliert hat, und weil andererseits sogenannte
> mk Züge sehr wohl z.T. Charakteristiken schon seiner
> Quellen sein könnten.[6]

Since Mark has largely rewritten his sources, the task of
separating tradition and redaction is more accurately perceived
as an effort to distinguish those sections of the gospel that
have been lightly reworked from those that have been heavily
rewritten or even created *in toto* by the author. There is no
consistently sharp polarity between tradition and redaction in
the gospel--all one can do is to weigh the evidence and hope
that a concentration of characteristics emerges that strongly
suggests either the Markan or non-Markan origin of the material.
In many cases, no doubt, the text will contain so rich a mixture
of Markan and non-Markan language that any distinction between
tradition and redaction will be impossible.

Annen perceives the problem clearly when he observes that
some portions of the 'tradition' are actually Mark's retelling
of the tradition, and that some of Mark's 'characteristic'
language may have also been characteristic in parts of the
tradition. Perhaps the best example of the latter is the use
of καί parataxis in Mark, a nearly ubiquitous feature of the
gospel that is certainly one of Mark's outstanding traits but

one which in many cases could easily have been present in pre-
Markan tradition influenced by a Semitic environment. Καὶ
parataxis is so common in both tradition and redaction that it
carries little weight as an indicator of Markan composition.
As Annen has observed:

> Für die Unterscheidung von Tradition und Redaktion wirft
> diese Vorliebe für καί allerdings wenig ab. Denn diese
> Eigenart prägt das ganze Evangelium, traditionelle und
> redaktionelle Texte. Es könnte sehr wohl sein, dass
> schon die Vorlage des Mk in dieser Weise erzählte;
> es handelt sich dabei wohl um semitischen Spracheinfluss.[7]

In the analysis of Mark 8:1-10 the observation of καί parataxis
is of little help in the search for Markan redaction: the
portion of the pericope containing the fewest signs of Markan
redaction (vv. 3-10) contains at least one instance of καί
parataxis in every verse, while the verses which show the most
prominent signs of Markan composition (vv. 1-2) contain not a
single καί. Furthermore, since καί parataxis is equally prominent
in both feeding stories, a far more interesting question in the
comparison of the two stories is Mark's use of δέ; with all the
discussion of καί parataxis in the literature it is easy to
overlook Mark's judicious use of this connecting particle.[8]

Mark 8:1-2

As we intimated above, Markan redaction is most obvious
within the Feeding of the Four Thousand in the two introductory
verses. One of the most striking features of these verses is
the occurrence of a Markan compositional technique that has
been called the Markan insertion technique by John R. Donahue.[9]
The insertion technique is essentially the use of what at first
appears to be the redundant or tautological repetition of
phrases to frame material inserted between the repeated elements.
Donahue proposes three criteria to describe this common feature
of the gospel: "(a) the second repeated phrase is superfluous--
it could be omitted without harming the sense of the passage
in which it is found, (b) the verbal correspondence is exact
or very close, and (c) the other synoptic writers change the
tautology."[10] As one might gather from the name "insertion
technique," Donahue claims that the material inserted between
the repeated elements is often of major significance, frequently

dealing with major Markan themes: "A general survey of the
inserted material indicates that it contains much material
which is very important to the major themes of Mark's gospel:
the *exousia* of the Son of Man . . . , the role of the
disciples and their reaction to Jesus' activity . . . , the
suffering and death of Jesus . . ."[11]

The observation of this technique is an important
contribution to the discussion of the characteristics of Mark's
composition, but it must be reconsidered in the light of the
more exhaustive study of such repetitive devices in Mark by
Frans Neirynck.[12] In the light of Neirynck's study, we
recognize that Donahue has pointed to a particular subcategory
of the familiar Markan double-step expression, as Neirynck
calls it. Donahue is especially concerned to find pairs of
phrases with close to verbatim repetition, which we clearly
have in 8:1-2:

8:1 μὴ ἐχόντων τί φάγωσιν

8:2 οὐκ ἔχουσιν τί φάγωσιν.

Neirynck recognizes, though, that this is one of many instances
in Mark where the repetition involves a shift from the indirect,
narrative mode to the direct, discourse mode, or vice versa.[13]
Hence the repetition is not really a redundancy which can be
treated lightly, as Donahue seems to imply by his use of the
terms "superfluous" and "tautology," because the reader is
actually receiving information from two different sources:
the narrator and a character in the story. The fact that one
source repeats the information provided by the other is no
small matter. If a character in the story repeats something
already stated by the narrator, then the narrator is confirmed
as a reliable source of knowledge for the reader--the reader can
trust what he says. Similarly, if a character in the story makes
a pronouncement which has an immediate result or reaction
described in the same language by the narrator, then the reader's
respect for the character is heightened--the reader knows that
he or she is a character whose words bring immediate action or
response. In 8:1 the stage setting is provided by the narrator:
"In those days, when again a great crowd had gathered, and

they had nothing to eat, he called his disciples to him, and
said to them . . ." Then in 8:2 Jesus speaks, indicating in
direct speech his awareness of the situation described by the
narrator in v.1: "*They have nothing to eat* . . ." It is our
claim that this use of repeated phrases, especially with a
shift from the narrative mode to the discourse mode, is a
clear indication that the evangelist has composed the
introduction to this story.

Confirming this judgment are other indications of Markan
composition in 8:1-2. Εν ἐκείναις ταῖς ἡμέραις is not
mentioned in the literature as a strikingly Markan phrase, but
we should note that it occurs elsewhere in Mark in 1:9 and
13:17,24. The beginning of the pericope also contains a
definite Markan sylistic characteristic in the use of the
genitive absolute. Mark is especially fond of using the
genitive absolute to begin sentences, a practice that is a
Hellenistic departure from classical Greek.[14] Indeed, the
author uses a double genitive absolute: πολλοῦ ὄχλου ὄντος
καὶ μὴ ἐχόντων τί φάγωσιν, with αὐτῶν understood in the latter
phrase.[15] Πάλιν appears frequently in Mark and usually in an
iterative sense, as it does here.[16] It signals the beginning
of an episode that repeats something that has occurred
previously in the gospel; in this case it recalls for the
reader the earlier feeding episode. The characterization of
the crowd as an ὄχλος πολύς is common in Mark; the crowd that
habitually gathers around Jesus is an important feature of
many of the stories in the gospel. The presence of the crowd
in 8:1 recalls a similar gathering of ὄχλος πολύς in 6:34,
one of the introductory verses in the earlier feeding episode
and one which is itself generally regarded as a Markan creation.[17]
The repeated phrases about the crowd having nothing to eat both
use the verb ἔχω, a verb which C. H. Turner claims is used by
Mark with unusual frequency in places where one would expect
to find the verb εἶναι with the dative.[18] Also in 8:1 one
finds προσκαλέομαι, which has been recognized as a verb from
Mark's preferred vocabulary.[19] Another prominent characteristic
of the Markan style appears in 8:1-2: the historical present;

i.e., the use of the present tense in the midst of narrative
where one would often expect to encounter the aorist indicative.
In 8:1 the historical present (λέγει) is used to introduce the
statement of Jesus to his disciples in vv. 2-3. The use of
λέγω in introductory phrases--either in the present or imperfect
tense--is itself especially characteristic of Mark.[20] Also to
be noted is the observation of J. C. Doudna that the use of
ἐπί and the accusative with σπλαγχνίζομαι is singularly Markan;
customary Greek usage would lead one to expect the use of περί
and the genitive. Interestingly, this usage is found in both
8:2 and its corresponding verse in the first feeding story,
6:34, from which Doudna infers that both verses should be
credited to Mark's account.[21] Finally, we note the use of
ἤδη (v.2) with a time reference, a usage which occurs several
times in Mark.[22] All of this is to say that the familiar traits
of Markan composition are unmistakable in 8:1-2--we have every
reason to conclude that the evangelist has composed these verses
as an introduction to the story that follows, and as we proceed
in this study we will see this conclusion confirmed and reinforced by additional insights.

Our claim that the evangelist has composed 8:1-2 as the
introduction to this story should not be taken as a claim that
the story was without a recognizable introduction before Mark
endowed it with one. Surely the evangelist has rewritten the
original introduction which no doubt also had set the stage for
the following story by referring to the hunger of the crowd.
So the mention of hunger is probably pre-Markan while the
manner in which it is now expressed (with repeated phrases)
is most certainly Markan. Once we move past v.2 the prominent
Markan phraseology suddenly gives way and we encounter the
traditional story substantially as Mark found it in his
Vorlage. We know this because now we begin to find numerous
examples of language uncharacteristic of the evangelist that he
has allowed to remain in the story, not bothering to retell the
entire story in his own words. Clearly the evangelist has
rewritten the introduction with no small amount of skill,
ceasing his thorough rewriting of the introduction in the middle

of Jesus' speech in vv. 2-3 without being conspicuous about it--
the Markan introduction flows smoothly, without a break, into
the pre-Markan story.

Mark 8:10

Just as Markan composition is evident in the introductory
verses of the Feeding of the Four Thousand, it is also present
in its concluding verse. In 8:10, after dismissing the crowd,
Jesus embarks in the boat with his disciples and proceeds to
the region of Dalmanutha (location unknown). Then a short,
two-verse confrontation with the Pharisees occurs, after which
he journeys in the boat again "to the other side" (v. 13).
In order to perceive fully the redactional nature of 8:10 it is
necessary to recognize that the author uses the two references
to a boat voyage (vv. 10 and 13) as the frame for the encounter
with the Pharisees, while at the same time setting the stage
for the discourse in 8:14-21 which takes place in the boat
(v. 14b). Traveling to and fro in the boat is a frequent motif
in Mark 4-8; we will argue in greater detail below that all such
uses of the boat motif in the gospel are the work of the
evangelist.[23] Only two stories in Mark, the Stilling of the
Storm (4:35-41) and the Walking on the Water (6:45-52), actually
involve a boat in the course of their telling. In all other
cases the boat serves merely to transport the characters of
the story from one scene to another. In other words, most of
the references to the boat appear in the seams between stories,
precisely where redaction critics expect to find the signs of
the author's hand.

As we will see later, the boat journeys in Mark are
always conducted in two steps, an initial withdrawal in the
boat followed later by a return trip,[24] but there is absolutely
no indication that the travelers end up after each journey
exactly where they started. In fact, geographical imprecision
is one of the dominant features of these boat journeys: they
are replete with vague references to "the other side" (εἰς
τὸ πέραν) and numerous problematic place names (e.g., "the
district of Dalmanutha"). Nevertheless, the general outline of
each boat trip is always clearly discernible, making it quite

easy for the reader to follow the progress of each voyage.
In particular, it is always clear where the second leg of
each boat trip begins, but it is especially so in 8:13 where
the Markan iterative πάλιν[25] signals to the reader that an
action is about to be repeated a second time, namely a
departure in the boat for a 'return trip.' The language of
this two-part boat trip is the same as that found in the other
boat excursions in the gospel. In both parts of the trip the
travelers embark (ἐμβαίνω) in the boat (εἰς τὸ πλοῖον)[26] and
go (cognate of ἔρχομαι in the aorist) to (εἰς) a particular
locale, often simply to the other side of the lake (εἰς τὸ
πέραν). Besides the recurring language of the boat journeys,
one finds other signs of Markan composition in 8:10,13: the
familiar Markan εὐθύς[27] in v. 10 and the previously mentioned
use of πάλιν in v. 13.

The observation of the Markan composition of 8:10,13[28]
coheres very well with the careful and persuasive argument
by Snoy that the encounter with the Pharisees (8:11-12) was
itself composed by Mark, although the evangelist has made use
of a logion attributed to Jesus in 8:12 (cf. Matt. 12:39, 16:4;
Luke 11:29).[29] Snoy finds no reason to doubt that v. 12 is
derived from the tradition of the sayings of Jesus that was
available to Mark, but an examination of the language of 8:11-12
reveals that the wording of the narrative framework of the
logion and indeed the wording of the logion itself is typical
of the Markan literary style. When Snoy's conclusion is added
to our own conclusion that the two-part boat trip in 8:10, 13
is Markan, then we realize that 8:10-13 has been constructed by
the evangelist as an interlude between the feeding story in
8:1-9 and the major discourse on the leaven of the Pharisees
and Herod that follows in 8:14-21. Having reworked the traditional
logion of Jesus in 8:12, Mark uses it as the heart of this
little section (8:10-13).

In a similar fashion, the saying of Jesus in 8:15 lies
at the heart of 8:14-21, initiating and provoking the exchange
between Jesus and his disciples regarding leaven and bread. Here,
though, the one saying by Jesus leads into a string of sayings,
each a devastating rebuke aimed at the disciples (8:17-21). It

is almost universally agreed that 8:14-21 is a Markan
composition,[30] and discussions of this pericope often focus
on the function of the logion in the narrative. Many have
suggested that v. 15 is an insertion into the discourse--they
claim it awkwardly interrupts the flow of the narrative, and
its elimination only improves the sense of the text. However,
one can retain v. 15 as an original part of the passage and
still make excellent sense of the text, as we shall see later.
Furthermore, 8:15 bears the marks of the evangelist's
compositional style in a fashion similar to 8:12; both logia
are phrased in a particularly Markan manner. For now it is
sufficient to know that Mark has constructed both of these
pericopes (8:10-13 and 8:14-21) around a logion of Jesus which
has been rendered in a particularly Markan manner. With its
focus on misunderstanding leaven and loaves, 8:14-21 is
especially important as a recapitulation of chapters 6-8. In
particular, it is difficult to over-emphasize the importance
of 8:19-20 where Jesus recalls for the disciples, and at the
same time for the reader, the two feeding episodes in chapters
6 and 8. The narrator of the story skillfully places on the
lips of Jesus an interpretive clue for the reader: one is to
'recall' the feeding stories as *Zwillingsgeschichten*: twin
stories.

Mark 8:7

Having demonstrated the Markan composition of the
introduction and conclusion of the Feeding of the Four
Thousand, it remains for us to discuss one verse that appears
to have been interjected by Mark into the midst of the story
he found in his *Vorlage*. This interjection is 8:7, a clumsy
reference to the distribution of fish to the crowd. In one
short verse the fish are introduced, blessed, distributed, and
forgotten. Many commentators have noted the awkward way this
verse interrupts the flow of the story. It is the only
reference to fish in the whole story, quite unlike the
scattered references to fish in the earlier feeding story where
fish are mentioned in 6:38, 41 (twice), 43. It seems obvious

that someone has added this verse solely to harmonize this
story with the other story in which the fish have such a
prominent place.[31] If we could find indications of Markan
composition in 8:7 we would have good reason to argue that the
evangelist himself interjected this verse into the story. Such
indications of the author's hand are in fact present in 8:7, as
Van Cangh has observed. In v. 7 Van Cangh points out the
Markan fondness for diminutives (ἰχθύδια) and the use of εἶπεν
followed by an infinitive with the sense of "to command."[32]
We may add to these two features the Markan proclivity for the
use of ἔχω where one might expect to find εἶναι with the dative.[33]
The conjunction of these Markan traits in v. 7 justifies the claim
that the awkward insertion of this verse was conducted by the
evangelist himself, probably with the aim of harmonizing this
story with the earlier feeding story. Consequently, we may
attribute 8:7 to Markan redaction along with the other
redactional elements found at the beginning and end of the
Feeding of the Four Thousand.

Tradition in Mark 8:1-10

The observation of numerous characteristics of Markan
composition in 8:1-2, 7, 10 is sharply contrasted by the
discovery of numerous instances of language uncharacteristic
of Mark in the remaining verses of the story. Especially
noteworthy are the numerous *hapax legomena* in these verses,
as commentators have often observed. Also to be noted, however,
are other words or phrases which are very nearly *hapax legomena*,
occurring with great infrequency in the gospel. In short, we
are quite fortunate to have in the Feeding of the Four
Thousand a story in which Markan and non-Markan characteristics
are easily predominant within their respective boundaries,
enabling us to perceive clearly the outlines of the preserved
portions of the traditional story, the redactional introduction
and conclusion, and the one inserted verse.

The *hapax legomena* in Mark 8:1-10 are often noted:
προσμένω (v. 2); νῆστις, ἐκλύομαι, ἥκω (v. 3); ἐρημία (v. 4);
ἰχθύδια (v. 7); περίσσευμα (v. 8); μέρος, Δαλμανουθά (v. 10).[34]

Several of these occur in verses that we have claimed are
redactional, but these instances are easily explained. Mark
8:1-2 is thoroughly Markan, as we have maintained, but
the *hapax* προσμένω in 8:2 may be a vestige of the original
story--it may well have been present in the introduction of
the story as the author found it in his *Vorlage* and may have
been preserved when he composed his own introduction to the
story. The use of the *hapax* ἰχθύδια in 8:7 is not surprising
since Mark is fond of diminutives.[35] Finally, the fact that any
one geographical locale (τὰ μέρη Δαλμανουθά) appears only once
in the gospel is not at all surprising. This reference to
Dalmanutha, though, is particularly interesting since no one in
antiquity or modernity has been able to locate this town or
region.[36] This reference may have been a part of the traditional
story preserved by Mark, but perhaps not. We do know that Mark
provides us with some especially difficult geographical
references in the verses where a boat trip is under way, and we
suspect that Mark's geographical problems are of his own making
and were not inherited by him from his forebears.[37] Hence these
hapax legomena in verses that are on other grounds clearly
redactional are easily understood as either vestiges of the
tradition which Mark is rewriting or as wholly characteristic
instances of the Markan style. Such is not the case with the
other *hapax legomena* in 8:1-10.

　　The other *hapax legomena* in 8:1-10 indicate that Mark has
utilized a fixed source and that he has allowed vocabulary and
phraseology that is uncharacteristic for him to remain in the
story. An important example of this phenomenon is the unusual
use of ἐρημία in 8:4. Elsewhere Mark always uses the form
ἔρημος, either as a substantive (1:3, 4, 12, 13) or an
adjective (1:35, 45; 6:31, 32, 35), and when he uses it as an
adjective it always modifies τόπος. Obviously the author uses
ἔρημος with strict consistency. Indeed, most of these verses
are redactional in origin, for the ἔρημος τόπος is an important
motif in Mark.[38] We note, for example, that the ἔρημος τόπος
is mentioned three times in the introductory verses of the
Feeding of the Five Thousand (6:31, 32, 35). This makes the

uncharacteristic use of ἐρημία in 8:4 all the more striking.
As with the other *hapax legomena* in 8:1-10, here Mark simply
does not bother to replace a word that he would not normally
use with another that is more to his liking. On the contrary,
the wording of the traditional story is allowed to stand.
This is true, of course, with all of the *hapax legomena*
derived from the source and preserved by the author, but it is
more striking in the case of ἐρημία since one is well aware
of the author's habitual preference for ἔρημος.

Besides the *hapax legomena*, there are other expressions
in 8:3-6, 8-9 which are unusual for Mark and which support
the thesis that a pre-Markan source is discernible in these
verses. When Mark uses ἀποκρίνομαι to introduce direct speech,
he almost always uses λέγω in conjunction with ἀποκρίνομαι
(seventeen times). Mark 8:4 is one of only three instances where
λέγω does not accompany ἀποκρίνομαι in the introduction of direct
speech in the usual Markan manner.[39] Mark 8:4 also contains
the only use in the gospel of χορτάζω in the active voice ("to
feed"). The other three occurrences of the verb are in the
passive voice with the sense of "to be satisfied" (6:42, 7:27,
8:8). Far more common in Mark is the use of ἐσθίω (twenty-seven
times). Usually when the author talks about "feeding" someone
he uses the latter verb.[40] If we may make a premature
comparison of the two feeding stories, we observe that the
triple use of ἐσθίω in 6:36-37 is far more typical of Mark
than the use of χορτάζω in 8:4. The author usually describes
providing food as "giving something to eat" (δίδωμι φαγεῖν),
as we see in 6:37 (twice) and in the earlier redactional verse
5:43. Furthermore, the redactional introductions to both feeding
stories also use ἐσθίω; the crowd either has "no leisure to
eat" (6:31) or they have "nothing to eat" (8:1, 2). Another
verb that is uncharacteristic of Mark occurs in 8:5: ἐρωτάω.
It is widely recognized that the evangelist greatly prefers the
compound verb ἐπερωτάω (twenty-five times) to ἐρωτάω (three
times; cf. 4:10, 7:26).[41] Finally, we must also point out the
use of σπυρίς, which occurs only in 8:8 and later in 8:20
where the feeding story is recollected for the disciples.

Therefore, we may add to the *hapax legomena* in 8:1-10 these additional instances where the language of the story is quite unusual, if not totally unique, for Mark. The accumulated mass of these observations provides weighty evidence for the non-Markan origin of 8:3-6, 8-9. Perhaps just as significant as the sheer plenitude of non-Markan expressions is the frequency of language for which a favorite Markan alternative is well known. The author has allowed these uncharacteristic phrases to remain in the text, even though he probably would have used different language if he had composed the original story himself.

The implication of these observations is not difficult to see. There is a clear division between those verses of the Feeding of the Four Thousand that bear the stamp of Markan redaction (8:1-2, 7, 10) and those that contain a preponderance of strikingly non-Markan characteristics (8:3-6, 8-9).[42] Although it is often quite difficult to distinguish redaction from tradition in Mark, in this case a sharp distinction can be made. Apparently the author found this story in his *Vorlage* and incorporated it into his own composition. He rewrote it only slightly, concentrating his attention on the introduction, conclusion, and one brief interjection. While retelling the story he may have endowed it with a few of his own stylistic traits, but he preserves so many features of the *Vorlage* that he betrays the true origin of the story. At the heart of the narrative the numerous *hapax legomena* and other unusual expressions predominate, demonstrating the non-Markan origin of the story. Typically Markan characteristics are similarly predominant in those verses composed by the author. As we examine the language of the other feeding story it will prove helpful to have available this simple bit of knowledge: Mark inherited at least one feeding story from his sources, edited it slightly, and made a place for it in his gospel.

Excursus: The Boat Motif in Mark

In our discussion of pre-Markan cycles in Chapter 1, we were introduced to the important boat motif in Mark--between the various episodes in Mark 3-8 Jesus and his disciples are continually traveling in the boat on the Sea of Galilee. As we

saw, interpreters who maintain that a pre-Markan cycle(s) of
stories underlies the present text of Mark 3-8 invariably
argue that the references to boat trips linking these stories
together are the original pre-Markan connections between these
stories. The most vocal advocates of this claim among those
whose work we discussed are probably Keck and Pesch. They both
assert that the boat motif is a traditional connecting device
in Mark 3-6, but they both admit that the use of the boat motif
in Mark 8 is probably the evangelist's own work. As we pointed
out, neither exegete gives an adequate explanation of how he
is able to distinguish between a traditional use of the boat
motif and a similar Markan use of the same motif. If Mark
introduced some of the instances of the boat motif, what is to
say that he did not introduce all of them?

There have been other attempts to offer a systematic
explanation of the boat trips in Mark. Werner Kelber (*The
Kingdom in Mark*), for example, devotes special attention to
the explicit references to a lake crossing using the phrase
εἰς τὸ πέραν or the verb διαπεράω. [43] In so doing, he takes
pains to observe how the author uses the boat trips to
establish the setting for individual episodes. He claims
that if a boat voyage takes one to the eastern shore then one
may expect the following episode to involve Gentiles; if it
takes one to the western shore one can expect to encounter a
Jewish milieu and Jewish characters. [44] We agree with Kelber
that explicit references to crossing the lake are featured
prominently in the boat trips and that Jesus does encounter
both Jew and Greek in his travels, but we cannot agree that
these elements constitute the major motivation behind the use
of the boat motif. For the most part, such information plays
only an incidental role in the boat trips. Mark actually has
very little concern for the kind of geographical exactitude
that Kelber sees in the boat trips; when scrutinized, the
geographical references associated with the boat trips are either
vague, inaccurate, or contradictory.

Kelber begins his exposition by correctly observing that
there are six boat voyages in Mark. [45] Actually, we would prefer

to say that there are three voyages, each consisting of two
parts:

Boat Trip I	A.	4:1-2, 35-36	--Departure
		5:1-2	--Arrival
	B.	5:18, 21	--Departure
		5:21	--Arrival
Boat Trip II	A.	6:32-33	--Departure
		6:34-35	--Arrival
	B.	6:45-47	--Departure
		6:53-55	--Arrival
Boat Trip III	A.	8:9-10	--Departure
		8:9-10	--Arrival
	B.	8:13-14	--Departure
		8:22	--Arrival

Kelber puts heavy emphasis on the use of the terms εἰς τὸ
πέραν and διαπερἀω to "introduce the all-important crossing
motif."[46] Much to his credit, he avoids the common error of
interpreting πέραν to mean the east side of the lake on the
basis of an analogy to the phrase πέραν τοῦ Ἰορδἀνου (3:8).
In Mark, the phrase εἰς τὸ πέραν simply means "to the other
side."[47]

A slight confusion arises when Kelber refers to both a
"voyage motif" and a "crossing motif," two terms which he
apparently does not use synonymously. The former simply refers
to the use of boat voyages to link episodes together; the
use of the latter expression arises when Kelber argues that a
boat voyage is a full-fledged lake crossing only when
πέραν/διαπερἀω is used to describe it. If πέραν/διαπερἀω is not
used, then the voyage is merely a short excursion along one of
the shorelines. Such is the case with the boat voyages in
6:32-33, 34-35, and 8:9-10--πέραν/διαπερἀω is not used in either
so they are *not* lake crossings. The conclusion Kelber draws
from this voyage/crossing distinction is that Mark does not
always need the boat to cross the lake in order to establish
the setting for the next story. Sometimes the setting of the
next story requires him to keep the boat on the same side of
the lake, so he only has the boat move a short distance down the
shoreline. For our part, we would draw a different conclusion
from the same observations. The fact that two of the six voyages
do not mention a crossing indicates, we believe, that the
author is not really concerned with a crossing motif at all.

If anything, he is concerned only with a voyage motif and that
only as a means of shifting the setting between stories. The
voyage motif, as Kelber calls it, serves the author as a simple
means of moving from one episode to the next. Saying that the
boat went "to the other side" is simply a vague, nondescript
expression used to shift the stage scenery; the expression
has no profound significance in itself. Many of the stories
in Mark 4-8 do appear to have a particularly Gentile (e.g., the
Gerasene demoniac in 5:1-20) or Jewish (e.g., the healing and
resuscitation in 5:21-43) setting. However, Mark does not
seem to be overly concerned to link geographical locales with
ethnic groups. Besides, Mark never bothers to tell us explicitly
on what side of the Sea of Galilee events take place. Admittedly,
he does provide us with the names of several towns around the
lake, but these references are notoriously confused and
unreliable. Drawing inferences about the exact itinerary of the
boat trips is quite suspect, because exactness and accuracy is
simply not a concern of the author.

Two episodes that have been the focus of numerous attempts
to discover their exact geographical setting are, coincidentally,
the two feeding stories. Kelber follows what is actually a
variation of an ancient interpretation[48] by claiming that the
Feeding of the Five Thousand is a feeding of a Jewish crowd on
the western shore and that the Feeding of the Four Thousand is
a feeding of Gentiles on the eastern shore.[49] Unfortunately,
there is no evidence in the text itself to support this
widespread opinion. In neither story is there any mention of a
specific location near the Sea of Galilee--one is only told that
the setting is a lonely, desolate place (ἔρημος τόπος/ἐρημία).
In neither story is there a description of the language, culture,
or social status of the people who throng around Jesus--they are
merely a nondescript crowd (ὄχλος). There is no justification
for locating one story on the western shore and one on the
eastern shore, nor is there any justification for characterizing
one crowd as Jewish and the other as Gentile. Besides, such
considerations miss the central thrust of both stories, which is
neither the location on the lakeshore nor the ethnic origin of

the hungry crowd but the intense confrontation between Jesus
and his disciples. Sometimes exegetes argue that since the
disciples leave the scene of the first feeding in the boat
bound for Bethsaida, which is located on "the other side" of
the lake (6:45), this must imply that the feeding took place
across the lake from Bethsaida; i.e., on the western shore.
The fact that one must go to such lengths to infer the location
of the feeding incident proves our point conclusively--one
simply cannot tell by reading the feeding story itself where
the incident supposedly took place. Besides, what is one to do
when they land, not at Bethsaida on the eastern shore, but at
Gennesaret on the western shore (6:53)?

Kelber does not spend a great deal of time analyzing the
language of the boat voyages for the signs of Markan redaction;
he is more concerned to see how the boat motif functions in the
final literary composition, a legitimate and productive
endeavor. However, the claims of those who perceive pre-Markan
cycles behind the text of Mark 3-8 would seem to make analysis
of the language necessary. It is their contention that the
boat motif in these chapters was present at the pre-Markan
stage, although the evidence they offer to support this claim
is extremely scant. This paucity of critical examination of the
language of the boat trips is beginning to be remedied by the
recent appearance of some rigorous studies by Snoy and Annen.
After Annen's detailed analysis of the instances of the boat
motif in and around the story of the Gerasene demoniac (5:1-20),
he concludes that all such instances are the products of Markan
redaction. These include Mark 4:1, 35-36c, 5:1-2a, 18, 21, which
is virtually all of the framing material in Mark 4:1-5:21.[50]
Annen has therefore examined *Boat Trip I* on our chart above and
found it to be a Markan creation. *Boat Trip II* has been analyzed
by Snoy in his dissertation, the conclusions of which are
available in his published articles. After his rigorous
examination of the boat trips in Mark 6, Snoy concludes that the
references to the boat in 6:32, 45, 54 are all redactional.[51]
Most curiously, he argues for the traditional origin of 6:53,
claiming that here we have the original ending to the feeding

story. We will attempt to refute this claim later, because
we believe 6:53 is also redactional. For advocates of the
redactional composition of *Boat Trip III* we may turn to Keck
and Pesch, who, of course, deny the redactional origin of trips
I and II. Nevertheless, the language and content of all three
boat trips are utterly consistent, leaving one no choice but
to attribute their origin to a single author. *It is our thesis
that all instances of the boat motif in Mark were created by
the evangelist himself.* We will discuss the consistent, recurrent
language of the three boat trips after first providing a brief
description of these trips.

The boat is introduced into the narrative in the redactional
Sammelbericht in Mark 3:7-12. There the disciples procure a
boat for their master (3:9), but it is only put to use for the
first time in 4:1 where Jesus sits in the boat to address the
crowd. We should note here that the boat is used to set the
stage for a discourse of Jesus in its first and last appearances
in the gospel. The boat is first put to use as the floating
stage from which Jesus addresses the crowd in the parable
chapter; in its last appearance in Mark, it provides the setting
for a stinging censure leveled at the disciples (8:14-21). All
other occurrences of the boat motif in Mark lie between these
two discourses. The first boat trip in Mark gets under way in
4:35-36, where it is stated that they took leave of the crowd
and rowed off with Jesus, who was already in the boat. The
author here has chosen to ignore that he has already had Jesus
and the disciples withdraw from the crowd in 4:10. At that
point Jesus provided his disciples with private instruction,
a favorite motif in Mark. Consequently, we find the privacy
motif (4:10) in direct conflict with the boat motif (4:1-2,
35-36), the privacy motif dictating an internal organization
of the chapter which contradicts the external framework
constructed around the boat motif. Be that as it may, the
first trip begins in 4:35-36, and the first half of the trip
is completed in 5:1-2. After the exorcism of the Gerasene
demoniac, Jesus boards the boat for the second half of the
trip (what we might call the return trip)[52] in 5:18 and
actually makes the crossing in 5:21, thereby completing the

first boat trip. After a considerable interlude, the boat
reappears for the beginning of Boat Trip II in 6:32. There,
Jesus and the disciples journey to a desolate place which
provides the setting for the feeding incident. [53] After the
feeding, the second half of this boat trip begins with the
dismissal of the crowd, Jesus' retreat to the mountain, and
the disciples' departure in the boat (6:45-47). This boat
trip concludes in 6:53-55 where the disciples and Jesus, who
has since rejoined them, come to dock at Gennesaret. Here
again, the boat disappears from view for a period until it
reappears for the third and last trip immediately following the
Feeding of the Four Thousand. This time the boat trip is
reported quite succinctly. The first half of the trip is
narrated in its entirety in 8:9-10 and the narration of the
second half requires only 8:13-14, 22. With these verses the
boat motif vanishes from the gospel.

The boat motif is a vital element in the framework of Mark
4-8, especially with its intimate association with both
feeding stories, but it should be noted that our analysis
demonstrates that the boat motif does not frame both feeding
stories in the same manner. The first feeding story lies between
the two halves of the second boat trip, while the second
feeding story is concluded before the third boat trip even
commences. This observation contradicts the long-standing
scholarly maxim that "parallel boat trips" follow the two
feeding stories.

Having sketched the Markan use of the boat motif in Mark
4-8, we may now give a more detailed analysis of the language
of the boat trips (see Appendix 1):

1.   Five of the six sections in the three boat trips use
phrase ἐμβαίνω εἰς τὸ πλοῖον to describe the embarkation. The
one section which lacks this phrase (6:32-33, 34-35) simply
says that they went away in the boat (ἀπῆλθον ἐν τῷ πλοίῳ).
Without fail, the reader knows exactly when a boat voyage is
beginning.

2.   The disembarkation is narrated less often than the
embarkation, but when it is narrated the verb ἐξέρχομαι is
used, usually with the phrase ἐκ τοῦ πλοίου. Clearly the author

does not feel obliged to repeat every minute detail in every instance of a boat trip, but when a particular detail is described, the author is inclined to use consistent, familiar terminology to describe it.

3. Another recurrent feature of the boat trips is the gathering or dispersal of a crowd (ὄχλος). The crowd is often characterized as large (πολύς or πλεῖστος). They throng to see Jesus: once the crowd gathers and forces Jesus into the boat (4:1);[54] twice they gather around him after the completion of a boat trip (5:21, 6:53-55). Once they even gather while Jesus is still in the middle of a boat excursion out on the lake (6:33). Otherwise, instead of attracting a crowd, the boat trips often involve dismissing (ἀπολύω) or taking leave (ἀφίημι) of the crowd in order to begin the journey.

4. All sections of the boat trips except one employ a cognate of ἔρχομαι in the aorist to describe the voyage. The sole exception uses the verb διαπεράω in the genitive absolute, evocative of the Markan phrase εἰς τὸ πέραν. In four out of six instances the phrase ἐν τῷ πλοίῳ is also employed.

5. The author is always careful to designate a destination for each leg of the boat trips; sometimes the destination is described with two or three different phrases. Almost always the preposition εἰς is employed. We have already noted the problematic nature of most of these geographical references--they are often vague or confusing. The most common description of the destination is the frequent εἰς τὸ πέραν, which occurs five times in four voyages. The use of such vague, unspecified locales is a familiar Markan practice; one is always reading about going into "the house," going away to "the mountain," or traveling "on the way." Another indefinite geographical locale, the "lonely place," is the destination of the first leg of Boat Trip II (6:32). Even when a specific geographical location is named, the author has a tendency to detract from its specificity by speaking broadly of the entire region. For example, Jesus and his crew arrive not at Gerasa but in the less distinct "country of the Gerasenes" (5:1). Similarly, in 8:10 the boat proceeds not to Dalmanutha but to

the region thereof. Furthermore, the vagueness of these
references is only half of the matter. As a glance at the
commentaries or the critical apparatus of a Greek text will show,
the names Gerasa and Dalmanutha have given rise to many
conjectures and emendations. The problem with Gerasa is that
the town lay some thirty miles southeast of the lake. The
scribes copying the text did their best to change the name
to the name of a town lying closer to the lake, thereby making
a boat landing there a shade less incredible. Since the author
conveniently formulates the localization in Mark 5:1 in a
rather loose fashion ("the country of the Gerasenes"),
commentators have been able to propose that perhaps the citizens
of Gerasa governed a stretch of territory running down to the
Sea of Galilee.[55] This is an ingenious solution, but we
probably should simply admit that the author of this story
uses the name Gerasa without knowing where it is. The situation
with Dalmanutha is similar but not entirely the same, since the
town of Gerasa did exist, while no one in antiquity or in
modern times has been able to discover a town or region with
the name Dalmanutha. Various copyists, the first of which may
have been Matthew (Matt. 15:39), inserted a number of alternative
readings into the manuscript tradition, indicating their lack
of familiarity with the name. Only two conclusions seem
possible: either the author of Mark 8:10 knew something that no
one else knew, viz., the whereabouts of Dalmanutha, or else he
was as ignorant about its location as we are.[56]

One other major geographical problem occurs in the second
leg of the second boat trip. There the disciples embark in the
boat for a voyage to Bethsaida (6:45), Jesus joins them in the
middle of the lake, and they all come to port in Gennesaret
(6:53). Countless exegetes have attempted to explain why the
voyage originally destined for Bethsaida ends at Gennesaret
instead. Some advocate a naturalistic explanation: the boat
was simply blown off course in the storm and had to land
wherever it could. Others perceive the problem as a confusion
of traditions: the reference to Bethsaida was an element of the
traditional sea story, while the reference to Gennesaret was
derived from another piece of tradition,[57] so when the two

traditions are juxtaposed an apparent contradiction is created.
Our solution is far simpler: both references were composed by
the author of the gospel who has almost no concern for the
consistency of his geographical references. Indeed, consistent
geographical references may have been beyond his reach, since
he demonstrates little if any knowledge of the geography of
Palestine. If one adds to the geographical infelicities of the
boat trips such instances as the bizarre itinerary of Mark
7:31, then one has ample evidence of the dearth of familiarity
with and concern for precise, accurate geography in the gospel.

Looking back now, we see that if the author had exercised
just a little more care, no problem with the geography of 6:45
and 6:53 would ever have been noticed. Both verses contain the
now familiar double-step expression:

6:45 εἰς τὸ πέραν/πρὸς βηθσαϊδάν
6:53 ἐπὶ τὴν γῆν/εἰς Γεννησαρέτ.

The first phrase in either verse is sufficiently vague to
cause no problems. It is only when Mark tries to add concrete
detail, such as place names, that he gets into difficulty. If
he had used εἰς τὸ πέραν, ἐπὶ τὴν γῆν, and the name of only
one of the towns, all would have been well. Instead, he used
both names, which confuses the reader who happens to know and
care where Bethsaida and Gennesaret were located in the first
century C.E. Mark's use of the names of towns and cities
throughout the gospel lends a certain concreteness and
verisimilitude to the narrative, which may be the reason why
the author scatters such references among his otherwise vague
references. Although the place names sound more precise and
authentic than the indefinite allusions to "the other side,"
"a lonely place," "the house," and "the mountain," we are
forced to conclude that both the concrete place names and the
indefinite localizations are on a par with each other--all
function merely to provide artificial background scenery for the
episodes in the narrative.

6. In sections 1-5 of this excursus the major features of
the boat trips are discussed. These are the features found in
nearly every instance of the boat motif: embarking, disembarking,

the crowd, a cognate of ἔρχομαι in the aorist, and the destination. Sections 6-11 involve less prominent features of the boat trips, features that appear only two or three times in the six sections. One such feature is reference to the time of day during which the boat voyage takes place. Three times the time of day is mentioned; in each case it is late in the day.

7.   In two cases Jesus' teaching is featured prominently along with the boat motif. In 4:1-2 Jesus boards the boat in order to teach; in 6:34-35 he leaves the boat in order to teach. In both cases the familiar Markan use of ἄρχομαι as an auxiliary verb is present (ἤρξατο διδάσκειν), as well as the typically Markan use of the adverbial πολλά.[58] Of course, the teaching of Jesus is itself a recurrent, characteristic theme in the gospel.[59]

8.-9.   Since we are dealing with boat trips, one would expect to find some references to the body of water upon which the voyages take place. Mark is especially fond of calling Lake Gennesaret (Luke 5:1) or Lake Tiberius (John 6:1, 21:1) a "sea" (θάλασσα), terminology which Luke takes particular pains to avoid. Far more interesting than individual references to the sea, however, are the two occasions when a special effort is made to contrast the people on land (ἐπὶ τῆς γῆς) with those in the boat on the sea (ἐν τῆς θαλάσσης). On the first occasion, Jesus sits (alone) in the boat on the sea to teach the "whole crowd" which is on the shore (4:1-2). On the second occasion, the disciples are in the boat on the sea, and it is Jesus who observes them from the land in his privacy (μόνος; 6:47). The function of this contrast between land and sea (or is it between Jesus and his hearers/followers?) in these narratives deserves further investigation.

10.-11.   Πάλιν and εὐθύς are two ubiquitous features of the gospel that are universally recognized as indicators of Markan composition. Although he finds Mark's redactional activity to be quite minimal, even Pesch regards these as sure signs of the author's hand. We include them in our chart not because they are associated uniquely with the boat motif, but because they

conveniently furnish us with further confirmation that the
three major boat trips in Mark 4-8 were indeed conceived and
constructed by the author himself. One could easily expand our
chart with the addition of numerous other Markan characteristics
present in the boat trip narratives.

The Composition of the Feeding of the Five Thousand

An examination of the language of Mark 6:30-44 yields a
firm conclusion: the Feeding of the Five Thousand in its
entirety was composed by the author himself. When one examines
Mark 6:30-44 for the signs of Markan composition, they are
found to be present throughout the entire story. Non-Markan
characteristics in the story are nonexistent; Markan
characteristics are in total dominance. This is in sharp
contrast to the feeding narrative in Mark 8, where our study
revealed parts of the narrative in which Markan characteristics
were dominant (8:1-2, 7, 10) and others where rare or unusual
language betrayed a non-Markan origin (8:3-6, 8-9). In the case
of the Feeding of the Five Thousand, however, no such
distinction between redaction and tradition is possible--
the story is Markan from beginning to end.

Therefore, the study of the language of the two feeding
stories yields the conclusion that one story is derived from a
pre-Markan source and edited slightly, while the other is
wholly the author's creation. At this point in our study, we
have yet to broach seriously the issue of the relationship of
the two stories, but we are now in a position to do so. Nearly
every interpreter would admit that the manifest verbal agreements
between the two stories at least suggests the possibility of a
direct relationship between them. The results of our study now
raise this possibility to a certainty--the author obtained the
story now found in 8:1-10 from a source, and he used this story
as the model for his own composition in 6:30-44. Besides revealing the Markan literary style pervading 6:30-44, our study also
discloses the manner in which the author expanded, developed,
and modified the narrative in 8:1-10. Consequently, as we are
describing the Markan characteristics of 6:30-44, we will also

point out along the way how Mark transformed the traditional
story. By proceeding in this manner, we will be conflating
the results of two distinct stages of investigation, since the
conclusion that one story is dependent on the other is wholly
contingent upon the completion of the prior study of their
literary styles. The reasons behind the author's composition of
his own version of the feeding story will be discussed later.

The Introductory Verses to the Feeding of the Five Thousand

There is almost unanimous agreement among interpreters of
Mark that the introductory verses of the Feeding of the Five
Thousand were composed by the author himself.[60] On the other
hand, there is very little agreement where this editorial
introduction ends and the (supposedly) traditional story
begins. Most interpreters suggest that the original introduction to the story has been at least partially rewritten by
Mark, making it impossible to recover the pristine beginning.
Nevertheless, most interpreters do think they can discern where
the traditional story begins to appear in the present text; a
rapid survey of standard works finds exegetes who think that
the traditional story begins in 6:32, 6:33, 6:34, and 6:35.[61]
We would like to suggest that these scholars have such a
difficult time agreeing where Markan redaction ends and the
traditional story begins simply because the Markan redaction
does not end--the entire story is Mark's creation. Exegetes
have been perplexed by an introduction which leads the reader
gradually and smoothly into the heart of the story. They expect
rather to find a pericope with a sharp, distinct beginning, but
such does not exist here. Even 6:30 does not fit the common
conception of the first verse of a pericope since it is a
continuation of the section 6:6b-13. One exaggerates very
little when one says that no new episode occurs in 6:30ff.,
only the continuation of 6:6b-13.[62]

When we begin to examine the language and structure of the
introductory verses of the feeding story, we discover the same
feature that is so prominent in the introduction of the other
feeding story: the particular kind of double-step expression

that Donahue calls the Markan insertion technique (see
Appendix 2). The introduction of the feeding story in Mark 8
is constructed around a pair of repeated elements, one of
which is in the narrative mode, the other in the discourse
mode. *Two* Markan insertions, on the other hand, are used by
the author to compose the introduction to the story in Mark 6.
We find the repeated expressions in 6:31-32 and 6:35:

> 6:31 κατ' ἰδίαν εἰς ἔρημον τόπον
> 6:32 εἰς ἔρημον τόπον κατ' ἰδίαν

> 6:35a καὶ ἤδη ὥρας πολλῆς γενομένης
> 6:35b καὶ ἤδη ὥρα πολλή.

Both of these pairs also involve a shift from narrative mode to
discourse mode, or vice versa. In 6:31-32 the first of the
repeated phrases is in direct speech; it is a part of Jesus'
command to the disciples. The fulfillment of the command is
described by the narrator in the narrative mode (6:32). In the
second insertion, the narrator informs the reader that the
hour is late before the disciples inform Jesus of the same in
direct speech.

We should also note while we are discussing these double-
step expressions that the repeated phrases in 6:31-32 are
themselves double-step expressions:

> 6:31 κατ' ἰδίαν/εἰς ἔρημον τόπον
> 6:32 εἰς ἔρημον τόπον/κατ' ἰδίαν.

Neirynck lists both of these as examples of double local
statements; one could say even more specifically that they
are *double privacy statements*. Neirynck's list of double local
statements contains several other expressions which also
involve Jesus' withdrawal from the crowd and his search for
privacy:

> 7:17 εἰς οἶκον/ἀπὸ τοῦ ὄχλου
> 7:33 ἀπὸ τοῦ ὄχλου/κατ' ἰδίαν
> 9:2 εἰς ὄρος ὑψηλὸν/κατ' ἰδίαν/μόνους
> 9:28 εἰς οἶκον/ . . . κατ' ἰδίαν.[63]

In other words, one of Mark's favorite themes, Jesus' quest
for privacy, is often expressed with a favorite Markan

construction, the double-step expression.

Although the introduction of the feeding story in Mark 6 is appreciably longer than its counterpart in Mark 8, it is instructive to see how the same elements and techniques are used to form the insertions in both stories. For example, the repeated phrases in 8:1-2 concern the crowd not having anything to eat, which is exactly the situation portrayed by the narrator in the material "inserted" between the repeated phrases in 6:31-32 (see Appendix 2; also, Appendix 3). The insertions in 8:1-2 and 6:35 are both introduced with the Markan genitive absolute, and the inserted material in them functions as a vivid antithesis: in 8:1 the disciples are summoned by Jesus (προσκαλεσάμενος), while in 6:35 they are the ones to seize the initiative by approaching him (προσελθόντες). When either Jesus or the disciples speak, their speech is introduced with the characteristic Markan use of λέγω (8:1, 6:35). Another element inserted between the repeated phrases in 8:1-2 is the mention of Jesus' pity for the crowd; a similar statement phrased in the same peculiar, Markan way[64] is inserted between the insertions in 6:34.

In addition, there are other elements featured prominently in the two insertions in Mark 6 as a result of the author's development and expansion of the story in Mark 8. For example, the desert locale of 8:1-10 is mentioned only once in 8:4, but Mark changes this locale to the Markan "lonely place" (ἔρημος τόπος) and refers to it three times in 6:31-35. There the ἔρημος τόπος appears in the repeated phrases of the first insertion and in the inserted material of the second insertion. In a similar fashion, the solitary time reference in 8:2 becomes the repeated mention of the late hour in 6:35a and 6:35b. Another example of the transformation of 8:1-10 in the opening verses of 6:30-44 is the use of ἐσθίω. The concern in 8:1-2 for the crowd's need to have "something to eat" (τί φάγωσιν) is broadened in 6:30-44 to span vv. 31 to 37, the double use of ἐσθίω in 8:1-2 having been expanded to four instances in 6:31-37. The narrator's statement in 6:31 that the crowd (πολλοί) has had no opportunity to eat creates the

necessary background for the following verses, especially for
the sharp exchange between the disciples and Jesus over how
the crowd should obtain "something to eat" (τί φάγωσιν).[65]

If one insists upon distinguishing where the introductions
of the two stories end and where their main bodies begin, then
the boundary lines would have to be drawn between 6:35 and 36
and between 8:2 and 3. Perceiving the use of repetition and
insertion in both introductions has made this observation
possible. Once the Markan insertions in 6:35 and 8:1-2 have
been discerned, one observes further that immediately following
the insertions the two narratives instantly converge upon the
issue of dismissing the crowd:

6:35b/36 . . . καὶ ἤδη ὥρα πολλή/ἀπόλυσον αὐτούς . . .
8:2/3   . . . οὐκ ἔχουσιν τί φάγωσιν/καὶ ἐὰν ἀπολύσω
             αὐτούς . . .

Coincidentally, the author has chosen to establish a strong,
verbal connection between the two stories at the exact point
in 8:1-10 where the traditional story first becomes discernible:
Mark 8:3 (see Appendix 3). This significant verbal agreement
between the two feeding stories still must not be allowed to
overshadow the crucial difference between the stories that
Mark introduces here. In the traditional story, Jesus stresses
the seriousness of the situation to his disciples, thinking
aloud about what might happen to the crowd if they were to
return home unfed: "If I send them away hungry to their homes,
they will faint on the way; and some of them have come a long
way" (8:3). In 8:3 Jesus is moved with pity for the crowd and
is loath to dismiss them. In the other story, however, the
disciples are the first to speak, and it is they who raise
the question of dismissing the crowd. They are not possessed
with Jesus' compassion, and their thoughts on the subject are
uttered brusquely: "Send them away. . . ." (6:36). This
startling contrast between the attitudes of Jesus and the Twelve
has only begun to emerge at this point in the narratives. Until
this antithesis can be examined further, we are content to
point out the dexterity with which the author has modified the
traditional account. At this particular place in the narrative
he has skillfully preserved the theme and even a little of the

wording of the traditional story while deviating radically
from its original compassionate tone.

Having now compared the Markan introductions to both
feeding narratives, we may profitably compare the introductory
verses of 6:30-44 with the verses which end the same chapter:
6:53-56. It is generally agreed that 6:53-56 is a redactional
summary statement (*Sammelbericht*) not unlike the introductory
Sammelbericht in 6:30ff.[66] There are, in fact, a number
of verbal parallels between these editorial compositions, the
sum of which leads us to recognize that these compositions are
meant to frame the material in 6:30-56. As Snoy has observed:
"Dans la perspective du rédacteur, Mc 6,30-56 forme un
ensemble."[67] The verbal agreements in this framing material
have been recognized at least since Wendling:

6:34 καὶ ἐξελθὼν (sc. ἐκ τοῦ πλοίου vgl. 32) . . .	6:54 καὶ ἐξελθόντων αὐτῶν ἐκ τοῦ πλοίου
33 καὶ ἐπέγνωσαν αὐτοὺς πολλοὶ καὶ πεζῇ ἀπὸ πασῶν τῶν πόλεων συνέδραμον ἐκεῖ.	εὐθὺς ἐπιγνόντες αὐτὸν 55 περιέδραμον ὅλην τὴν χώραν ἐκείνην . . .
36 εἰς τοὺς κύκλῳ ἀγροὺς καὶ κώμας . . .	56 εἰς κώμας ἢ εἰς πόλεις ἢ ἀγρούς.[68]

Wendling has indeed pointed out most of the points of contact
between these sections: the presence of the boat motif
(ἐξέρχομαι); the recognition of Jesus by the crowd (ἐπιγινώσκω);
the gathering of the crowd (cognates of τρέχω); the mention of
cities, villages, and farms (πόλις, κώμη, ἀγρός). There are
two additional observations we should make, the first of which
is Mark's characteristic use of πᾶς or ὅλος in these sections.
Mark is quite fond of phrases like "all of Judea," "the entire
region," "all of the city," "the whole neighborhood," and other
similar expressions, as Schweizer has noted:

> Aber auch Wendungen mit determinierten ὅλος oder πᾶς, die
> die Wirkung Jesu auf alle Welt, das ganze Volk usw.
> beschreiben, sind oft in redaktionellen Abschnitten zu
> finden. Sie können auch die Wirkung der Verkündigung des
> Täufers auf "ganz Judäa" und "allen Jerusalemiten" oder
> die Predigt des Evangeliums an "alle Völker"
> beschreiben.[69]

In light of Mark's inclination to generalize or universalize
scenes by using ὅλος or πᾶς, it is not surprising to find that
one of the redactional compositions under consideration refers

to the crowd coming from "all of the cities" (πασῶν τῶν πόλεων; 6:33), while the other states that the crowd gathered from "the whole region" (ὅλην τὴν χώραν; 6:55). Such generalized, unspecific localizations are absolutely typical of Mark.[70]

Finally, we should comment upon the content of these framing devices. Here, though, instead of finding a common orientation, we see that the two compositions function as obverse portrayals of the ministry of Jesus: teaching (6:34) and healing (6:55-56).[71] Interpreters have often noted with some perplexity the strict exclusion of one kind of activity in each location, for throughout the gospel Jesus' words and deeds are usually very closely related. The mention of either teaching or healing without its complementary activity is less perplexing when one sees that 6:34 and 6:55-56 are actually components of a larger integral unit, 6:30-56. Therefore, once one perceives the true dimensions of the narrative unit within which both references occur, the supposed exclusivity of 6:34 and 6:55-56 disappears. That Jesus is active in both teaching and healing in 6:30-56 should not be surprising since this narrative is a continuation of 6:6b-13 where it is *the disciples* who teach (κηρύσσω; but cf. 6:30) and heal. Indeed, 6:30-56 begins with the disciples reporting to Jesus the results of their teaching (ὅσα ἐδίδαξαν) and healing (ὅσα ἐποίησαν), their own ministry of word and deed. The reader is told next to nothing about the actual conduct of the disciples' ministry of word and deed, much to the dismay of many. Rather, what the author does present to the reader is a portrayal of the disciples' dull, unfeeling reaction to Jesus' ministry of word and deed. Their cold insensitivity to the crowd in 6:30-44 and their inability to recognize their master in 6:45-52 destroys whatever positive connotations the reader may have read into 6:12-13, 30--whatever good they might have done in their own ministry of word and deed, it is clear that they have no part in or understanding of Jesus' ministry of word and deed. The narrator's portrayal of the disciples is utterly clear: "Their hearts were hardened" (6:52).[72]

To this point we have slighted another vital element in the organization of 6:30-56: the boat motif. As we have observed in

our discussion of the boat trips in Mark 4-8, Boat Trip II
lies wholly within 6:30-56 and serves to bind together and to
frame the feeding story and the sea story. The use of three
boat trips in Mark to tie stories together is the author's
own work, we claimed, and we have surely seen no evidence to
contradict that supposition in the case of 6:30-56. Whether we
wish to speak of comparable *Sammelberichte*, complementary
instances of Jesus' ministry of word and deed, or the beginning
and end of Boat Trip II, the result is the same: the opening
and closing verses of 6:30-56 frame this integral narrative
unit and bind it together into a whole.

Markan Characteristics in the Narrative
of the Feeding of the Five Thousand

In the preceding section of this study we anticipated to
a certain extent the observations and conclusions about the
Markan composition of the narrative to be discussed in this
section. Nevertheless, it is the following detailed
investigation that enables us to conclude that this passage
is indeed a Markan composition and allows us to observe how the
author uses 8:1-10 as a model for the composition of his own
version of the feeding story in 6:30-44.

Mark 6:30

As we have mentioned, the Markan origin of the first few
verses of this unit is almost universally acknowledged. With
regard to v. 30 Taylor states: "The vocabulary suggests that
it is a Markan construction, since all the words, except
οἱ ἀπόστολοι, are common elsewhere in the Gospel. . . ."[73]
The use of συνάγω, especially in the historical present, is
common in redactional introductions to pericopes.[74] Also
common in introductory sentences in Mark is the practice of
naming Jesus, often with the phrase πρὸς τὸν Ἰησοῦν or πρὸς
αὐτόν.[75] The verb ἀπαγγέλλω is regarded by Taylor as Markan;
Taylor also considers the use of ὅσα with ποιέω as a Markan
trait. Both of these traits find a striking parallel in 5:19:
ἀπάγγειλον αὐτοῖς ὅσα . . . πεποίηκεν.[76] Mark 6:30 concludes
with the familiar Markan theme of teaching, although here is one
of the few instances in the gospel where the teaching of the dis-

ciples is mentioned.[77] What the disciples report to Jesus is:
πάντα--"all that they had done and taught." As we have noted,
Mark has a special liking for πᾶς and ὅλος, which is evident in
the present narrative where πᾶς appears nò less than five times:
6:30, 33, 39, 41, 42.[78]

As Taylor has stated, only the use of ἀπόστολοι in v. 30
is unusual for Mark. It is the only place in the gospel where
the Twelve are called apostles, with the possible exception of
3:14, where the manuscript evidence is uncertain. Of course,
the verb ἀποστέλλω is used in the commissioning of the disciples
in 6:7, so ἀπόστολος in 6:30 could very well be intended in the
ordinary sense of "emissary" or "commissioned agent." It is
often suggested that the disciples of Jesus are called
"apostles" here to distinguish them from the disciples of John
who appear in 6:29. This suggestion has merit, but we would like
to suggest that the use of ἀπόστολος in 6:30 implies a
distinction of far greater significance than that between Jesus'
disciples and John's. First of all, though, we must recognize
that there are two prominent characters in 6:6b-29 who
commission "apostles": Jesus and King Herod. Jesus commissions
his emissaries in 6:6b-13; Herod commissions (ἀποστέλλω)
emissaries twice in 6:14-29, once to arrest John (6:17) and
once to have him beheaded (6:27). A rich, intricate contrast is
therefore established between Jesus and his "apostles" and King
Herod and his "apostles."

Mark 6:31

This verse is introduced by λέγω in the historical
present, a familiar Markan construction; the imperative δεῦτε
is also a Markan expression, according to Taylor.[79] Although it
is not a special characteristic of Mark, the use of the emphatic
pronoun ὑμεῖς should be noted.[80] This pronoun is used twice in
the feeding story, once in 6:31 and again in 6:37. The use of
the emphatic pronoun thrusts the disciples into the spotlight,
which becomes especially critical in 6:37 when Jesus informs
them that *they* are to feed the crowd. Next in v. 31 we find the
phrase κατ' ἰδίαν εἰς ἔρημον τόπον with which we encounter the
first of the two Markan insertions in 6:31-35 (see Appendix 2).
We have already discussed in length the Markan use of this

compositional technique. Consequently, we need only observe
that the individual expressions, κατ'ἰδίαν and ἔρημος τόπος,
are both as typical of Mark as the insertion technique itself.[81]

The bulk of the material inserted between the repeated
phrases in vv. 31 and 32 lies in a parenthetical statement
introduced by γάρ (v. 31b), a favorite Markan construction:[82]
"For many were coming and going, and they had no leisure even
to eat." One of the major discussions of this Markan
characteristic is the article by C. H. Bird on "Some γαρ
Clauses in St. Mark's Gospel."[83] Bird's article contains a
number of helpful insights into Mark's use of these explanatory
comments, but he advocates the rather peculiar thesis that
these γάρ clauses are often allusions to familiar Old
Testament passages. One need not go to such lengths to find the
significance of these parentheses; usually they are used to
interject the narrator's commentary into the narrative, and if
the comment is meant to "allude" to anything outside of the
immediate context, it usually "alludes" to another section of
the gospel. As Snoy states: "On peut voir en ces passages des
sortes de parenthèses, sans cependant leur donner la portée
symbolique profonde que Bird leur attribue. . . .À plusieurs
reprises, *Mc.* emploie γάρ *à l'intérieur* de notices rédactionnelles,
pour en relier des phrases distinctes; ainsi par exemple en
I,22; VI, 31; . . ."[84] In the case of 6:31, Bird himself
recognizes an echo of earlier passages in the gospel where a
crowd (πολλοί) clusters around Jesus.[85] For example, 2:15c
contains a similar γάρ parenthesis: ἦσαν γάρ πολλοὶ καὶ
ἠκολούθουν αὐτῷ. From the context of 2:15c one must conclude
that the πολλοί here are the πολλοὶ τελῶναι καὶ ἁμαρτωλοί in the
preceding phrase (2:15b) Another verse that bears a striking
resemblance to 6:31b is 3:20, where such a (large) crowd
gathers "that they could not even eat." Here the "they" is
quite indefinite, but from the context one must conclude that
this refers to the crowd (ὄχλος)--the only alternative would
be the disciples, but they are absent. Having been alerted to
these important counterparts to 6:31b,[86] we are in a much
better position to understand this parenthetical comment.

Quite simply, the crowd (οἱ πολλοί) has been coming and going, and they--the crowd--have had no opportunity to eat. The narrator divulges to the reader the insight into the needs of the crowd that the reader must have in order to comprehend fully the events which are about to unfold. Indeed, later in the narrative the hunger of the crowd will become a vital issue (6:36-37), but at this point in the narrative it is sufficient for only the narrator and reader to be aware of the problem. Thus our judgment that 6:31b refers to the hunger of the crowd is confirmed by the course of events that follow; also, we should remember that an identical situation is depicted in 8:1, where again (πάλιν) a crowd gathers and has nothing to eat.

Not only is 6:31b a typical Markan parenthesis, the vocabulary it employs is also Markan, as one might expect. The Markan preference for compounds of ἔρχομαι is well known: in 6:30-44 ἔρχομαι occurs once (6:31), ἀπέρχομαι three times (6:32, 36, 37), προέρχομαι once (6:33), ἐξέρχομαι once (6:34), and προσέρχομαι once (6:35).[87] Other Markan vocabulary in 6:31 includes ὑπάγω, which occurs three times in the narrative (6:31, 33, 38), and ἐσθίω, which occurs six times (6:31, 36, 37 [twice], 42, 44).[88]

Mark 6:32

This verse has been discussed thoroughly in our excursus on the boat motif in Mark and in our discussion of the editorial introduction to the feeding story. The mention of the journey in the boat utilizes the usual language; the phrase εἰς ἔρημον τόπον κατ' ἰδίαν marks the termination of the first Markan insertion in 6:30ff. We only wish to point out additionally the verbal parallel in 1:35, the first place in the gospel where a retreat to the ἔρημος τόπος is related: ἀπῆλθεν εἰς ἔρημον τόπον.

Mark 6:33

In 6:32 Jesus and the disciples go away in the boat to a lonely place; 6:33 continues to use third person plural verbs, but it is clear that there has been a change in the subject of these verbs. The "they" in v. 33 is no longer Jesus and the

Twelve but the faceless crowd (πολλοί) that watches the progress
of the boat from the shore. This use of the impersonal plural
is common in Mark; many interpreters point to its use in 6:33
and later in the narrative in 6:43.[89]

We have already discussed the parallels between this
verse and the redactional verses at the end of Mark 6: the
crowd's recognition of Jesus (ἐπιγινώσκω); their running to meet
him (cognate of τρέχω); the use of πᾶς/ὅλος. We should note also
the second of three uses of ὑπάγω in the feeding story (see v.
31).

Mark 6:34

With ἐξελθών the first leg of Boat Trip II is completed--
Jesus disembarks and immediately meets the omnipresent
thronging crowd (ὄχλος πολύς).[90] The statement of Jesus'
compassion for the crowd is expressed in the same peculiar
manner as in 8:2. The comment that the crowd is like sheep
without a shepherd has always attracted attention; it recalls
a number of familiar Old Testament passages where the imagery
of the shepherd and the sheep is used, and it raises some
interesting possibilities for the interpretation of the
following feeding story. Turner has correctly observed the Markan
preference for ἔχω here, since one would expect εἶναι with
the dative to be used instead, as the Septuagint consistently
does.[91] The phrase in v. 34--ὡς πρόβατα μὴ ἔχοντα ποιμένα--is
a typically Markan rendering of the Septuagint phrase ὡς
πρόβατα οἷς οὐκ ἔστιν ποιμήν (Num. 27:17, 1 Kgs. 22:17, 2 Chr.
18:16, Jdt. 11:19). In its use of ἔχω, the description of the
crowd as sheep μὴ ἔχοντα ποιμένα matches the corresponding
description in 8:1: μὴ ἐχόντων τί φάγωσιν. Interestingly, the
imagery of the sheep and the shepherd occurs in one other place
in Mark: the prediction after the Last Supper that the shepherd
will be struck down and the sheep scattered (14:27).

The remainder of the verse is also quite Markan. The mention
of teaching is a familiar Markan characteristic, especially when
accompanied by the ἄρχομαι auxiliary. The use of πολλά here
probably should be understood adverbially, another Markan
trait.[92] Similar phrases may be found in Mark 1:45 and 4:1-2:

1:45 ἤρξατο κηρύσσειν πολλά

4:1-2 ἤρξατο διδάσκειν . . . καὶ ἐδίδασκεν αὐτοὺς . . .
       πολλά

Mark 6:35

This verse has been discussed in detail above. It contains
the second insertion found in 6:31-35, beginning and ending
with a declaration of the late hour. As we have pointed out,
the use of the genitive absolute is Markan and occurs also with
the insertion in 8:1-2. Inserted between the repeated references
to the late hour is an action that is antithetical to the action
in 8:1-2--here the disciples approach Jesus with their demand,
but in 8:1-2 Jesus commands their attention. Other Markan
characteristics are not lacking: the use of λέγω;ὅτι recitative;
and, once again, the ἔρημος τόπος.[93]

Mark 6:36-37

We will consider these two verses together since they
constitute a short dialog between the disciples and Jesus.
These verses correspond to 8:3-4, the first two discernible
verses of the traditional story (see Appendix 3). Both 6:36
and 8:3 begin immediately with the issue of dismissing
(ἀπολύω) the crowd, but different characters raise the issue
in the two stories. While the disciples demand that Jesus
dismiss the crowd in 6:36, the corresponding verse in Mark 8
has Jesus hypothetically considering the adverse effects of
such an action--a stark contrast between callousness and
sympathy. This contrast and others have been wrought by the
evangelist, who has reworked the material in 8:3-4 and created
out of it the dialog we now have in 6:36-37. In a way, the
author introduces dialog into a story that previously had none.
To see this we must isolate the traditional story momentarily,
removing it from its context in the gospel for closer
examination. In its preserved form, the traditional story
begins with Jesus musing aloud about the hungry crowd. The
response of the disciples is natural and innocent; they merely
respond with the rhetorical question: "How can one feed these
men with bread here in the desert?" Jesus then seizes control
of the situation, determines the amount of provisions at hand,

and begins to feed the crowd. Both Jesus and the Twelve speak
their lines and play their parts, but there is no sharp
debate or vigorous dialog in vv. 3-4. In fact, there is no
dialog here, at least not in any meaningful sense of the word.

The debate created by Mark in 6:36-37 stands in bold
contrast to the serious but nevertheless peaceful setting of the
traditional story. The new dialog begins with the disciples'
demand that the hungry crowd be sent away to buy food for
themselves. Jesus' sharp reply places the burden squarely
on the shoulders of the disciples: "*You* give them something to
eat." The disciples are aghast; they think Jesus wants them to
spend their own money to feed the crowd! Shocked, they respond
incredulously: "Shall *we* go and buy bread with (our) two
hundred denarii, and give it to them to eat?" The author has
carefully used the four verbs ἀπέρχομαι, ἀγοράζω, δίδωμι,
and ἐσθίω to build the dialog up to this "querulous question":[94]

6:36	ἀπελθόντες ἀγοράσωσιν		φάγωσιν
6:37b		δότε	φαγεῖν
6:37d	ἀπελθόντες ἀγοράσωμεν	δώσωμεν	φαγεῖν

Earlier the crowd had preempted the disciples' holiday (6:31);
now the crowd threatens to devour their treasury as well.

Several features of 6:36-37 enhance the sharpness of the
words between the disciples and Jesus. First, we should make
the elementary observation that one reason there is sharper
interaction in 6:36-37 than in 8:3-4 is simply that there are
more spoken lines in 6:36-37; the author has transformed the two-
line script of 8:3-4 into the three spoken lines in 6:36-37.
Also, the exchange between Jesus and his disciples is now
characterized by the imperative mood. The disciples order
Jesus to send the crowd away, and his reply is equally stringent,
employing the Markan εἶπεν with the sense of "to command."[95]
Another salient feature of this dialog is Mark's use of the
adversative δέ. Mark's fondness for καί parataxis is well
known, but too seldom is his judicious use of δέ appreciated,
especially in redactional verses where intense conflict or
disagreement is involved. Zerwick and Snoy have noted the
Markan use of the adversative δέ in "Gegenrede":

> Die Gegenrede (die nicht Antwort auf eine Frage ist) wird
> mit δέ eingeleitet, und dabei liegt in ihr ein negatives
> Element, eine Ablehnung, ein Tadel, ein Einwand, ein
> Widerspruch: 6,37.38. . . .

> Pour conclure, nous dirons donc que la particule δέ,
> relativement rare dans l'ensemble de *Mc.*, est aussi
> employée que la particule καί dans les dialogues. . . .
> Nous avons d'ailleurs relevé plusieurs cas d'emploi
> de δέ dans les versets rédactionnels où il est question,
> comme en X, 24a, 26a, d'une réaction inadéquate à une
> parole de Jesus: ainsi en I, 45; VII, 36; IX, 32,
> 34 . . .; cfr aussi XIII, 5a dans l'introduction
> rédactionnelle du discours eschatologique . . .; voir
> encore dans un contexte narratif I, 32.[96]

The adversative δέ occurs once with 6:36-37 and again in the
first verse following this dialog, in both cases introducing
a statement by Jesus. Being the only two occurrences of δέ in
6:30-44, they add subtle emphasis to the tension and disharmony
between the disciples and Jesus.[97] One other feature of 6:36-37
accentuates the conflict between the characters: Jesus' use of
the emphatic pronoun ὑμεῖς (cf. 6:31). Jesus tries to get the
disciples to assume responsibility for the care of the "sheep,"
but they are offended at what they understand to be a demand
calculated to empty their wallets.

Even after this discussion of how the author has transformed 8:3-4 into 6:36-37, there are still many other Markan
traits to be pointed out in 6:36-37. Already in v. 31 we noted
the Markan preference for cognates of ἔρχομαι (here, ἀπέρχομαι)
and the verb ἐσθίω; κύκλῳ is also Markan.[98] The farms and
villages of v. 36, along with the cities mentioned in v. 33, all
reappear in the concluding verse of the chapter (6:56)--the
author has an unmistakable liking for this triad. In our
discussion of 8:4 we discussed the Markan tendency to accompany
ἀποκρίνομαι with a form of λέγω; here ἀποκρίνομαι is followed
by the aorist εἶπεν, which is used with the sense of "to
command." This command (εἶπεν . . . δότε αὐτοῖς . . . φαγεῖν).
finds a striking parallel in 5:43: εἶπεν δοθῆναι αὐτῇ φαγεῖν.
Another Markan characteristic in the dialog is λέγω in the
historical present (cf. 6:31); also Markan is the specific
reference to two hundred denarii, but this claim will require
some explanation.

Several exegetes have commented on the prominence in Mark
of numbers and other concrete details, often in places where
Matthew and Luke do not bother to preserve them. In his
thorough investigation of the language of Mark, Turner devoted
a section to "The use of numbers in St. Mark's Gospel"[99] in
which he attempted "to shew that it is Marcan usage to note
numbers, and Matthaean and Lucan usage to tend to omit them. . . .
That Mark is fond of numerals is then a matter of fact which
this instalment of my Notes is intended to prove. . . ."[100]
Rigaux has observed:". . .the author excels when he is dealing
with *concrete matters*. He uses 11 words to designate 'house'
or its parts, 10 to signify 'garments' and 9 for foods. He
likes numbers(36 times)."[101]

Numbers are featured quite prominently in 6:30-44. The
traditional story already contained several numbers: seven
loaves, seven baskets, "about four thousand" diners. These are
changed by the author to five loaves, twelve baskets, and
exactly five thousand diners. All other numbers and concrete
details in 6:30-44 are Markan embellishments added to the
traditional story. New to the story are the references to the
two hundred denarii (6:37) and the two fish (6:38, 41 [twice],
43). The disciples' fear that they will have to relinquish two
hundred denarii to feed the hungry crowd finds a poignant echo
in 14:5, where certain bystanders (the disciples?) lament the
loss of three hundred denarii' worth of ointment, for the
money could have been "given to the poor."[102] The two fish are
equally new to the story. The traditional story originally
contained no reference to fish; Mark 8:7, we noted, is an
editorial addition. Therefore, what was originally a story
about bread has become in 6:30-44 a story about bread *and* fish.
It is inaccurate, consequently, to call 6:30-44 a *Brotvermehrung*
--every time the five loaves are mentioned the two fish are
mentioned also, and every action performed with the five loaves
is performed also with the two fish. The two fish are even
mentioned once when there is only an indirect reference to the
five loaves (κλάσματα; 6:43).[103] It is fair to say that the
single-strand traditional story, a bread meal, has been transformed by the author into a dual-strand story, a meal in which

bread and fish are carefully balanced. We now recognize that
the insertion of 8:7 into the traditional story is a weak effort
to endow the story with a hint of the duality of its companion
narrative. In comparison to its mate, though, it remains
decisively unbalanced on the side of the bread, but the modest
reference to fish in 8:7 is at least sufficient to insure that
the reader will note a superficial similarity in the two
accounts.

One of the numbers in the traditional story that has been
changed by the author is the number of persons fed by Jesus. In
8:1-10 a single estimate of the size of the crowd is provided:
approximately four thousand (8:9). In his own composition, the
author not once but twice states the exact number of people
present. The first enumeration is in his peculiar description
of the crowd's seating arrangement by rank and file (6:39-40).
Their formation is rectangular, one hundred by fifty in length
and breadth, a punctilious five thousand in number. The same is
expressed in 6:44 where the diners are said to be "five
thousand men"--no more, no less. The use of such numerical
precision by the author makes his composition crisp, vivid, and
lifelike. Although he leaves the traditional story relatively
untouched, he makes it look "bare and colourless"[104] in
comparison to his own composition.

Mark 6:38

This verse concludes the dialog of 6:36-37, but we will
consider it separately since the author begins to follow the
traditional story more closely at this point. The author will
continue to follow the traditional account closely through the
rest of the narrative, making it even easier to perceive the
modifications he incorporates into his own composition. We see
first that he uses the adversative δέ in v. 38 to reinforce the
conflict between the disciples and Jesus in their dialog. The
non-Markan ἠρώτα in 8:5 is replaced by the familiar λέγω in the
historical present (cf. 6:31). The historical present of λέγω
is also substituted for εἶπαν. The question πόσους ἄρτους ἔχετε
employs ἔχω as it did in 8:5, but, unlike its counterpart in
8:5, the question in 6:38 is encompassed by other Markan traits.
Here the question is introduced with the historical present of

λέγω and followed by a typically Markan asyndetic construction:
. . . ἔχετε; ὑπάγετε ἴδετε.[105] The verb ὑπάγω is also from the
Markan vocabulary (cf. 6:31). Next, the phrase in 8:5 using the
copulative δέ and the aorist verb εἶπαν is replaced by καί
parataxis and the historical present: καί γνόντες λέγουσιν. . . .
The same construction is also found in another section of the
gospel composed entirely by the evangelist: καί γνοὺς
λέγει. . . .(8:17).[106] Mark 6:38 concludes with the first of
several references to the five loaves and two fish.

Mark 6:39-40

These two verses correspond to the short statement in
8:6a that Jesus directly commanded the crowd to be seated on
the ground. In the evangelist's own composition, Jesus speaks
not to the crowd but to the disciples, telling them to seat the
crowd[107] "upon the green grass," another of Mark's colorful
details. The non-Markan verb in 8:6 (παραγγέλλω) is exchanged
for a Markan verb (ἐπιτάσσω),[108] but the author does retain the
traditional story's use of ἀναπίπτω. Another Markan characteristic
in vv. 39-40 is the use of πᾶς, the third such occurrence of
this word in 6:30-44 (cf. 6:30).

The most prominent feature of these two verses is the
unwieldy threefold description of the crowd. Their seating
arrangement is:

   συμπόσια συμπόσια
     πρασιαί πρασιαί
       κατὰ ἑκατὸν καί κατὰ πεντήκοντα
   company by company
     group by group
       one hundred by fifty

Such use of distributive doubling [109] is not unlike Mark; the
same construction is used in 6:7 and 14:19:

   6:7   καί ἤρξατο αὐτοὺς ἀποστέλλειν δύο δύο
   14:19 καί λέγειν αὐτῷ εἷς κατὰ εἷς.

Moreover, Mark has a fondness for series or groups of three.[110]
On this basis alone, we should not be surprised that he uses
distributive doubling to create, albeit artificially, a threefold audience out of the single, unified crowd in the

traditional story. There is, however, an additional reason why
the author wants a threefold crowd in his story, a reason
involving the episode preceding 6:30-44 in the gospel (6:14-29).
This episode is often called "The Death of John the Baptist,"
a rubric that exercises extraordinary control over how one
perceives the story. To be sure, John is beheaded in the course
of the story, but the main scene of the narrative is a feast
at which Herod the King is host. Accordingly, it would be more
descriptive of the entire narrative to call it "The Banquet of
Herod." The guests at Herod's banquet also constitute a threefold group, consisting of courtiers, military officers, and
leading citizens of the region (6:21):

τοῖς μεγιστᾶσιν αὐτοῦ

τοῖς χιλιάρχοις

τοῖς πρώτοις τῆς Γαλιλαίας.

Following "The Banquet of Herod" (6:14-29) is a story that could
aptly be called "The Banquet of Jesus": The Feeding of the Five
Thousand. Here the host is Jesus, who fulfills the host's
responsibility by saying the blessing before the meal and by
breaking the bread to initiate the meal. As befits an oriental
banquet, Jesus' guests are all men (ἄνδρες; 6:44),[111] as were
the guests at Herod's banquet table. Nonetheless, the
similarities in the two banquets cannot mask the stark contrast
between them. This contrast is symbolized vividly in the uses
to which the two hosts put their serving vessels: Herod's
banquet concludes with the grisly spectacle of the Baptist's
head on the serving dish, while Jesus' banquet concludes
innocently with the gathering of the leftover food in baskets.
Although the accounts of the two banquets are abruptly juxtaposed
in the narrative and, we believe, were meant to be compared, it
is as if there were an immeasurable gulf separating the
blundering butchery of Herod from the innate benevolence of
Jesus.

Mark 6:41

Two Markan characteristics in this verse are the use of
ἀναβλέπω and πᾶς,[112] but perhaps the most important observation
to be made concerning this verse is the observation of the
balance between the bread and fish. Everything done with the

bread is done also with the fish.[113] Remembering that Mark 8:7
is an editorial addition to the traditional account, we are not
surprised to find that 8:7 has no genuine counterpart in 6:30-
44. The fish that are only mentioned in passing in 8:7 are
thoroughly integrated into the author's new composition. In
6:41, Jesus takes the bread *and* the fish, looks up into heaven,
and says the blessing. Then he distributes both the bread and
the fish. At this point a certain unavoidable awkwardness
troubles the author. In early Christian literature the verb
κλάω (or a cognate) is always used for the breaking of bread,
and Mark conforms to that practice.[114] Although one speaks of
"breaking bread," one does not use such language to describe
the distribution of other foods, so the author must turn to a
verb like μερίζω ("to divide, apportion") to describe the
distribution of fish. Thus the bread is broken, the fish
divided, and the duality of bread and fish preserved, in spite
of a certain loss of elegance in the wording of the verse.

Generations of scholars have focused on this verse and its
counterpart in 8:1-10 as the heart of the feeding stories. Its
similarity to the language of the Last Supper is always noted,
and numerous hypotheses have been proposed suggesting that
perhaps the feeding stories were originally a part of a
eucharistic celebration, or perhaps were originally non-
eucharistic stories but were given a eucharistic flavor, etc.
Especially rich food for thought is the different terminology
used in the two feeding stories for the blessing preceding
the meal. Mark 6:41 employs εὐλογέω whereas 8:6 employs
εὐχαριστέω. If one assumes that the feeding stories are
"eucharistic," then it is quite natural to suggest, as many
have, that these two terms indicate two different streams of
eucharistic tradition, perhaps Jewish and Hellenistic respectively. If one does not operate with the presupposition that
the feeding stories are "eucharistic," and if one has concluded,
as we have, that one feeding story is a Markan transformation
of the other, then a far more elementary conclusion may suffice.
If the evangelist is rewriting a traditional story and wants his
story to be different then he must introduce differences. Our

discussion of the language of 6:30-44 has been to a large extent
a cataloging of the changes wrought by the evangelist in the
traditional story. Some details introduced into the narrative
by the author have no counterpart in Mark 8. In other cases,
Mark simply changes details already present in his model. A
short list of these contains most of the major features of both
stories:

1.	Seven loaves	becomes	five loaves *and* two fish
2.	The ground	becomes	green grass
3.	To give thanks (εὐχαριστέω)	becomes	to bless (εὐλογέω)
4.	Seven baskets (σπυρίς)	becomes	twelve baskets (κόφινος)
5.	Their contents (περίσσευμα)	becomes	their contents (πλήρωμα)
6.	Four thousand	becomes	five thousand *men*

The change from εὐχαριστέω to εὐλογέω is no more outstanding
than the other changes; they are all changes carried out by
the author to make his narrative distinctive from the traditional
story.[115]

Mark 6:42-44

   In several discussions of Mark's fondness for the
impersonal plural, 6:42-43 is cited as a notable example (cf.
6:33). More impressive here, though, are the clearly visible
changes made in the traditional story by Mark. Fortunately,
although the evangelist introduces several new expressions in
these short verses, he still adheres closely to the outline of
his *Vorlage*, making the modifications easy to see. Mark 6:42
repeats 8:8a verbatim with the addition of a single word: the
familiar Markan πᾶς (cf. 6:30). The next verse follows the
outline of 8:8b closely but changes nearly all of the
vocabulary. The *hapax legomenon* περίσσευμα is exchanged for a
word from the Markan vocabulary: πλήρωμα;[116] "seven" is
exchanged for "twelve"; the term for basket is changed from
σπυρίς to κόφινος.[117] The only feature in 6:43 without parallel
in 8:8b is, of course, the explicit reference to the fish. This
phrase (ἀπὸ τῶν ἰχθύων) is appended awkwardly to a statement
that originally referred only to broken pieces (κλάσματα) of

bread.[118] By the addition of such an inelegant phrase, however,
the author is able to establish a rough parity of bread and
fish in this verse. Finally, the approximate size of the crowd
in 8:9a is changed to a precise statement that five thousand
men (ἄνδρες) were in attendance at Jesus' "banquet."

Mark 6:45 and following: Concluding remarks

We will cease our discussion of the Markan characteristics
in Mark 6:30ff. with the comments above. This decision is
somewhat arbitrary--we must stop somewhere--since Markan
composition continues at least through the transitional verses
6:45-47, as we have noted in our discussion of the boat motif.
There is no clear dividing line between the feeding story and
the following sea story. The former flows smoothly into the
latter, a skillful transition created by the evangelist. It is
impossible to tell how the original feeding story ended since
the account in 8:1-10 has an editorial conclusion. It may have
contained a reference to dismissing the crowd--we cannot be
certain. Certainly the departure from the scene in the boat,
which is used in both accounts, is the author's invention. It
is especially interesting to see how he shifts his actors in
6:45-47, moving them from one stage setting to another. In just
a few verses the disciples are sent away on a boat trip, the
crowd is dismissed, Jesus departs to the mountain to pray,
night falls, and the next episode begins to unfold. The author's
intention in creating this unity of feeding and sea stories will
be explored further in our next chapter.

Our discussion of Mark 6:30-44 has, we believe, demonstrated
the predominance of Markan characteristics in this narrative,
thereby necessitating the conclusion that this passage is a
Markan composition. It is clear also that the author follows the
model story derived from his *Vorlage*, the story that is preserved for us in 8:1-10. Time after time we discovered the
evangelist expanding and transforming the traditional story.
Features of the traditional story he found congenial were
preserved and sometimes developed; other features of the story
that are obviously non-Markan were frequently abandoned in
favor of Markan terminology and syntax. By definition, the

discovery of the numerous Markan traits in 6:30-44 is at the
same time the discovery of the narrative's numerous connections,
associations, and echoes with other sections of the gospel.
The stylistic tendencies of this narrative correspond to those
found in other sections of the gospel known to have been
composed by the evangelist. In particular, we discovered as we
proceeded just how well the Feeding of the Five Thousand fits
into its context in the gospel. We discovered that it develops
and transforms the story in 8:1-10, it continues the action
begun in 6:6b-13, it contrasts with the banquet in 6:14-29, it
leads into the episode in 6:45-52, and it complements to a
certain extent the summary in 6:53-56. Such is the author's
handiwork. Examining more closely how the feeding stories fit
into their contexts and how they interact with each other will
be the task of our next chapter.

CHAPTER III

THE FEEDING STORIES IN THE CONTEXT

OF THE GOSPEL OF MARK

In Chapter 1 we discussed various attempts to uncover
pre-Markan cycles of stories lying behind Mark 4-8. The
repetition that features so prominently in these chapters of
the gospel is best explained, it is often argued, as the
accidental product of repetitious tradition. As a result, very
few attempts have been made to find an intelligible purpose
behind the repetition. With our discovery now of the role
played by the author in the creation of the doublet of feeding
stories, the search for an intelligible purpose for the
repetition in Mark 4-8 becomes mandatory. Now that we know that
the author has composed one feeding story using the other as a
model and has placed his own version first in the gospel, we
must ask why he did this. What is the function of the two
feeding stories in their immediate context and in the gospel as
a whole? Moreover, do the other pairs of stories in Mark 4-8
that are often perceived as doublets function similarly? We will
attempt to answer these questions in the present chapter.

The Doublet of Feeding Stories

Points of tension and conflict between the feeding stories
have always been perceived by astute interpreters. Often the
response has been to label such disharmonies as illusions
created by the chance repetition of the "same story." With our
discovery of the author's role in the creation of this doublet,
such explanations may now be retired. If there are tensions
and conflicts between the two narratives, as indeed there are,
then the evangelist must bear full responsibility for them; they
are there because he has put them there. It is our task now to
explore these tensions and conflicts in greater detail. In so
doing, there is no need to look beyond the disharmonies that
have long been perceived by interpreters of the feeding stories.
We have no startling new observations to make here about the
tension between the narratives, only a new attitude toward the
old observations. Since the author has created one of the two

stories, tensions between them are his creation and must not be attributed to the happenstance of repetitious tradition. We are no longer free to evade features of the text intended by the author.

As we observed in our discussion of the language of the stories, Mark takes special care to rework the innocent discussion of 8:3-4, creating the antagonistic debate of 6:36-38. Numerous features of 6:36-38 cooperate to accent the antagonism between Jesus and his disciples. By comparison, the "dialog" in the original, traditional story is calm and innocuous. We were very careful to state that the accurate discernment of the original tone of the speech in 8:3-4 requires that the story be removed from its context in the gospel. Observing how the author transforms the grave but tranquil scene in 8:3-4 into the dispute in 6:36-38 necessitates following the chronology of composition instead of the chronology of the gospel narrative. We have seen how the author transformed 8:1-10 into the story in 6:30-44. Now it is time to see how the author's composition functions as a finished, connected narrative. On the one hand, redaction criticism has demonstrated that 8:1-10 contains the chronologically older, traditional narrative. Literary criticism, on the other hand, is concerned with the finished literary work and its own internal chronology, according to which the author's own composition (6:30-44) is the "older" story, since it occurs first in the gospel.

The simple observation that we read the traditional story in Mark's gospel only after we have read the author's own version is crucial. When we read the gospel straight through, we encounter the story in Mark 8 not as the original pre-Markan version of the feeding story but as the second feeding episode in the gospel, and we read that second account in light of the previous account in Mark 6. Stated another way, redaction criticism demonstrates that Mark 6:30-44 is an outgrowth of 8:1-10, but from a literary critical perspective Mark 6:30-44 is the backdrop against which the events of 8:1ff. are portrayed. Interestingly, the author has chosen to control how the reader understands 8:1-10 not by significant internal changes in the traditional story but by manipulating the context within which it is read.

Following the hints uncovered in our investigation of 8:3-4 and 6:36-38, we may conclude with assurance that the crux of both feeding stories is the interaction between Jesus and the disciples. We have noted, in particular, Mark's transformation of an innocent, rhetorical question in 8:4 into the "querulous question" (Taylor) of 6:37. However, when we confront these verses in their proper context in the gospel, our perception of them is radically different. Having been introduced at length to the disciples' acrimonious obtuseness in 6:30-44,[1] we perceive 8:4 as a further indication of their incredible blindness and stupidity. Just two chapters earlier they had handed over five loaves and two fish to Jesus, they themselves had distributed them to the crowd at Jesus' command, and they had gathered the leftover fragments of food--they should know very well how one is to "feed these men with bread here in the desert," but they do not. The innocent, rhetorical question in the traditonal story has been subtly transformed into an eloquent self-condemnation by virtue of the preceding feeding episode.

The incredible obtuseness of the disciples in 8:4 is universally recognized. It has been customary for interpreters to assume that the author cannot have meant to portray the disciples in such a negative light. They prefer to think that the stupidity of the disciples is an illusion accidentally created by the repetition of two versions of the same traditional story. The comments made by Branscomb and Gould are typical:

> Had the tradition meant to describe two separate incidents, the disciples would certainly not have been described as so astonished on the second occasion.

> The objection is valid; the stupid repetition of the question is psychologically impossible.[2]

Such conclusions are not possible for us; our study forces us to conclude that Mark intends to cast the disciples in such a negative light. Interpreters like Branscomb and Gould are correct in their observation of the stupid obtuseness of the disciples in 8:4, but we must reject their claim that this is not the portrait of the disciples that the author wishes to paint.[3]

Clearly Mark 8:4 is the crucial verse for the interpretation of the two stories *as a doublet*. Perhaps it would be helpful to

to observe that the disciples' question fits the criteria
proposed by Wayne Booth for the detection of "stable irony"
in a text.[4] Stable irony, according to Booth, is irony that
is *intended*--it is "deliberately created" and not produced
accidentally or unconsciously; *covert*--the meaning intended by
the author does not reside on the surface of the text but must
be reconstructed by the reader; *stable*--once the reconstruction
of the meaning is accomplished it is not undermined by further
ironies; and *finite*--"the reconstructed meanings are in some
sense local, limited."[5] The key, of course, is the presence in
the text of a disharmony or incongruity that gives the reader
pause. Often the reader discovers the narrator or a character
in the narrative "saying something he does not mean." As a
result, the reader is obliged to delve beneath what is said
to seek out what is meant. Booth outlines in four steps the
process by which readers reconstruct the intended meaning
hiding behind an irony, which we may discuss using Mark 8:4 as
an example.

"*Step one*. The reader is required to reject the literal
meaning."[6] The first step in the reconstruction of the meaning
of an irony is the realization of its incongruity or disharmony.
Its literal meaning is at odds with what one knows to be "true"
in the context of the literary work. In the case of 8:4, the
incongruity arises in the implication of the disciples' question
that no one, or at least no one *they* know, can feed such a
crowd in the desert. The reader must reject this implication in
the disciples' question because the reader remembers a prior
occasion upon which Jesus fed a slightly larger crowd with
slightly fewer provisions.[7] Not only was the crowd fed, but
the disciples were participants in and eyewitnesses to the
feeding. Their question is on its face incomprehensible. How
could they *not* know "how to feed these men with bread here in
the desert"?

"*Step two*. Alternative interpretations or explanations are
tried out."[8] One of the more popular interpretations of 8:4 is
that any supposed incongruity arising here is the result of
repeated traditions--the disciples only appear to be obtuse.

However, our discovery of the Markan composition of 6:30-44 has made this supposition untenable. The portrayal of the disciples implied in the doublet of feeding stories is intended by the author and is not an accidental product of repetitious traditions. Remaining are other alternative interpretations much less palatable to defenders of the disciples. The disciples either could have lost all memory of the prior incident--a kind of mass amnesia--or they could have been incognizant of the earlier feeding even as it was happening. Neither is particularly flattering for the disciples, but these do seem to be the only possible explanations.

"*Step three*. A decision must therefore be made about the author's knowledge or beliefs."[9] At this point we avail ourselves of what we have learned about the author's intentions elsewhere in his work. In view of the rest of this literary work, what is he likely to be saying here? In the first feeding story, we already have a suggestion of the disciples' obtuseness in the brusque manner they order Jesus to send away the crowd. Admittedly, there is no indication here that the disciples do not comprehend the actual act of feeding the crowd. Nevertheless, that the disciples did fail to understand "the loaves" is stated explicitly by the author in a somewhat obtrusive parenthetical comment in 6:51-52: "And they were utterly astonished, for they did not understand about the loaves, but their hearts were hardened." The disciples' lack of perception and understanding in the sea story of 6:45-52 is explained by reference to their lack of perception and understanding in the feeding story of 6:30-44. Mark 6:52 also finds an echo in 8:17 where Jesus himself accuses the disciples of hardheartedness; i.e., failure to perceive, understand, see, hear, and remember. Mark 6:52 summarizes the first feeding story; Mark 8:14-21 summarizes both feeding stories. Consequently, the supposition that Mark intends the disciples to appear obtuse and dull-witted in 8:4 can scarcely be questioned.

"*Step four*. . . . we can finally choose a new meaning or cluster of meanings with which we can rest secure."[10] The true significance of the disciples' question is by now evident. They

condemn themselves with their own words by unwittingly admitting
that they possess no awareness of what Jesus has done and can
do. They are his disciples, but their lack of understanding
hinders their sharing in any significant, lasting way his
ministry. Even worse, they do not perceive that they are not
equal partners in Jesus' ministry. Try as he might, Jesus seems
unable to pierce their shell of incomprehension (6:36-38, 8:2-3,
8:14-21). All of this is skillfully communicated to the reader
by the author's use of irony.

Of the many guises a storyteller may choose to tell his
tale, Mark has chosen the guise of the omniscient narrator who
is able to give the reader penetrating insights into both master
and disciples. In 8:4 Mark presents the reader with a puzzle
created out of stock, traditional material by the simple,
effective expedient of creating the one principal narrative
that precedes it. The author offers the reader a sample of
irony in 8:4, irony that the reader is able to see through in
order to perceive the intended meaning lying behind it. As all
successful ironists must, the author offers not only the irony
but the tools with which to perceive and understand it.

Excursus: Irony in Mark

As one might expect from the title of his book (and from
his previous work),[11] Booth is largely concerned with irony as
a rhetorical device in literature. He demonstrates eloquently
how authors may use this delightful technique to insinuate their
intended meanings to alert readers. Irony is an especially
seductive ploy since it tends to create a comfortable, secure,
self-congratulating community of readers who have successfully
deciphered the author's ironies. The author's purposeful use
of irony and the reader's accurate discernment of it is an
"astonishing communal achievement,"[12] Booth observes. Just such
a "communal achievement" invariably occurs in Mark 8:4 where
countless interpreters have been staggered by the realization
of the author's intended meaning lying below the surface of
the text. Regrettably, many of those who have accurately
perceived the author's intended meaning in 8:4 have recoiled
from it and have sought to deny it. There exist other superlative

examples of irony in Mark, however, that are irresistible and undeniable, as Booth himself has observed. The prominent example cited by Booth is the crucifixion scene where irony has often been detected. Booth's perceptive comments deserve to be quoted at length:

> Often the predominant emotion when reading stable ironies is that of joining, of finding and communing with kindred spirits. The author I infer behind the false words is my kind of man, because he enjoys playing with irony, because he assumes *my* capacity for dealing with it, and--most important--because he grants me a kind of wisdom; he assumes that he does not have to spell out the shared and secret truths on which my reconstruction is to be built.
>
> Even irony that does imply victims, as in all ironic satire, is often much more clearly directed to more affirmative matters. And every irony inevitably builds a community of believers even as it excludes. The cry "Hail, King of the Jews," an example cited by Thomas Hobbes, was intended initially to satirize Christ's followers who had claimed him as king; presumably the chief pleasure for the shouting mob was the thought of the victims, including Christ himself. But what of Mark as he overtly reports the irony ironically in his account of the crucifixion?
>
> It is true that Mark may in part intend an irony against the original ironists, but surely his chief point is to build, through ironic pathos, a sense of brotherly cohesion among those who see the essential truth in his account of the man-God who, though *really* King of the Jews, was reduced to this miserable mockery. The wicked and foolish insolence of those who mocked the Lord with the original "Hail" is no doubt part of Mark's picture, but it is surely all in the service of the communion of Saints.
>
> And there is a curious further point about this community of those who grasp any irony: it is often a larger community, with fewer outsiders, than would have been built by non-ironic statement. Ironists have been accused of elitism. For Kierkegaard, irony "looks down, as it were, on plain and ordinary discourse immediately understood by everyone; it travels in an exclusive incognito. . . . [It] occurs chiefly in the higher circles as a prerogative belonging to the same category as that *bon ton* requiring one to smile at innocence and regard virtue as a kind of prudishness." But it seems clear that Mark's irony builds a larger community of readers than any possible literal statement of his beliefs could have done. If he had said simply, "Those who gathered to mock Jesus did not know that he was in fact King, king not only of the Jews but

of all mankind, quite literally the Son of God,"
a host of unbelievers would draw back, at least
slightly. But the ironic form can be shared by
everyone who has any sympathy for Jesus at all,
man or God; even the reader who sees him as a
self-deluded fanatic is likely to join Mark in
his reading of the irony, and thus to have his
sympathy for the crucified man somewhat increased.[13]

Booth's insightful comments cause us to wonder to what
extent irony is used elsewhere in the gospel of Mark. Certainly,
we believe that the author uses irony in Mark 6-8, but, far
beyond that, we believe that careful study of the irony in Mark
would go far to explain the elusive notion of the Messianic
Secret throughout the gospel. Traditionally, the Messianic
Secret has been viewed as a historical or theological problem,
but if one shifts to a literary critical perspective, then the
observation of the Messianic Secret in Mark may be accurately
regarded as the observation of irony in the gospel. Since Jesus,
the Messiah, is the central figure in the story, most of the
irony in the gospel touches on him. Too seldom is the literary
critical observation made, though, that there is no Messianic
Secret for the reader of Mark.[14] In the very first verse of the
gospel the author reveals to the reader that Jesus is the
Messiah, the Son of God. Periodically in the gospel this proclamation is reaffirmed by the supernatural testimony of demons
and heavenly voices (1:11, 24, 34, 3:11-12, 5:7, 9:7), to say
nothing of Jesus' own messianic demeanor. The author interjects
the irony of the Messianic Secret into the story when Jesus'
divinely sanctioned power and authority is manifested to the
reader but scorned and rejected by characters in the story, or
when Jesus attempts to hide or to suppress discussion of matters
that have already been revealed to the reader. Repeatedly the
reader is given the information he needs in order to see through
the author's irony. Fortunately for the author, irony occurs in
a wide spectrum of language ranging from everyday speech to the
finest literature. Consequently, hearers and readers are
accustomed to deciphering irony with little thought given to the
process. The readers of Mark find most of his irony easily
comprehensible, so much so, in fact, that there has been too
little explicit recognition of it. Historical and theological

concerns have dominated the study of the gospel, so the Markan ironies have been analyzed under these essentially alien categories. The result has been universal agreement that the Messianic Secret is a vital feature of the gospel, but nearly universal disagreement over what it is. "It," we suggest, is a rhetorical device, the use of irony to narrate "the gospel of Jesus Christ, the Son of God." If so, the work by Booth (and others) may prove to be quite helpful in our endeavor to understand the gospel of Mark.[15]

Conclusions

We may now summarize briefly our insights into the doublet of feeding stories. Most significant is the realization that Mark 6:30-44 (or 6:30-56) functions as the primary backdrop against which the events of Mark 8:1ff. are portrayed. By constructing the Feeding of the Five Thousand as he has, the evangelist induces the reader to perceive a portrayal of the disciples in 8:1-10 that is not present when the traditional story is viewed in isolation from its present context. The disciples are the victims of their own ironical question in 8:4; they have no concept of the self-condemnation implied by their words. Thanks to the author's insistent portrayal of the obtuseness of the disciples, the reader has no difficulty comprehending the import of the disciples' revealing query in 8:4.

As a result of our exploration of the ironic tension created by the author between these stories, we have begun to develop a new definition of the term "doublet." In the case of the feeding stories, we have argued that it is inappropriate to use the term "doublet" with the sense of variant pre-Markan accounts of the same story. As we have seen, however, it still makes sense to use the term to describe pairs of narratives intended by the author to be read together as a matched pair of stories.[16] The author has expended considerable energies to create this particular doublet, requiring us to regard these stories with equal seriousness *as a doublet*. There are two other pairs of stories in Mark 4-8 that the evangelist has constructed as doublets, and these we will discuss below.

The Doublet of Sea Stories

We have already devoted considerable attention to the doublet of feeding stories in Mark; in the following pages we will continue this line of investigation with discussions of the tandem sea stories (Mark 4:35-41, 6:45-52) and healing stories (Mark 7:31-37, 8:22-26). Before proceeding any further, though, we should recall an observation we made earlier about the dual structure present in each of these six stories. Such duality is particularly noticeable in the first member of each doublet, stories which involve, respectively, a calming of wind *and* sea (4:35-41), a banquet of bread *and* fish (6:30-44), and a healing of a man who is deaf *and* mute (7:31-37). The following chart sets forth these dualities:

	Wind	*Sea*
4:37	λαῖλαψ μεγάλη ἀνέμου	καὶ τὰ κύματα ἐπέβαλλον εἰς τὸ πλοῖον
4:39	ἐπετίμησεν τῷ ἀνέμῳ	καὶ εἶπεν τῇ θαλάσσῃ
	ἐκόπασεν ὁ ἄνεμος	καὶ ἐγένετο γαλήνη μεγάλη
4:41	καὶ ὁ ἄνεμος	καὶ ἡ θάλασσα ὑπακούει αὐτῷ

	Bread	*Fish*
6:38	πέντε	καὶ δύο ἰχθύας
6:41	λαβὼν τοὺς πέντε ἄρτους	καὶ τοὺς δύο ἰχθύας
	κατέκλασεν τοὺς ἄρτους	καὶ τοὺς δύο ἰχθύας ἐμέρισεν
6:43	ἦραν κλάσματα	καὶ ἀπὸ τῶν ἰχθύων

	Deaf	*Mute*
7:32	φέρουσιν αὐτῷ κωφὸν	καὶ μογιλάλον
7:33	ἔβαλεν τοὺς δακτύλους αὐτοῦ εἰς τὰ ὦτα αὐτοῦ	καὶ πτύσας ἥψατο τῆς γλώσσης αὐτοῦ
7:35	ἠνοίγησαν αὐτοῦ αἱ ἀκοαί	καὶ ἐλύθη ὁ δεσμὸς τῆς γλώσσης αὐτοῦ
7:37	τοὺς κωφοὺς ποιεῖ ἀκούειν	καὶ τοὺς ἀλάλους λαλεῖν

Duality is also featured in the second members of these three doublets, but their dualities vary somewhat from their partners'. Dualities of wind *and* sea, and bread *and* fish are present also in 6:45-52 and 8:1-10, but in both cases there is an imbalance in the duality, one element being featured more prominently than the other. In 6:45-52 the duality of wind and sea is maintained, but the latter feature is represented by Jesus' walking on the sea (περιπατῶν ἐπὶ τῆς θαλάσσης in vv. 48 and 49), which is clearly the predominant motif in the present version of the story. In 8:1-10 the imbalance is on the side of the bread, which, as we have seen, was originally the only food mentioned in the story. Duality is also maintained in 8:22-26 but in an entirely novel way. In this story Jesus heals a man with a different, single ailment--blindness. Although he has only one ailment, duality is still introduced by means of a double cure in which Jesus brings sight to the man in two successive stages (8:23, 25). The recognition of the duality in each of these six individual stories is vital to the proper appreciation of the function of each doublet in the text of Mark 4-8.

In the case of the doublet of sea stories, there are some additional striking similarities with the doublet of feeding stories besides their shared duality. In both sea stories, as well as in both feeding stories, the focus of the action is on the disciples of Jesus. The sea stories also complement each other with regard to who seizes the initiative. In the first sea story, as in the first feeding story, the disciples seize the initiative and demand action of Jesus, and their cry in 4:38 is no less a "querulous question" than 6:37. In the second sea story, as in the second feeding story, the initiative lies entirely with Jesus, who comes to the disciples walking on the sea. The disciples' reaction again reveals their blindness--they take for a phantom him who had already demonstrated to them his power over wind and wave two chapters earlier. Indeed, the disciples' failure to understand Jesus or to perceive the scope and nature of his ministry is the dominant theme in both the feeding stories and the sea stories. One only needs to recall 6:52, which associates the disciples' astonishment at the sea miracle with their dull-witted failure to understand "the loaves."

We will make no attempt in this study to separate tradition from redaction in the sea stories as we did with the feeding stories. We suspect that such an undertaking would not succeed the way it does with the feeding stories, because the doublet

of sea stories was created in a different manner than the
doublet of feeding stories. Besides, in the present discussion
it is sufficient to recognize that both sea stories have been
shaped by Mark and paired as a doublet. Unlike the feeding
stories, there is probably no single story that serves as the
model for both sea stories, since two quite distinct motifs--
the calming of a storm and walking on water--seem to be
involved. Interpreters have long been aware that these two
motifs seem to be awkwardly conflated in 6:45-52.[17] There are
some verses in which the wind storm seems to be the primary
concern (vv. 48b, 51b), but for the most part the walk on the
sea is the dominant motif of the story. The precise verbal
agreement in 4:39 and 6:51 (καὶ ἐκόπασεν ὁ ἄνεμος) has prompted
some to suggest that 4:35-41 and 6:45-52 are variant, traditional
accounts, but this should instead be regarded as an indication
of the evangelist's compositional activity in both stories.[18]
The rigid duality of wind and sea in 4:35-41 and the hopelessly
tangled duality of wind and walking on the sea in 6:45-52 both
manifest the evangelist's hand.

More important for the present discussion is the recognition
of how the sea stories cooperate as a doublet. The first sea
story presents the disciples in an extremely negative light, not
at all unlike the portrayal in 6:30-44. Fearing for their lives,
they rouse Jesus from a sound sleep only to rebuke him for his
insensitivity to the crisis. Jesus silences the wind and calms
the waves, and, turning to the disciples, he accuses them of
cowardice and unbelief. The episode concludes with the disciples
still afraid and muttering among themselves: "Who then is this,
that even wind and sea obey him?" (4:41). This concluding,
unanswered, rhetorical question is doubly important for the
reader of the gospel. First, it reveals to the reader that the
disciples have not even begun to fathom this person whom they
call "teacher" in their time of peril (4:38). At the same time,
the unanswered question stands as a guidepost for the reader,
indicating in the starkest possible manner the central question
addressed by Mark's gospel: "Who then is this. . . .?" Ever
since Mark 1:1 the reader has known that the person of Jesus
Christ, the Son of God, is the focus of the gospel. Mark 4:41

provides the reader with one formulation of the multifaceted question that the author will be answering for the reader as the story progresses. The answer to the question is at this early stage of the story not fully revealed, but by the gospel's end the reader, with help from the author, should be in a position to provide his own answer.

With the first sea story well in mind, we may turn to its companion story in 6:45-52. (The first sea story, we have noted, occurs in Boat Trip I in Mark, while the second sea story occurs in Boat Trip II.) The introductory verses of the second sea story are designed in part to recall for the reader the earlier boat trip in 4:35ff., this being especially true of the reference to the opposing wind in v. 48. In this narrative Jesus' mastery over the sea is displayed in a different manner, by his walking on the sea. In what may be a feature preserved from an original sea epiphany,[19] it is stated that Jesus intended to "pass by them." This comment makes very little sense, it is often remarked, if the intention of the water-walking was to rescue the struggling boaters. It makes a great deal of sense, however, if Mark wants to use the story to demonstrate the disciples' exceptional obtuseness. This is exactly what happens in 6:45-52. Having witnessed previously Jesus' extraordinary power over wind and sea, they mistake for a ghost a being passing by them, through the wind, on the sea. The original epiphantic ἐγώ εἰμι is undermined--Jesus may reveal himself but the disciples do not perceive. We repeat: "their hearts were hardened" (6:52).

As a result of these observations, we realize that Mark is once again manipulating how we perceive one story by stationing a comparable story as a backdrop for it. Analogous to his modification of the traditional feeding story, a new element is added to the traditional *Seewandeln*--the wind--in order to make it resemble the preceding sea story, while the preceding sea story is utilized to control how the reader perceives the *Seewandeln* of the second story. Just as 6:30-44 controls how one perceives the disciples' question in 8:4, 4:35-41 controls how one perceives the disciples' mistaken identification and fear in 6:49-50. What once may have been a proper, understandable

reaction to a disturbing nocturnal apparition is now an
inexcusable demonstration of spiritual blindness. Although he
does not discuss explicitly the manner in which 4:35-41 controls
how the reader perceives 6:45-52, nonetheless Snoy has astutely
observed how Mark has reinterpreted the traditional story that
probably lies behind 6:45-52:

> Ce faisant, *Mc*. modifie profondément et inverse, pour
> ainsi dire, le sens traditionnel de la marche sur les
> eaux. Le miracle comme tel, malgré l'absence de
> développement littéraire du récit, veut illustrer
> le caractère surhumain de la personne de Jésus et sa
> puissance quasi divine sur les éléments. . . . Pour
> le rédacteur, cela a moins d'importance que sa
> conception de la messianité cachée de Jésus qu'il
> développe tout au long de son évangile, et il se sert
> donc de la marche sur les eaux dans le sens de cette
> théorie; au lieu de manifester qui est Jésus, le
> miracle a l'effet contraire, parce que les disciples
> ont "l'esprit bouchée" et, tout comme les paraboles,
> il devient une "énigme" (VII, 17), incompréhensible
> par définition. Comme le phénomène a cependant par
> lui-même une portée théophanique, pour neutraliser
> celle-ci en quelque sorte et simultanément pour
> accentuer la transcendance de celui qui s'y
> manifeste, *Mc*. doit presque nécessairement recourir
> au motif de l'inintelligence des disciples.[20]

For his part, E. Wendling long ago focused on the visual imagery
used in 6:45-52 to portray the disciples' lack of perception
and understanding, a use of language similar to that used in
8:22-26:

> Eine innere Ähnlichkeit besteht nämlich auch zwischen
> 6:49 und 8:24. In beiden Fällen handelt es sich um
> eine optische Täuschung. Der halbgeheilte Blinde
> sieht alles in nebelhaften Umrissen; er hält die
> Menschen zunächst für Bäume; da sie sich aber--
> wunderbarerweise--bewegen, kommt er zu dem Schluss,
> dass es Menschen sein müssen. Die Jünger im Schiff
> sehen im Dunkel der Nacht eine Gestalt sich auf dem
> Wasser bewegen und ziehen aus dieser wunderbaren
> Tatsache den (unrichtigen) Schluss, dass es ein
> Gespenst ist. Während der Mann von Bethsaida seinen
> Irrtum sofort korrigiert, muss den Jüngern Jesus
> selbst die Wahrheit sagen: ἐγώ εἰμι, denn ihr Herz
> ist verstockt (6:52) und mit sehenden Augen sehen
> sie nicht (vgl. 8:18). So weist also schon die
> Konzeption der nächtlichen Erscheinung auf dem See
> in die Richtung von 8:14-26, und die Erzählung
> 6:45ff. ist, wie die beiden Heilungen 7:31ff. 8:22ff.,
> symbolisch zu verstehen. . . .[21]

We can only agree with Wendling that the disciples are "blind"
in 6:45-52--they still seem incapable of resolving the question
they posed in 4:41. Wendling's comment that the blindness of
6:49 corresponds to the blindness of the blind man in 8:24 is
also on target and leads us most conveniently into a discussion
of the third doublet in Mark 4-8: ". . . die beiden Heilungen
7:31ff. 8:22ff., symbolisch zu verstehen. . . ."

The Doublet of Healing Stories

The two healing stories in 7:31-37 and 8:22-26 possess as
much or more verbal similarity than any two stories in Mark,
including the two feeding stories. Our discussion of this
doublet will be facilitated by a synoptic comparison of these
stories:

Mark 7:31-37	Mark 8:22-26
7:31 καὶ πάλιν ἐξελθὼν ἐκ τῶν ὁρίων Τύρου ἦλθεν διὰ Σιδῶνος εἰς τὴν θάλασσαν τῆς Γαλιλαίας ἀνὰ μέσον τῶν ὁρίων Δεκαπόλεως.	8:22 καὶ ἔρχονται εἰς βηθσαϊδάν.
7:32 καὶ φέρουσιν αὐτῷ (κωφὸν καὶ μογιλάλον), καὶ παρακαλοῦσιν αὐτὸν ἵνα ἐπιθῇ αὐτῷ τὴν χεῖρα.	καὶ φέρουσιν αὐτῷ (τυφλὸν) καὶ παρακαλοῦσιν αὐτὸν ἵνα αὐτοῦ ἅψηται.
7:33 καὶ (ἀπο)λαβόμενος αὐτὸν (ἀπὸ τοῦ ὄχλου κατ' ἰδίαν) ἔβαλεν τοὺς δακτύλους αὐτοῦ εἰς τὰ (ὦτα) αὐτοῦ καὶ πτύσας ἥψατο (τῆς γλώσσης) αὐτοῦ,	8:23 καὶ (ἐπι)λαβόμενος τῆς χειρὸς τοῦ τυφλοῦ ἐξήνεγκεν αὐτὸν (ἔξω τῆς κώμης), καὶ πτύσας εἰς τὰ (ὄμματα) αὐτοῦ, ἐπιθεὶς τὰς χεῖρας αὐτῷ, ἐπηρώτα αὐτόν, Εἴ τι βλέπεις;
7:34 καὶ ἀναβλέψας εἰς τὸν οὐρανὸν ἐστέναξεν, καὶ λέγει αὐτῷ, Εφφαθα, ὅ ἐστιν Διανοίχθητι.	8:24 καὶ ἀναβλέψας ἔλεγεν, Βλέπω τοὺς ἀνθρώπους, ὅτι ὡς δένδρα ὁρῶ περιπατοῦντας.
7:35 καὶ εὐθέως ἠνοίγησαν αὐτοῦ αἱ ἀκοαί, καὶ ἐλύθη ὁ δεσμὸς τῆς γλώσσης αὐτοῦ, καὶ (ἐλάλει ὀρθῶς).	8:25 εἶτα πάλιν ἐπέθηκεν τὰς χεῖρας ἐπὶ τοὺς ὀφθαλμοὺς αὐτοῦ, καὶ διέβλεψεν, καὶ ἀπεκατέστη, καὶ (ἐνέβλεπεν τηλαυγῶς) ἅπαντα.

7:36 καὶ (δι) ἐστείλατο
αὐτοῖς
ἵνα μηδενὶ λέγωσιν·
ὅσον δὲ αὐτοῖς
διεστέλλετο,
αὐτοὶ μᾶλλον περισσότερον
ἐκήρυσσον.
7:37 καὶ ὑπερπερισσῶς
ἐξεπλήσσοντο λέγοντες,
Καλῶς πάντα πεποίηκεν·
καὶ τοὺς κωφοὺς ποιεῖ
ἀκούειν καὶ τοὺς ἀλάλους
λαλεῖν.[22]

8:26 καὶ (ἀπ) ἐστειλεν αὐτὸν
εἰς οἶκον αὐτοῦ λέγων,
Μηδὲ εἰς τὴν κώμην
εἰσέλθῃς.

The obvious verbal parallels in these two stories, which are
underlined in the synopsis above, strongly suggest that both
stories were composed by the same person.[23] Just as significant
as the verbal agreements themselves is the fact that the
agreements follow the same order in both stories, with two
instructive exceptions. The exceptions are the phrases used
for Jesus' healing touch in 7:32, 33 and 8:22, 23:

7:32 ἐπιθῇ αὐτῷ τὴν χεῖρα ⟍ 8:22 ⟋ αὐτοῦ ἄψηται

7:33 ἥψατο . . . αὐτοῦ ⟋ 8:23 ⟍ ἐπιθεὶς τὰς χεῖρας αὐτῷ

The verbal agreements here are clear, but they form a crisscross
pattern instead of facing each other in the synopsis as happens
with every other verbal agreement.

Not only is there extensive verbal *agreement* between these
stories, there is also a striking correspondence or correlation
in the *differences* between the stories--the distinguishing
features of both stories often face each other in the synopsis
and are in a sense correlative or complementary. (The correlative differences in 7:31-37 and 8:22-26 have been indicated in
our synopsis by the use of parentheses.) For example, different
maladies are introduced at the same point in each story (7:32
and 8:22); also, different expressions are used for the same
familiar, Markan motif of withdrawal from the crowd for the
sake of privacy (7:33 and 8:23). In other places we find
different cognates of the same verb used (7:33 and 8:23; 7:36
and 8:26); such characteristics of the stories are simultaneously
similarities and dissimilarities. Since the maladies treated in
the two stories are different, Jesus' healing touch is applied
to different parts of the body and the resulting cures manifest
themselves in different ways. Nevertheless, the naming of the

different parts of the body occurs in the same place in each
story (7:33 and 8:23), and the two cures are described in a
similar fashion, with a verb followed by an adverb (7:35 and
8:25). The observation that the outstanding similarities and
dissimilarities of the two stories face each other in the
synopsis necessitates the conclusion that the stories were
composed by the author as a matched pair: the similarities
invite us to compare the stories while the dissimilarities
force us to recognize the integrity of each story as a distinct
episode within the Markan narrative.

Although we will not attempt to recover pre-Markan
tradition lying behind this doublet as we did in the case of
the doublet of feeding stories, we may observe that both
doublets manifest the same striking combination of verbal
agreements and correlative differences, which leads us to
suspect that both doublets were composed in a similar manner.
In both cases the author has endowed the stories with enough
verbal agreements to insure their comparison and sufficient
differences to establish the distinctiveness of each individual
story. Moreover, there is another major feature of the healing
stories that recalls the formulation of the other doublets we
have examined; namely, their clear duality.[24] Analogous to the
first members of both of the other two doublets in Mark 4-8,
7:31-37 relates a dual miracle: Jesus heals a man who is both
deaf *and* mute. The duality of 8:22-26 is also clear but totally
unlike that of 7:31-37. Here only one cure is performed--the
giving of sight to a blind man--but it is performed in two
distinct stages. The significance of Jesus' double healing
touch in both 7:31-37 and 8:22-26 will be explored in greater
detail below.

The one ingredient missing from these stories that is
featured prominently in the other doublets is the role played
by the disciples. The only characters in either story are Jesus
and the man he heals in private. Since the disciples do not
appear in either story, we are alerted immediately to the fact
that this doublet does not function as a demonstration of the
disciples' obtuseness as do the others. Nevertheless, the

doublet does provide an indirect commentary on the disciples'
lack of perception by exhibiting individuals who *are* able to
hear, speak, and see. The key to this insight is the
recognition that the major function of 7:31-37 and 8:22-26
in Mark is to frame the intervening verses in 8:1-21, the
culmination of which is a devastating criticism by Jesus of
the disciples' stupidity, expressed principally in terms of a
failure to "see" and to "hear" (8:18). In contradistinction to
the healed men in 7:31-37 and 8:22-26, the disciples persist in
their deafness, dumbness, and blindness.

It is especially important to recall where we are in the
course of the gospel when we arrive at 8:13-21. Mark 8:13 marks
the beginning of the second half of the third and last boat
trip in Mark. In the first boat trip, the calming of wind and
sea took place. In the second boat trip, the companion sea
story occurs. Now for a third time Jesus and his disciples
are about to play out a scene in the boat on the lake. Is it
not natural for the reader to wonder at this point if the
disciples will conduct themselves any differently in the third
sea story than in the first two? Just as this narrative recalls
the earlier sea stories, it also recalls the two prior feeding
stories. Of course, the second feeding has just been narrated
(8:1-10) so it should still be fresh in the reader's memory,
but, more importantly, 8:14, 16 marks the third time in the
gospel that a shortage of bread arises as a problem. The mention
of a lack of bread in 8:14, 16 recalls for the reader the
situation of the two feeding stories where thousands were fed
with just a few loaves and fish. The reader asks: will the
disciples show more perception here than they did in their
previous two opportunities? Unfortunately, they do not seem to
have profited either from the experiences on the lake or with
the hungry crowds--they are as dull-witted as ever.[25] In a
certain sense, then, inasmuch as the doublet of sea stories and
the doublet of feeding stories are both remembered here, the
function of the doublet of healing stories is to frame and
interpret the other two doublets. Threads from all three doublets
are intertwined in 7:31-8:26.

It is important to realize also that 8:13-21 pulls together other material from the preceding chapters of the gospel.[26] Besides alluding to previous shortages of bread and other boat trips, the introductory verses of this section contain Jesus' warning to beware of the leaven of the Pharisees and the leaven of Herod (8:15). We are not surprised to find Markan asyndeton and duality in this verse:

8:15 ὁρᾶτε

βλέπετε

ἀπὸ τῆς ζύμης τῶν Φαρισαίων

καὶ τῆς ζύμης Ἡρῴδου.[27]

This verse has often been regarded as an awkward insertion into the text, inasmuch as the disciples continue to speak in v. 16 of their lack of bread (v. 14) as if Jesus had not spoken to them.[28] One can make excellent sense of the pericope, however, without dropping v. 15; indeed, we would spoil the evangelist's careful composition if we were to do this. One helpful distinction we may make is that between what the narrator tells us and what the characters in the story tell us. The background to 8:13-21 is provided by the narrator, who informs us that the following episode will take place on a boat (v. 13) and will concern bread (v. 14). Only then does the dialog begin with Jesus' warning about the leaven of the Pharisees and Herod. This logion may be a Markan rendering of a traditional logion of Jesus concerning leaven, but as it is presently formulated it is understandable only in the context of Mark's gospel. The association of Pharisees and Herod has been a factor in the story ever since 3:6, where Pharisees and Herodians begin to plot Jesus' death. In the chapters following that reference, the Pharisees and Herod are either contrasted generally with Jesus or are placed in direct opposition to him. Mark 8:15 refers to no specific characteristics, attitudes, or practices of the Pharisees and Herod, but Mark's consistently derogatory portrayal of them, coupled with the usually negative connotations associated with leaven, enables the perceptive reader to comprehend the metaphor. According to the evangelist, Jesus' benevolent teaching and healing activity may be accurately characterized as "giving bread" (7:27, cf. 2:16-17, 2:24-26),

and the contrasting hostile activity of the Pharisees and Herod
may fairly be regarded as "leaven." Indeed, when Jesus speaks
of leaven in 8:15, the disciples correctly perceive that he is
engaged in bread-talk, although they have not the slightest
inkling of what Jesus is really talking about, persisting in
their worry about their lack of provisions. The reader of the
gospel, who has followed the intrigues of the Pharisees and
Herod from the beginning, has a reliable intuitive feeling
for what the "leaven" refers to--the reader has seen these
characters in action.[29] (If we were to include 8:11-12 among
the introductory verses of 8:13-21, as perhaps we should, then
the section is introduced with a succinct demonstration of the
Pharisees' enmity in addition to references to the boat and to
bread.) To the disciples the metaphor is opaque; so much so, in
fact, that interpreters have attempted to overcome the utter
discontinuity between v. 15 and v. 16 by eliminating v. 15.
They fail to see that the discontinuity between these verses is
not between distinct, divergent pieces of tradition but between
the thoughts of the characters in the story. What we have here
is the same kind of play on words and associated misunderstanding
that we find repeatedly in the gospel of John (e.g., John 3:34,
6:33-35).[30] The disciples misunderstand the bread-talk of v. 15
as a reference to loaves of bread; they are oblivious to the
true significance of Jesus' words. Jesus responds to them in
v. 17, pointing out that if they are talking about real bread
then they obviously do not understand--their hearts are
hardened (8:17). The rest of the discourse employs a variety of
expressions for sense perception and intellectual understanding
to stress the magnitude of the disciples' obtuseness. After a
final attempt to get them to recall and discern the significance
of the doublet of feeding stories, the section concludes with
Jesus' plaintive rhetorical question: "Do you not yet understand?" (8:21). Precisely *what* the disciples are to understand
is left unspecified; in fact, the evangelist never spells it out
explicitly anywhere in this part of the gospel. The interpreter
of the gospel must admit that even he does not know for sure
what the disciples should understand. We may safely state at

the very least that what they should understand has something
to do with the person of Jesus. Fortunately, the reader does
have the portrayal of Jesus prior to this point in the
narrative to rely on, and it allows the reader to feel
reasonably sure that he has some genuine insight into the
story's protagonist. We need only recall the numerous
occasions upon which the divinely sanctioned power and
authority of Jesus is seemingly manifested to the disciples
only to have them indicate that they fail to see or understand.
Such epiphanies are not lost upon the reader. Nevertheless,
the full revelation of who Jesus is is, at least for the
reader of Mark, contingent upon the completed reading of the
entire gospel.

We have already commented on the predominance of the
language of deafness, dumbness, and blindness in 7:31-8:26.
The tragedy of this section is that Jesus is able to heal two
strangers with these afflictions but is unable to penetrate the
spiritual deafness, dumbness, and blindness of his closest
associates. In several places in this section there are significant parallels of language that strengthen the implied
contrast between the doublet of healing stories and the
incredible stupor of the disciples depicted in the intervening
verses. Noteworthy is the construction of the warning in 8:15
using two verbs for "to see." The disciples are admonished to
"look out for" (ὁρᾶτε), to "beware of" (βλέπετε), the leaven
of the Pharisees and Herod. That they do neither is clear from
the following verses. This is in direct contrast to the man in
8:22-26 who comes gradually to an awareness of his surroundings
(βλέπω) by first seeing (ὁράω) men as trees. Moreover there is
a prolixity to the description of the man's ability to see that
parallels the profusion of terms used to describe the disciples'
blindness in 8:13-21. In 8:23-25 no less than five verbs are
employed to describe the man's newly acquired vision: βλέπω,
ἀναβλέπω, ὁράω, διαβλέπω, and ἐμβλέπω.[31] Another repetition of
familiar language occurs in 8:18 where it is stated that the
disciples have eyes but do not see, ears but do not hear. This
one verse simultaneously contrasts the disciples' obtuseness
with both stories of the doublet.

To this point we have concentrated on the disciples'
deafness and blindness to the neglect of their third affliction
--dumbness, or the inability to speak properly (λαλέω ὀρθῶς--
7:35)--but this too is a feature of 8:13-21. It is, in fact,
their dumb muttering about a lack of bread that first reveals
to Jesus that they still do not "perceive or understand" (8:17).
This is quite consistent with other episodes in the gospel
where the disciples reveal their lack of perception by what
they say. We became well acquainted with the disciples' self-
condemning utterances in the previous doublets (e.g., 4:38, 41,
6:37, 8:4), and their verbal ineptness will continue in
following chapters (e.g., 8:32, 9:6, 9:33-34, 10:35, 37, etc.).
Especially striking are those instances where the author goes
out of his way to indicate that their words are clumsy, foolish,
and insensitive (e.g., 9:6 and 10:38). Dumbness, no less than
deafness or blindness, is indeed an affliction that besets the
Twelve.

A contrast is drawn between the doublet and the intervening
verses in another intriguing way. Both healing stories, on the
one hand, involve Jesus healing a man with a double touch. In
8:13-21, on the other hand, Mark has very carefully presented
to the reader the third example of a boat episode and the third
example of a lack-of-bread episode. In spite of this repetition
of familiar circumstances, the disciples are as uncomprehending
as ever. The antithesis is inescapable. Jesus' ability to
confer hearing, speech, and sight by a double touch fails in the
case of the disciples. They have already had dual opportunities
for achieving insight and understanding in the previous doublets,
and now a third opportunity arises, but they remain as insensate
as ever. Mark 8:22-26, in particular, unhappily reminds us of
the disciples' inability to obtain even the smallest measure of
perception. The man in this story obtains partial sight before
obtaining full vision, an acquisition of perception in
successive stages. The disciples, to the contrary, do not
increase in perception from one stage to the next. The blind
man was fully healed after two touches, but even after three
"touches," the disciples are as blind as they were in the
beginning.

The Doublets in Mark: Concluding Remarks

We are now in a position to make some final remarks on
the function of the three doublets in Mark 4-8. Besides the
recognition that the themes of all three doublets are gathered
in 8:13-21, revealing the author's intent to have the reader
recall them collectively, we should note also that the three
doublets overlap in the structure of Mark 4-8, forming a chain-
like structure:

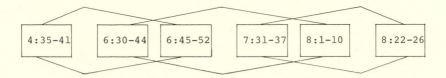

The theories suggesting the author's use of pre-Markan cycles of
stories in Mark 4-8 invariably break down this structure in
order to reconstruct what is supposedly the original pre-Markan
order of these stories. The presence of doublets is taken as an
indication of repetitious tradition, the doublets often being
regarded as markers of the beginnings or endings of cycles. In
other words, the doublets in these chapters are taken as signs
of the original discontinuity and disunity of these stories
instead of being perceived for what they now are--unifying
elements that tie these chapters together into an indissoluble,
harmonious whole. It all depends upon the interpreter's
orientation. If the interpreter is intent on explaining the
duality in these chapters by appealing to pre-gospel tradition,
then the doublets will be regarded as invitations to fragment
the text into its original component units. If, however, the
interpreter is intent on understanding how these stories function
in the gospel as we now have it, he will discover the manner in
which these stories work together to tell the author's story.
The one approach regards the doublets as a license to fragment
the text; the other approach discovers the doublets to be the
means by which the text is given its cohesiveness and integrity.
It is no small confirmation of the latter approach to discover
that the evangelist has had the major role in the actual creation
of doublets, primarily with the doublet of feeding stories.
All the facts seem to demand the immediate abandonment of all

talk about double, pre-Markan traditions in Mark 4-8.

Another confirmation of the discovery that the doublets give Mark 4-8 its unity is the recognition that this is exactly the kind of compositional technique of which Mark is quite fond. Whether we want to speak of duality, progressive double-step expressions, Markan insertions, intercalation, the sandwich technique, inclusio, framing, or doublets, we are essentially talking about a single compositional technique: the use of repeated elements to frame and elucidate intervening material. Mark does this on a very small scale, in the so-called Markan insertions or double-step expressions, and he does it on a large scale, with intercalated stories and doublets. The function of this technique varies from instance to instance. In the case of the three doublets in Mark 4-8, we observe that the author creates an ironic tension between both sea stories and both feeding stories, a tension that is entirely absent from the healing stories, whose function is, rather, to stand together as an antithetical framework to the imperception of the disciples in 8:1-21. Perhaps the most interesting thing we have learned about Mark's framing technique is that he is unafraid of overlapping these constructions. In this way he is able to tie his stories together into a connected whole. We suspect, moreover, that the entire gospel is composed in this fashion.

The Feeding of the Five Thousand in Its Immediate Context: The Intercalation of 6:6b-13/14-29/30ff.

We have now discussed briefly the function of the three doublets in Mark 4-8. There is, of course, much material lying between these stories that is of importance for the proper understanding of these chapters in the gospel. An exhaustive examination of this material will have to be postponed for future work, but we should at least examine in greater detail the intercalation in Mark 6. The intercalation of the Banquet of Herod between the beginning (6:6b-13) and end (6:30ff.) of the disciples' mission has long been noted.[32] Little significance has been attached to this observation, other than the oft-repeated platitude that the author inserts 6:14-29 to fill the gap between the beginning and end of the mission. As Nineham puts it, "to fill in the gap between the sending out of the

twelve (vv. 6b-13) and their return (vv. 30-34) St. Mark tells
the story of the beheading of John the Baptist by Herod (vv. 17-
29)."[33] To say that the story is used "to fill the gap" is,
however, merely to use a circumlocution for the term intercalation (or sandwich technique, or *Schachtelung*). That the
author has "filled the gap" between 6:6b-13 and 6:30ff. is
obvious. The question is why he did this. What is the significance of this organization of the narrative? What is the
author attempting to communicate to the reader by organizing
his material in this way? We suggest that the abrupt juxtaposition of seemingly disparate material in 6:6b-44 does
indeed have significance. We need only to look at other
instances of intercalation in Mark to see that this is a
credible suggestion.

Another well-known instance of intercalation in Mark is
found in 11:12-14/15-19/20-25, the insertion of the incident
at the temple into the midst of the episode of the cursed fig
tree. Here we have the same sort of association by intercalation
of seemingly unrelated, disparate episodes. Because of the
intimate way they are associated, though, the reader is
emboldened to attempt to make sense of 11:12-25 *as a whole*.
As it so happens, it is not difficult to perceive the implications of this montage. Above we cited Nineham's opinion that
the function of 6:14-29 is merely "to fill in the gap"; he is
typical of the considerable number of exegetes who have failed
to perceive the significance of 6:6b-13/14-29/30ff. while
easily recognizing the significance of 11:12-14/15-19/20-25.
Nineham states:

> As we have already seen, St. Mark's understanding of
> the temple cleansing emerges in part from the way he
> has sandwiched it between the two parts of the fig
> tree story. The temple and its worship stand for
> Jewish life and religion; the Messiah comes to it
> and when he finds that the outward foliage of
> ceremony hides no fruit of righteousness, his
> only possible reaction is one of judgement and
> cleansing. . . . Jesus' action is therefore seen
> as that of the messianic king on his great final
> visit to his Father's house and people, and, as
> such, it embodies God's *ultimate* judgement upon
> the life and religion of Israel.[34]

Nineham is no less astute in his observations of the significance of intercalation in other instances. The intercalation
of the trial of Jesus (14:55-65) into the denial of Peter
(14:53-54, 66-72) is not hard to fathom--this intercalation
makes it possible for Jesus to give a piercingly clear
confession of his identity (14;62) at the same time that Peter
is disavowing his own identity as a follower of Jesus (14:68,
70, 71):

> The explanation of the intertwining of this story
> with the story of Peter's denial lies probably in
> v. 62 where Jesus for the first and only time
> publicly proclaims his true, heavenly status and
> the glorious destiny awaiting him. He does this
> not only in the moment of his deepest humiliation
> and weakness, when he is completely at the mercy
> of his enemies, but also at the moment when he is
> denied and deserted by the last of his human
> supporters. . . . [The story of Peter's denial]
> serves as a foil to Jesus' self-revelation in
> v. 62. . . .[35]

If these interpretations of other intercalations in Mark are
correct, and we believe they are, then it would seem highly
appropriate to redouble our efforts to make sense of the
intercalation in Mark 6. Before allowing the judgment to
stand that 6:14-29 serves merely to fill the gap between 6:13
and 6:30, we should examine this material once more.

Mark 6:6b-13

This section begins the mission of the disciples which is
completed in 6:30ff. with their report to Jesus about what they
had "done and taught" and with the subsequent events near or on
the sea. As we already noted, the mission's seemingly auspicious
beginning is totally obliterated by the disciples' failure to
"understand the loaves" (6:30-44) and to perceive who Jesus is
(6:45-52).[36] We may be entitled to see in 6:12-13, 30 an
indication that the mission began well enough, but it is inappropriate to conclude from these verses that it also ended
well.[37] The disciples may be able to teach and heal, but their
antagonism to Jesus (6:36-38) and their utter inability to
comprehend him (6:49-50) betrays a serious disjunction between
their ministry and his. While Jesus teaches (6:34) and heals
(6:55-56) they are intractable and blind.

The conclusion to be reached as a result of these observations is that the action begun in 6:6b-13 continues in 6:30 and beyond with the feeding and sea stories. We may add one more observation to substantiate this continuity in the text. We note, first of all, that Jesus takes pains to instruct the disciples on how to prepare for and how to conduct their mission. This instruction especially concerns how they are to dress and what provisions they are to take. We note, in particular, that they are admonished to take no bread and no money (6:8). Perhaps Jesus' command is to be taken even more strictly if, as Swete suggests, "the order is ascensive: 'no bread, no bag to carry what they could buy, no money to buy with.'"[38] How well do the disciples fulfill this part of their mission charge? The author gives us an implicit answer in 6:30ff. The heart of 6:30-44 is the controversy over bread and money between Jesus and the Twelve (6:36-38). After the disciples' insistence that the crowd be sent away to buy their own bread, Jesus responds by ordering his disciples to feed the crowd themselves. This command makes no reference to buying food, but it provides the opportunity for the disciples' peevish response which is intensely concerned about the amount of money required to buy food for such a crowd: "Shall we go and buy two hundred denarii worth of bread, and give it to them to eat?" We must suggest that the implication of this verse is that the disciples have two hundred denarii that they are unwilling to spend on the crowd. They think that Jesus' command to feed the crowd is a command to empty their wallets. It will not suffice to offer the apology for the disciples that this amount of money is more than the disciples would have had and less than they would have needed to feed the crowd, thereby reading into this passage the meaning of John 6:7, where the two hundred denarii are mentioned only as a hypothetical figure which would not suffice to feed the crowd.[39] *All* of the other gospel writers-- Matthew and Luke as well as John--have chosen to soften the disciples' miserliness as portrayed in Mark 6:37. Matthew and Luke have chosen to drop the reference to the denarii altogether (Matt. 14:13-21, Luke 9:10-17); John alone retains it,

but he makes it clear that the two hundred denarii is only a
hypothetical sum. It is particularly inappropriate to read John
6:7 into the Markan account. In the context of Mark, we must
insist that Mark 6:37 be taken at face value. There is no
clear indication anywhere previously in Mark that the disciples
were without such funds, indeed, the gospel's repeated
admonitions about lures of wealth may be intended to suggest
quite the opposite.[40] The scandal of 6:37 is that the
disciples have disregarded Jesus' admonition of 6:8. Having
been commanded at the outset of their mission to take no money,
they now worry about having to spend a considerable sum on a
hungry crowd. Upon hearing their financial deliberations, Jesus'
response is swift: "How many *loaves* have you? Go and see."
"Five," they reply, "and two fish." Ordered in 6:8 to take
neither bread nor money on their travels, they complete their
mission with both contraband elements on hand. They would not
part with the money to feed the crowd, but they are willing to
relinquish their modest store of provisions to feed five thousand men. Just as John's account represents a softening of the
scandal of the disciples' monetary resources by making the sum
only hypothetical, the scandal of their possession of bread
and fish is eliminated there by having a small boy provide the
food. Is it too much to suggest that John has accurately perceived the unflattering portrait of the disciples in Mark
6:36-38 and has been able to rescue them even while maintaining
the references to two hundred denarii, five loaves, and two
fish?

The disciples' possession of bread and money in 6:37-38,
after having been expressly ordered not to carry such, is yet
another indication of the failure of their mission. Whatever
they may have in common with Jesus and his mission, they are
ultimately callous to his wishes and blind to the significance
of his teaching and mighty deeds. From the standpoint of Mark's
narrative technique it is interesting to note the function of
6:6b-13 as a backdrop for 6:30-44 just as 6:30-44 is a backdrop
for 8:1-10. In both cases the way one perceives a particular
episode in the narrative is controlled by the details related
to the reader in a prior episode. We have therefore discovered

a continuous thread running through 6:6b-13, 6:30-44, and 8:1-10. When the second feeding incident occurs the disciples again have bread on hand; this takes on a new significance when we link this information with 6:37 and 6:8. We may even follow the thread further into 8:14 where it is stated that the disciples lack bread through their neglect (ἐπιλανθάνομαι). The virtue enjoined upon them in 6:8 has now become a vice in their eyes; their lack of bread in 8:14 occurs through inadvertence and not through conscious choice. They do not realize that what they have "neglected" is really obedience to the command of 6:8. They continue to fret over their lack of bread (8:14, 16), oblivious to the fact that Jesus has prescribed such austerity as a way of life for his ἀπόστολοι.

Mark 6:14-29

The major feature we wish to focus on in this section of the intercalation is the impact this unit has on the reader's perception of the identity of Jesus. The identity of Jesus, the protagonist of Mark's story, is a matter of concern beginning with the first verse of the gospel where one is told that Jesus is the Christ, the Son of God. What these titles mean to the author is, of course, unknown at first, but the reader has every right to expect to be informed what this affirmation means in the course of the story. It is fair to say that the gospel serves to interpret and dramatize the affirmation of its first verse. The author uses a number of techniques to keep the identity of Jesus before the reader as a lively issue. First, a variety of christological titles are applied to Jesus throughout the gospel; to "Christ" and "Son of God" we may quickly add "Son of Man," "Lord," and "Son of David."[41] Second, there are instances such as 4:41 and 6:3 where the question of Jesus' identity is raised but given no concrete answer. The reader is handed the unresolved question and the obligation to solve it himself. Third, as we have seen in the doublets of Mark 4-8, the author graphically portrays the incomprehension and blindness of the disciples vis-à-vis Jesus. Exactly what they are to comprehend or perceive when they confront Jesus is not always clear, but the recurrent

blindness of the disciples prods the reader to attempt to
discover what the disciples are missing.

We could continue to discuss at length the narrative
techniques used by the author to interject subtly the question
of Jesus' identity into the story. However, the tactic that is
most noticeable in 6:14-29 is the introduction of character
models with which to compare Jesus. In the narrow compass of
three verses--6:14-16--we are introduced to King Herod, John
the Baptist, Elijah, and a "prophet." Mark 6:14-16 furnishes
the reader with a sumptuous tableau of personages and
encourages the reader to compare them to Jesus. The importance
of this tableau to the author is affirmed by its reappearance
in 8:28, implying that the characters named in these passages
are of some importance in the understanding of who Jesus is.[42]

The first figure to appear in 6:14-16 is King Herod
(Antipas). We have already discussed the comparison between
Herod and Jesus implied by the juxtaposition of their respective
banquets in 6:14-29 and 6:30-44. We observed, for example, the
threefold group of diners that each host feeds (6:21, 39-40) and
the novel uses to which they both put their serving vessels
(6:28, 43). Naturally, both banquets were attended by men only
(6:21-22, 44). In addition we noted the parallel actions of
Jesus and Herod in commissioning their emissaries or "apostles"
(6:7, 17, 27, 30). Once we begin to talk about commissioning
emissaries, however, we move from the imagery of the oriental
banquet to another cluster of images that is pervasive in the
gospel: the imagery of kingship and kingdom. Fastidious
commentators are careful to note that Herod was not really a
king (6:14, 22, 25, 26, 27) and that he did not have a
legitimate kingdom to offer the dancing girl (6:23). Matthew
and Luke give him his correct title: Tetrarch (Matt. 14:1, Luke
3:19, 9:7). Why then does Mark insist on calling him "king"?
We could regard this as a satire on Herod's kingly pretensions,
if we were able to assume that the story was originally
intended for readers who knew that Herod Antipas was deposed
by Caligula in 39 C.E. because of Herod's aspiration to have the
title of king.[43] The text of Mark itself does not lend support

to this assumption. One could also conclude that calling Herod a
king is simply one of the many errors of fact in a story drawn
from Mark's *Vorlage*.[44] Even if this is a factual error preserved
from Mark's source, the question remains: why did Mark allow
the stress on the title to remain? As the story stands now in the
text of Mark, what meaning should we attach to the insistence
that Herod is a king? We suggest that the sharp emphasis on the
kingship of Herod functions to make the comparison between
Herod and Jesus in 6:14-44 an implicit comparison of kingly
figures. Their parallel actions in hosting banquets and
commissioning apostles induces the reader to compare and contrast
Herod and Jesus; the emphasis on the kingship of Herod encourages
one at least to contemplate in what ways and to what extent it
is appropriate to speak of Jesus with kingship language. Elsewhere in the gospel, Jesus is linked quite explicitly with the
notions of kingship and kingdom. It is entirely accurate to
speak, as John Donahue has, of a "Royal Christology" in Mark:
Jesus is the herald of the Kingdom (1:14-15) and, for those
who have eyes to see and ears to hear, he is the Christ, the
King of the Jews (15:2, 9, 12, 18, 26, 32).[45] Although Jesus is
not specifically referred to as king in Mark 6, it is no small
matter that his actions are deliberately set over against those
of King Herod. Mark 6:14-29 is the only place in the gospel
where the deeds of a publicly recognized king are set forth.[46]
By juxtaposing the deeds of Herod with the deeds of Jesus, Mark
adroitly demonstrates the ways in which King Herod and Jesus are
similar while simultaneously contrasting their kingly behavior.

King Herod's first act in 6:14-29 is to hear the gossip
about Jesus' identity--is he John the Baptist, Elijah, or a
prophet of old?--and to give his own opinion: he is John the
Baptist *redivivus*.[47] Jesus has already referred to himself
earlier in this chapter as a prophet (6:4); now he is identified
with no less than three prophetic figures. In addition to
comparing Jesus with the King, the reader is compelled to
compare him with these prophets. The implicit question that
arises now is what qualities or characteristics does Jesus have
that lead people to see in him either John the Baptist, Elijah,
or another prophet? The evangelist does not provide an explicit

answer to this question, but reliable deductions may be made
from the way he has fashioned his story. Right now we wish to
stress the point that the images of both the *king* and the *prophet*
are juxtaposed to Jesus' activity in Mark 6 and linger in the
reader's mind as he reads the feeding story and the sea
story. If we may be allowed to turn to John's gospel yet
another time, is it not possible that John has accurately
perceived the prophet/king imagery in Mark 6 and preserved it in
his own gospel? In John there is no comparison of Jesus to King
Herod or to the three prophets,[48] but there is the epilogue to
the Feeding of the Five Thousand wherein it is plainly stated
that the crowd perceived Jesus to be "the prophet who is to come
into the world" and consequently wished to make him king (John
6:14-15).[49]

What is the significance for the reader of Mark of Herod's
conclusion that Jesus is John *redivivus*? On the one hand, the
reader is able to dismiss at once this false conclusion, since
the reader knows from reading the gospel that Jesus and John
are two distinct individuals. At the beginning of the gospel,
Jesus and John appear together in the scene where Jesus is
baptized in the Jordan by John (1:9). The reader knows that
these men are not the one and same person, so the reader
perceives the error in Herod's conclusion as soon as it is
uttered. On the other hand, one cannot escape the conclusion
that there is some striking similarity or resemblance providing
the basis of the false identification of Jesus as John. Indeed,
Jesus and John are constantly paired in Mark's gospel; they are
almost twins or *Doppelgänger*.[50] The gospel begins with the
preaching of both John (1:4, 7) and Jesus (1:14). John is
described as an Elijah-like figure wearing camel-hair and leather
girdle (1:6; cf. 2 Kgs. 1:8), but allusions to the Elijah
stories in the book of Kings are also applied to Jesus. In
particular, Elijah's forty-day sojourn in the wilderness during
which time he was fed by an angel is echoed in Mark 1:12-13.[51]

The opening verses of Mark also appear to link John with
Jesus in a master-disciple relationship. Jesus submits to John's
baptism of repentance and is clearly the anticipated disciple of

John (the one who comes from his following--ἔρχεται ὀπίσω
μου)[52] who is his superior (ὁ ἰσχυρότερός μου). Even though
John is delivered up (παραδίδωμι)[53] and removed from active
participation in the narrative already in 1:14, his ghost
haunts the entire gospel. As late in the gospel as 11:27-33,
where Jesus is asked to defend his abrogation of the temple
cultus,[54] Jesus refuses to explain the basis of his ἐξουσία
unless his opponents explain to him the basis of John's
ἐξουσία. They refuse to talk about John; Jesus refuses to talk
about himself. The questions about both John and Jesus are left
unanswered in the story, but the reader is not at a loss for
answers. To understand either John or Jesus, in Mark's opinion,
is to understand his counterpart, and by this point in the
story the alternative of "from heaven" or "from men" (11:30)
presents no real puzzle for the perceptive reader.

Mark 6:14-16 does far more than simply associate Jesus with
John the Baptist. More specifically Jesus is identified with a
dead (6:14), *beheaded* (6:16) John the Baptist, injecting an
ominous threat into the story of Jesus. If Jesus' counterpart
met such a heinous end, should we not contemplate the same
possibility for Jesus?[55] Since we know as early as 3:6 that
persons associated with Herod are plotting to kill Jesus, John's
cruel death through Herodian intrigue in 6:14-29 serves to
foreshadow Jesus' own fate. Indeed, if we look ahead in the
story to the account of Jesus' hearing before Pilate and his
subsequent execution, we perceive that there is a striking
parallel between the account of John's death at the order of
Herod and Jesus' execution at the consent of Pilate. Austin
Farrer has pointed out this parallel vividly;

> Herod, like Pilate, is lukewarm and would spare
> the preacher if he could. But, like Pilate, he is
> subject to a pressure which in the end he fails to
> resist. In both stories the dénouement turns upon
> a feast-time boon. On an occasion arising out of
> the celebration of his birthday Herod offers his
> little daughter any boon she likes to ask. On
> occasion of the Passover Pilate offers the people
> the freedom of any prisoner for whom they like to
> intercede. The two offers look entirely different
> but the boons actually demanded turn out to be
> comparable. Moved by her mother, the girl asks,

> not for the expected trinket, but for the
> Baptist's death; moved by the priests the
> people decline to ask for Christ's life and
> demand Barabbas's instead. Pilate and Herod
> are both trapped by their princely promises;
> Jesus and his precursor are both executed
> (vi. 14-28, xv. 6-15).[56]

We began by comparing the kingly deeds of Herod and Jesus in
Mark 6; then the judgment by the Baptist's murderer that Jesus
is the Baptist prompted us to survey the duo of John and Jesus
in Mark's gospel. Now we must add to this growing web of
character portrayals in Mark the similar deeds of Herod and
Pilate.

All of the references we have discussed to this point
concerning the *Doppelgänger* John and Jesus have demonstrated
rather clearly their close association and comparable fates.
There is still one passage in Mark that is far more enigmatic:
9:11-13. This passage involves two figures, Elijah and the Son
of Man, ciphers for characters in the gospel that the reader
should be able to identify: John and Jesus. The organization of
this passage is garbled, as countless commentators have
observed,[57] but it is possible to make some sense of it. The
essential insight to be gained here is that "Elijah" has come
and that his fate was like the fate destined for the "Son of
Man."

After the disciples' incomprehension of Jesus' word about
the resurrection of the Son of Man in 9:9-10, the issue of the
coming of Elijah is raised abruptly in v. 11. Jesus confirms that
"Elijah does come first to restore all things," a clear allusion
to the eschatological expectation of the coming of Elijah before
the appearance of the Messiah.[58] After confirming that the
expectation of Elijah is a valid one, Jesus suddenly begins to
talk about the fate of the Son of Man: "And how is it written
of the Son of Man, that he should suffer much and be scorned?"
Then, abruptly, we jump back to Elijah again: Elijah has already
come and has met his fate, as it was written of him. It is
probably impossible to untangle these verses; everything said is
purposely allusive and oblique. The use of the cipher-names
(Elijah, the Son of Man) obscures the passage, as do the
references to unknown (apocryphal?) writings in 9:12c, 13c.

Nonetheless, is there not something to be learned even from the tangled, oblique state of these verses? Even in their obliqueness, do they not clearly imply that the fates of "Elijah" and the "Son of Man" are intertwined? The mystery of the fate of the Son of Man is now extended to include the fate of Elijah. Walter Wink speaks rightly of an "Elijianic secret" attached to the Messianic Secret in Mark.[59]

Just as with the Messianic Secret in Mark, there is no Elijianic secret *for the reader of Mark*; the author has equipped the reader with the information necessary to penetrate both of these "secrets." Regarding the Son of Man in Mark, the author's parenthetical comments in 2:10, 28 make it clear that third person references to the Son of Man actually refer to Jesus himself. The predictions of the passion and resurrection of the Son of Man in 8:31, 9:12, 31, 10:33 may be strange, enigmatic utterances to the disciples in the story, but they are transparent to the reader. Similarly with the figure of Elijah, the reader who recognizes Mal. 3:1 in Mark 1:2 and 2 Kgs. 1:8 in Mark 1:6 suspects from the beginning that John is an Elijah-like figure. Now Mark 9:13 makes this certain. The Elijah who has already come and met his fate can only be the "Elijah" who was executed in 6:14-29. If the "Son of Man" is Jesus, the "Elijah" must certainly be his *Doppelgänger*, John the Baptist.

The identification of John with Elijah opens up a whole new line of inquiry into the identity of Jesus in Mark, for if John is to be identified with Elijah, should we not expect to find Jesus identified with Elijah's disciple and successor, Elisha? There do seem to be, in fact, some latent similarities between Jesus and Elisha. Jesus, like Elisha, is portrayed as a disciple of an "Elijah" (1 Kgs. 19:19-21, Mark 1:7-9), and only after "Elijah" leaves the scene do either of them begin their own careers (2 Kgs. 2:11-18, Mark 1:14-15). In the succession narratives in both 2 Kgs. 2:1-18 and Mark 1:9-15 there is an emphasis on the successor's receiving "the spirit" in the vicinity of the Jordan river: Elisha receives a double portion of his master's spirit, and Jesus has the spirit descend on him in the form of a dove. Both men go on to become famous wonderworkers, both of them at one time feeding a multitude with

just a few loaves of bread, leaving food to spare (2 Kgs. 4:42-
44, Mark 6:30-44, 8:1-10). Gerhard Hartmann has gone so far as
to suggest that the structure and sequence of the miracle
stories in Mark are modeled after the miracles of Elisha in 2
Kings.[60] This suggestion probably asserts too much, as his
critics have maintained,[61] but it is important to realize that
both Elijah and Elisha imagery seems to be present in Mark.
Inasmuch as Elisha is never mentioned explicitly in the gospel,
we must regard the Elisha imagery as secondary in importance to
the more prominent Elijah imagery.

We are ready now to examine the other personages present
in 6:15 and 8:28; Elijah and "a prophet like one of the
prophets." The latter designation is somewhat obscure, to be
sure, but in the context of the gospel there can be little
doubt that this evokes the image of the eschatological
"prophet like Moses" expected by some Jews and Samaritans on
the basis of Deut. 18:15-22.[62] Simply on the basis of this
widespread speculation in the milieu of early Christianity about
the coming of a prophet like Moses, we are tempted to suggest
that the references in 6:15 and 8:28 serve to associate Jesus
with a Mosaic model. Even so, there is further evidence in Mark
to indicate that the personages referred to in 6:14-15 and
8:28 are actually John, Elijah, and "a prophet like Moses."
The key here is the combined evidence of Mark 1:7-11 and 9:2-8,
the two episodes in the gospel where Jesus receives the
commendation of the heavenly voice.[63] The primary figures in
attendance alongside of Jesus in these episodes (not counting
the disciples in 9:2-8) are, in the first episode, John the
Baptist, and, in the second episode, Elijah and Moses, the same
figures referred to, we claim, in 6:14-15 and 8:28. In 9:4
the order of appearance--"Elijah with Moses"--often attracts
attention. Why is the order not reversed according to the order
in which these figures appear in the Hebrew scriptures or,
indeed, according to the order in which they are named in 9:5?[64]
Finding the answer may be as simple as turning to the final
verses of Malachi. The last two verses of Malachi in the
Masoretic text (Mal. 3:23-24 MT) are, of course, the major text
in the Old Testament referring to the eschatological appearance

of Elijah.[65] In the Masoretic text an admonition to "remember
the law of my servant Moses" (Mal. 3:22 MT) immediately precedes
the promise of the coming Elijah. In other words, an exhor-
tation to heed the law of Moses is juxtaposed to the promise of
Elijah's coming, a pairing that could encourage reference to
Moses and Elijah in the same breath. In some manuscripts of
the Septuagint, on the other hand, the order is reversed, with
the statement about Elijah (Mal. 3:22-23 LXX) preceding the
statement about Moses (Mal. 3:24 LXX). Hence the order of
"Elijah with Moses" in Mark 9:4, the same order, we might add,
that is found in 6:15 and 8:28.

Besides clarifying for us exactly what personages are
referred to in 6:14-15 and 8:28, the narratives in 1:7-11 and
9:2-8 serve the valuable function of telling us the author's
opinion of these figures as they relate to Jesus. This confirms
the validity of our decision to consult 1:7-11 and 9:2-8 in
order to clarify 6:14-15 and 8:28. Standing alone, 6:14-15 and
8:28 are neutral. They provide no evaluation of the prophetic
figures mentioned, nothing that indicates to the reader what
he should think about these figures as he compares them to
Jesus. Obviously we are to compare Jesus with these figures, but
what conclusions should we reach as a result of such comparison?
To find the author's evaluation of these figures as they relate
to Jesus, we must move, as we have, from 6:14-15 and 8:28 to
1:7-11 and 9:2-8, where the authorial evaluation of John, Elijah,
and Moses vis-à-vis Jesus is revealed. The conclusion the author
wants us to draw is easily summarized: Jesus is their superior
and he is to be heeded above them.

In 1:7-11 John's announcement of the one from his following
who will prove superior to him is juxtaposed to the account of
John's baptism of Jesus, the descent of the spirit upon Jesus,
and the voice from heaven proclaiming Jesus as the Beloved Son.
The author does not state explicitly that Jesus is the "mightier"
one, but in light of the events of 1:9-11 the reader can hardly
come to any other conclusion. Similarly in 9:2-8, when Peter
makes the nonpartisan suggestion that three tents be erected,
one for Jesus, one for Moses, and one for Elijah, his foolish
utterance[66] is smothered by the voice from the cloud which

repeats the acclamation of 1:11: "This is my beloved Son;
listen to him" (9:7). The latter command--"listen to him"--does
more than merely proclaim the preeminence of Jesus over Moses
and Elijah. It also echoes the passage in Deut. 18 concerning
the "prophet like Moses": "The Lord your God will raise up
for you a prophet like me from among you, from your brethren--
him you shall heed" (Deut. 18:15).[67] To say that Jesus is the
one to be heeded is to speak of him with language appropriate
for the prophet like Moses. Mark 9:7 thereby furnishes additional
support for our conclusion that the references to "a prophet"
in 6:15 and 8:28, together with the appearance of Moses himself
in 9:4-5, are all designed to evoke for the reader the image of
the prophet like Moses promised in Deut. 18.

The insight that the author has interjected the models of
Elijah/Elisha and the prophet like Moses into his story in
6:14-15 has important implications for how one perceives the
feeding story in 6:30-44. Often in the interpretation of the
feeding stories in Mark, reference is made to the memorable
feeding stories of the Old Testament, chief of which are the
accounts of the manna and quail in the wilderness associated
with Moses (Exod. 16, Num. 11) and Elisha's feeding of one
hundred men with twenty loaves (2 Kgs. 4:42-44). It is
frequently suggested that at some point in the transmission of
these stories--perhaps even in their original composition--
they were purposely endowed with characteristics designed to
recall the familiar Old Testament stories.[68] Such suggestions
are impossible to support with conclusive internal evidence
inasmuch as we are dealing with ambiguous allusions and do not
have the author's explicit admission of dependence on the Old
Testament texts. Nevertheless, judging simply from the
experience of modern interpreters of Mark, it seems inevitable
that anyone with a passing familiarity with the stories in Exod.
16, Num. 11, and 2 Kgs. 4 will discern echoes of those stories
in Mark 6:30-44 and 8:1-10. The essential points of contact
were pointed out long ago by David Friedrich Strauss, and, as
Van Cangh observes,[69] his successors have scarcely been able to
improve upon his remarks:

And here the fourth Evangelist, by putting into
the mouth of the people a reference to the manna,
that bread of heaven which Moses gave to the
fathers in the wilderness (v. 31), reminds us of
one of the most celebrated passages in the early
history of the Israelites (Exod. xvi), which was
perfectly adapted to engender the expectation
that its antitype would occur in the Messianic
times; and we in fact learn from rabbinical
writings, that among those functions of the first
Goel which were to be revived in the second, a
chief place was given to the impartation of
bread from heaven. If the Mosaic manna presents
itself as that which was most likely to be held
a type of the bread miraculously augmented by
Jesus, the fish which Jesus also multiplied
miraculously, may remind us that Moses gave the
people, not only a substitute for bread in the
manna, but also animal food in the quails
(Exod. xvi. 8, [12,] 13; Num. xi. 4ff.). On
comparing these Mosaic narratives with our
evangelical ones, there appears a striking
resemblance even in details. The locality in
both cases is the wilderness; the inducement
to the miracle here as there, is fear lest the
people should suffer from want in the wilderness,
or perish from hunger; . . . But there is another
point of similarity which speaks yet more
directly to our present purpose. As, in the
evangelical narrative, the disciples think it
an impossibility that provision for so great a
mass of people should be procured in the
wilderness, so, in the Old Testament history,
Moses replies doubtingly to the promise of
Jehovah to satisfy the people with flesh (Num.
xi. 21f.). . . . If we search for an intermediate
step, a very natural one between Moses and the
Messiah is afforded by the prophets. We read of
Elijah, that through him and for his sake, the
little store of meal and oil which he found in
the possession of the widow of Zarephath was
miraculously replenished, or rather was made to
suffice throughout the duration of the famine
(I Kings xvii. 8-16). This species of miracle
is developed still further, and with a greater
resemblance to the evangelical narrative, in the
history of Elisha (2 Kings iv. 42ff.). As Jesus
fed five thousand men in the wilderness with
five loaves and two fishes, so this prophet,
during a famine, fed a hundred men with twenty
loaves, (which like those distributed by Jesus
in John, are called barley loaves,) together
with some ground corn. . . . The only important
difference here is, that on the side of the
evangelical narrative, the number of the loaves

is smaller, and that of the people greater;
but who does not know that in general the
legend does not easily imitate, without at
the same time surpassing, and who does not
see that in this particular instance it was
entirely suited to the position of the Messiah,
that his miraculous power, compared with that
of Elisha, should be placed, as it regards the
need of natural means, in the relation of five
to twenty, but as it regards the supernatural
performance, in that of five thousand to one
hundred?[70]

We must admit that we find the intuitive accuracy and
cogency of these comments undeniable. In opposition to this
stance, however, one could legitimately protest that the Old
Testament allusions in Mark 6:30-44 and 8:1-10 are too obscure
to be regarded as direct borrowings from the Old Testament--if
Mark (or the story teller before him) had wanted the reader to
catch Old Testament allusions to Moses and Elisha he could
have been more direct and explicit. Our study of 6:14-16/8:28
and 1:7-11/9:2-8 now provides the element of explicit reference
to the Old Testament worthies that has to this point been
missing from discussions of the Old Testament derivation of the
feeding stories. This is not to say that the one, "correct,"
exhaustive interpretation of the feeding stories is one that
regards them as repetitions of Old Testament stories. On the
contrary, our study of the feeding stories has demonstrated
conclusively that the controversy between Jesus and the disciples
is the central focus of both stories. However, the comparison of
Jesus to the Elijah/Elisha and Moses models encouraged by 6:14-
16/8:28 and 1:7-11/9:2-8 also legitimates to a certain extent
the countless intuitions that Mark 6:30-44 and 8:1-10 portray
deeds performed by a Moses-like or Elisha-like figure.

Having begun with the dual tableaux of 6:14-16 and 8:28, we
have since developed a considerably larger aggregate of inter-
locked evidence. Our final assemblage of evidence consists of
the dual tableaux of personages like Jesus in 6:14-16 and 8:28,
the dual attestations of Jesus' Sonship and unique superiority
in 1:7-11 and 9:2-8, and the dual feeding episodes in 6:30-44
and 8:1-10. The explicit clues provided in 6:14-16 and 8:28
demand that the reader compare Jesus with John, Elijah, and

Moses, and these models are employed by the author in several
significant episodes in the gospel. The full extent to which
these models are employed by Mark cannot be addressed in this
study.[71]

An interesting tangential issue raised by this study is
the question of the extent to which the miracle stories in the
gospels were modeled after Old Testament stories. Interpreters
like Bultmann have expressed skepticism at attempts to establish
direct links between the gospel miracle stories and the miracle
stories of the Old Testament. Bultmann's position is, of course,
that the development of the gospel miracle stories was not a
literary process but a process of popular oral tradition.[72]
Our analysis of the composition of Mark 6:30-44 demonstrates,
to the contrary, that at least this one story was created by
"ein literarischer Prozess," modeled as it is after the fixed
text now preserved in 8:1-10. Moreover, the author's insistence
that Jesus be compared with Old Testament figures has led us to
perceive at least a few instances in which he has implanted
direct allusions in his text--definitely a literary process.
For our part, we are open to a reexamination of the possibility
that significant portions of the gospel may be authorial
creations utilizing Old Testament texts and personages as models.

To conclude briefly, we have discovered Mark 6:14-16 to be
a helpful guide provided for the reader as he attempts to
comprehend the figure of Jesus in the gospel. It provides the
reader with a ready-made array of models with which to compare
Mark's protagonist: Herod, John, Elijah, Moses. The process of
comparison encouraged by 6:14-16 cannot follow narrowly defined
paths, for the author has not given the reader strict guidelines
dictating exactly what the reader should think about this multitude of characters.[73] The reader is given a great deal of
freedom within the boundaries of the text to construct his own
comparisons. The comparison process encouraged by 6:14-16 can
only be a loose and free activity--more of a matter of serendipity
than close-order drill. One simply cannot pursue the thread of
each comparison all the way through the gospel, because the logic
of each comparison inevitably breaks down or begins to conflict

with other comparisons. For example, Jesus is compared with
both John *and* Elijah, but the reader later learns that John
is Elijah . . . so is this comparison really one of Elisha-
Jesus with Elijah-John? Or, to take another path, we note that
Jesus is compared to both Herod, John's murderer, and to John,
the murdered one. Let us now add to that knot the similarities
between Pilate and Herod. Dare we consider an extension of
this comparison to include Pilate, Herod, *and* Jesus?[74] Clearly
we are not dealing here with precise, analytical descriptions
of Jesus. Rather, what we have are random musings about Jesus
encouraged--or demanded--by the author. Mark 6:14-16 is a
guidepost for the reader's imagination, an invitation to pursue
the figure of Jesus down diverse paths.

Eating with Jesus: The Meals in Mark

Once our attention is drawn to it, we recognize immediately
the frequency with which references to food and eating are to
be found in the gospel. The gospel is full of references to
eating, drinking, cups, loaves, foods, feasts, banquets, fasting,
hunger, and leaven.[75] The author enjoys interpreting the events
of his story with the language of the dinner table: an exorcism
may be called "taking bread from children and giving it to dogs"
(7:27); the deeds of the Pharisees and Herod may be called
"leaven" (8:15); Jesus' passion may be described as "drinking
the cup" and "being baptized" (10:35-40, 14:36; cf. 7:4).
Conversely, the author also interprets meals by means of non-
culinary metaphors: eating with tax collectors and sinners is
described as a doctor healing ill patients (2:15-17); the disciples' failure to fast is called a celebration with the bridegroom
(2:18-20); the bread and cup of the Passover meal is called
body and blood (14:22-25). We are repeatedly denied the luxury
of taking the references to food and eating in Mark as literal,
straightforward references. Rather, meals in Mark are constantly
associated with metaphor--various episodes in the story may be
interpreted by means of meal-metaphors or the meals themselves
may be interpreted with non-meal-metaphors.

We should also recognize that the meals in Mark are almost
always controversial affairs, and usually the controversy

revolves around the disciples of Jesus.[76] Often they are caught
in the middle of a debate between Jesus and his opponents over
Jewish meal customs. In Mark 2:15-17, for example, the disciples
are questioned about Jesus' practice of eating with tax
collectors and sinners. Before they are able to respond, Jesus
himself answers the question, having overheard the query. The
disciples are given no opportunity to demonstrate their grasp
of the significance of Jesus' eating habits. Later they will be
given a chance to display their understanding of Jesus' meals,
but instead they will only display their abysmal lack of
understanding. Their failure in 2:15-17 to provide a quick,
ready apologia for their master's practices foreshadows future
meals in Mark.

　　More typical than this example, though, are the several
instances in which Jesus is questioned about the disciples'
eating habits. In 2:18-20 he is asked why they do not fast as
do the disciples of John and the disciples of the Pharisees; in
2:23-28 Jesus is questioned about his disciples' act of plucking
and eating grain on the Sabbath; in 7:1-8 he is queried about
their failure to observe regulations concerning washing the
hands before eating. It is in these instances that the disciples
are most clearly caught in the middle between Jesus and his
opponents. In these instances it is the disciples who are eating
and conducting themselves improperly, at least according to
Pharisaic ideals (2:18, 24, 7:1, 3, 5), but it is Jesus who
defends their actions. Nowhere are they given a chance to defend
themselves and to demonstrate that they too comprehend the justification for their deeds so readily provided by Jesus. Indeed,
the reader who perceives their consistent failure to understand
Jesus and his conduct elsewhere in the gospel is led to suspect
that, if called upon, the disciples would *not* adequately defend
their unorthodox behavior. Because they do not understand what
they are doing when they (presumably) imitate the conduct of
Jesus, they are in the position of the man who, when discovered
working on the Sabbath by Jesus, was warned that if he understood what he was doing, he was blessed, but if not, he was
"accursed and a transgressor of the law" (Luke 6:5 Codex D).

Besides these instances in which the disciples are caught
in the middle of a meal-controversy between Jesus and his
opponents, there are several instances in which there is a
direct conflict between Jesus and his disciples in the context
of a meal. We have already discussed at length the centrality
of such conflict in the feeding stories (6:30-44, 8:1-10) and
in related material in Mark (e.g., 8:13-21). There are other
instances as well in which a meal provides the setting for an
unmediated confrontation between master and disciples; e.g.,
10:35-40, 14:3-9, and 14:12-26. In these episodes the disciples
show most vividly that they do not comprehend Jesus and do not
understand "the loaves" (6:52). In other words, the disciples
fail to grasp the significance of Jesus' eating with and providing food for others from the beginning of the story to the
very end. While the disciples fail to grasp the significance of
eating with Jesus, the reader is gradually made aware of what
the disciples are missing. The reader is never given a precise,
analytical description of the significance of eating with Jesus,
but the reader does learn along the way that eating with Jesus
can be health to the ill (2:17), a celebration for wedding
guests (2:19), a meal of holy food (2:25-26), food for
thousands (6:30-44, 8:1-10), or a sharing of body and blood
(14:22-25).

In the history of the interpretation of the gospel the
account of the Last Supper has been regarded as the preeminent
meal in Mark (14:12-26). Usually this attitude is shaped more
by the intense scholarly interest in the origin of the
Christian Eucharist than by a careful, unprejudiced examination
of all the meals in Mark. As our brief description of the meals
demonstrates, the Last Supper is in fact one of many meals in
the gospel. The earlier meals prepare for and lead up to this
one last meal, making it crucial not to overlook or minimize
the significance of these earlier meals. Often the verbal
similarities between 6:41, 8:6, and 14:22 are noted and used to
justify the discovery of "eucharistic" overtones in the two
feeding stories. Regrettably, to argue in this fashion is to
stand the gospel on its head. *As the author has structured his*
work, Jesus' last meal with his disciples in Mark 14 presupposes

the earlier feeding stories and not vice versa. Here we are
making a conscious decision to adhere to the internal
chronology of the author's story, according to which the last
meal is preceded by, and read in the light of, the previous
meals in Mark.[77] This means that by the time we arrive at
the Passover meal in Mark 14 in our reading of the gospel, the
issue foremost in our mind will be the ongoing dinner table
conflict between Jesus and the Twelve and not the traditional
scholarly questions of the historical origin of the story, the
ipsissima vox of Jesus, and the variance of traditions in Mark
14:22-25, Luke 22:15-20, and I Cor. 11:23-26. These may be
legitimate scholarly concerns, but they are not Mark's concerns.
When we take care to read the account of the last meal of
Jesus and his disciples in light of the previous meals in Mark,
we are struck by the recurrence of the dominant theme of
discipleship failure in this account. To be sure, we are by
now accustomed to portrayals of the disciples' ineptness and
misunderstanding at the dinner table, but here their failure
assumes shocking proportions. Even before the Passover meal is
prepared, we are told that one of the disciples, Judas
Iscariot,[78] has allied himself with the plot to kill Jesus
(14:1-2, 10-11). After the preparation of the meal, but still
before the familiar words of 14:22-25, Jesus announces solemnly
that he will be delivered up by one of his own disciples. The
prophecy is repeated twice, in different words, to the
astonished disciples:

14:18   εἷς ἐξ ὑμῶν παραδώσει με,

         ὁ ἐσθίων μετ' ἐμοῦ. . . .

14:20   εἷς τῶν δώδεκα,

         ὁ ἐμβαπτόμενος μετ'ἐμοῦ εἰς τὸ τρύβλιον.

The scandal of the prophecy is dual: Jesus will be delivered up
by one who is both a disciple and a table intimate. Corresponding
to the prediction in 14:18-21 of Jesus' being delivered up by
a disciple is the prediction in 14:27-31 that *all* the disciples,
and especially Peter, will be "scandalized" and scattered. Of
course, the latter unit does contain the comment in 14:28
concerning Jesus leading or preceding (προάγω) the disciples

to Galilee, which may be intended as an optimistic expression
of hope for the disciples' future. However, this is not certain;
the verse is remarkably ambiguous. In any case, we must insist
that, on the whole, the failure of the disciples is the
dominant theme in 14:27-31 and that the two units in 14:18-21
and 14:27-31 conspire to shroud 14:22-26 with the severest
failure of discipleship imaginable: scandalization (14:27),
renunciation (14:30), and outright, treacherous betrayal (14:18-
21). This is the true import of the Last Supper narrative for
the evangelist Mark.

In our discussion of Jesus' last meal in Mark, we have
taken care to render the technical term παραδίδωμι rather
strictly as "to deliver up" or "to hand over."[79] Even though
the verb does not necessarily bear the connotation of betrayal,
it has been customary to refer to Jesus' being handed over to
the Jewish authorities as his "betrayal"[80] insofar as his
παράδοσις was brought about by an intimate companion. We must
suggest the possibility, on the other hand, that the evangelist
Mark is responsible for endowing the term παραδίδωμι with the
connotation of betrayal by being the first to link one of the
Twelve with Jesus' being delivered up. The only earlier
references we have to Jesus' παράδοσις are the references in
the letters of Paul, none of which can be regarded with
certainty as a reference to a betrayal by one of Jesus'
disciples.[81] The suggestion that Mark is the first to attribute
Jesus' παράδοσις to one of the disciples cannot be proven
conclusively, but such an action on the part of the evangelist
would be in total agreement with Mark's consistent denigration
of the disciples. In the other gospels there is a concerted
effort to divorce Judas from the Twelve, to make him a scapegoat,
and to make sure that he receives his just deserts. In Mark
there is little to distinguish Judas' betrayal from the flight
of the other eleven--they all abandon Jesus, each in his own
way. Judas' distinguishing characteristic is simply the boldness
and shrewdness with which he abandons Jesus. He safely renounces
Jesus with a kiss rather than with a curse like Peter (14:45,
14:71), and he is even paid for his trouble (14:11). No mention
is made of repentance or of a horrible fate which befell him
later.

So forcefully does Mark present this παράδοσις of Jesus by one who is a disciple and a table intimate that this feature becomes an indelible element of the tradition. Later gospel writers cannot ignore it; they can only acknowledge it and attempt to temper or moderate Mark's shocking, scandalous accusation that one of the Twelve, one who ate with Jesus himself, handed him over. Matthew, Luke, and John all temper the shock of Judas' infamous deed by dissociating him from the other disciples and by heaping defamation and doom upon him. He is called a devil (John 6:70-71) and a thief (John 12:4-6); several times it is stated that he was possessed by Satan or the Devil (Luke 22:23, John 13:2, 26-27). Matthew says he returned the blood money unspent and died by his own hand (Matt. 27:3-10); Luke says he spent the money on land and died a horrible, but natural, death (Acts 1:15-26). Mark, for his part, says only that Judas delivered Jesus up--nothing is said about his base character or his awful fate. Mark does not even draw a sharp line between Judas and the others. To be sure, a special woe is pronounced upon the man who will deliver up the Son of Man (14:21), but the abandonment and renunciation by the other disciples is scarcely less contemptible. The woe pronounced in 14:21 appears to fall upon Judas; yet the others are equally under a solemn curse inasmuch as they, and Peter in particular, have demonstrated that they are ashamed of the Son of Man and his words (8:38), having failed abysmally to deny themselves, to take up their crosses, and to follow Jesus (8:34).[82] For Mark, the Last Supper is the last of many meals in which the disciples have failed to grasp the significance of Jesus and his ministry. Here the failure of their discipleship reaches its climax, and from their ranks now emerges the one disciple who will become the instrument by which Jesus' death is precipitated. It is scarcely possible for modern readers of the gospel even to begin to imagine the original scandal created by Mark's claim that "Judas Iscariot, one of the Twelve, delivered Jesus up." "Judas Iscariot," in modern parlance, is an epithet, a synonym for villain and traitor. When we encounter Mark's claim, we recognize this

epithet and think merely that the author has finally brought
the archvillain onto the stage. We fail to see that the
author's emphasis is not on the traitor's name but on the
fellowship of which he is a part: he is "one of the Twelve"!
The scandal of Mark's Last Supper narrative is that Jesus' own
disciples will abandon him and one will even deliver him up.
The Markan Last Supper narrative must not be removed from the
context of the ominous predictions of 14:18-21 and 14:27-31, for
the entire narrative has been constructed as a natural outgrowth of the feeding stories in Mark 6 and 8 and the discipleship failure depicted there. That the discipleship of the Twelve
ends so ignobly in Mark 14 is not surprising in view of the
incredible obtuseness of the disciples narrated already in
Mark 6-8.

By attempting to perceive the Markan narrative of the Last
Supper in the light of the feeding stories and not vice versa,
we are swimming against the prevailing current of interpretation
regarding the relationship of the feeding stories and the Last
Supper narrative. It is widely accepted that the feeding stories
are to be read in the light of the Last Supper narrative and
the familiar Christian practice of the Eucharist. Hence one
encounters countless claims that the feeding stories are
"eucharistic."[83] The stories are "eucharistic," it is said,
because they are somehow reminiscent of the early Christian
Eucharist or were perhaps first told in the context of the
early Christian cult meal. We will refrain from defining the
adjective "eucharistic" more carefully because such restraint
is also practiced by those who indulge in its use. The term,
as commonly used, is so vague as to be nearly meaningless.
What is actually meant when it is said that the feeding stories
are eucharistic is that the language of Mark 6:41, 8:6, and
14:22 contains verbal parallels and that the perceptive reader
of the gospel will need to make sense of this repetition. Is it
so clear, though, that 14:22 and its context should be regarded
as the logical antecedent of the narratives containing 6:41 and
8:6? Is this not in fact a violation of the gospel's internal
logic, according to which the narratives containing 6:41 and
8:6 precede and lay the basis for the narrative containing
14:22?

The issue at stake here is the issue of how to read the feeding stories so as to perceive accurately the author's intended meaning. The method usually adopted by advocates of the eucharistic interpretation of the feeding stories involves constructing a hypothetical original reader in order to see how he would have understood these stories. This hypothetical reader is invariably a Christian who, we can assume, was familiar with the traditions of the Christian Eucharist. When such a reader encounters the feeding stories, it is argued, there is an instant recognition that these stories contain eucharistic overtones. There are, however, several problems with this procedure.

First, the hypothetical original reader is often a thinly disguised stalking-horse for the modern interpreter. The knowledge and perceptions attributed to the original Christian reader are too often indistinguishable from the knowledge and perceptions of the interpreter who has hypothesized the original reader. Indeed, it would appear that some modern interpreters perceive eucharistic overtones in these stories and attempt to legitimate their perceptions by claiming that the original readers would have seen the same thing. It is even clearer that the "reader" reading the feeding stories is actually the modern exegete when, as happens so often, the conclusion that the feeding stories are eucharistic is used as an entree into extensive speculation into the original eucharistic *Sitz im Leben* of these stories.[84] Such are the concerns of a modern exegete, not of the original readers. We would not go so far as to say that it is illegitimate for a modern interpreter to bring to bear on the feeding stories his knowledge of the early Christian Eucharist, but when this is done it must be done openly and knowingly.

We have already alluded to the second problem with the eucharistic interpretation: it is superficial and vague. To say that the feeding stories bear echoes of the Eucharist is to say very little. As we have noted, what is actually under discussion here are the verbal parallels between Mark 6:41, 8:6, and 14:22, but do such parallels justify the use of the adjective

"eucharistic"? To attach this label to the feeding stories is
not to interpret them. One still needs to examine how the
feeding stories function in the gospel, especially in conjunction with the Last Supper narrative. Moreover, we are not even
sure that a reader familiar with the Christian Eucharist must
feel compelled, upon the first reading of the gospel, to regard
the feeding stories as eucharistic. Could not such a reader
possess the self-discipline to read the stories in the gospel
in their proper order, abstaining momentarily from a eucharistic
interpretation of the feeding stories, in order to see what the
author was attempting to say by the way he organized his gospel,
a gospel in which feeding stories precede and prepare for the
Last Supper?

The third problem is implicit in all the criticisms above:
the eucharistic interpretation of the feeding stories tends to
violate the author's text by reading it out of order. It can
scarcely be overemphasized that the Feeding of the Five
Thousand and the Feeding of the Four Thousand precede and
prepare for the Last Supper narrative in Mark. To read casually
the former stories in the light of the latter is simply to
overturn the gospel. Fidelity to the text demands that we work
with the text the author has given us and, barring accidental
displacements or authorial instructions to disregard the present
order of the text, that we read it in the order it is presented
to us. We share with the advocates of the eucharistic interpretation their enthusiasm for considering how a reader perceives
the feeding stories in Mark, but whereas their "reader" is
distinguished by knowledge extrinsic to the text--knowledge of
eucharistic traditions--we prefer to examine how a reader
operating with the intrinsic knowledge provided by the text
itself would read the feeding stories. Far greater authority
must be accorded the text itself to inform, control and mold
its reader. We prefer to allow the text to educate and guide its
own reader, rather than insisting on inventing a hypothetical
reader characterized primarily by knowledge and experience
external to the text.[85] To see how the text molds its own reader
involves seeking out those features of the text that shape the

reading experience of *every* perceptive reader, ancient or
modern. This approach restores to the text its rightful
measure of autonomy. The fundamental datum imposed on us by
the text of Mark with regard to the feeding stories and the
Last Supper is, we repeat, the priority of the feeding stories
over the Last Supper. To illustrate our remarks we will discuss
briefly the work of two advocates of the eucharistic interpretation, Van Cangh and Quesnell.

Van Cangh has endeavored to uncover layers of tradition
underlying the feeding stories in Mark.[86] Following closely the
work of Van Iersel,[87] he utilizes two major presuppositions in
his work: the feeding stories are independent stories from pre-
Markan tradition and they are "eucharistic." For Van Cangh,
understanding the feeding stories is not a matter of seeing
how they function in the context of Mark's gospel, but a matter
of analyzing the modifications made in the stories in the pre-
gospel tradition. The key to Van Cangh's effort to uncover the
layers of tradition lying below the surface of the feeding
stories is the detection of imbalances and tensions within the
stories. Primarily Van Cangh focuses upon the tension between
the loaves, which are reminiscent of the Eucharist, and the
fish, which are not. From the observation of the supposed
tension between eucharistic loaves and non-eucharistic fish Van
Cangh is able to propose a five-stage development for the
feeding stories.[88]

1. The original miracle story,[89] which involved both
bread and fish.

2. The "eucharistic reinterpretation"[90] of the original
miracle story. Here the language of the Eucharist was introduced,
stressing the role of the bread while diminishing the role played
by the fish. The story was then used in "eucharistic catechesis."[91]

3. "The reintroduction of the fish."[92] In part, this was
carried out to reestablish the parallelism between the bread and
fish lost when the story was given its eucharistic flavor in
Stage 2.[93] Also, this modification reestablishes the story as a
legitimate miracle story instead of primarily a piece of edifying
eucharistic catechesis.[94]

4. Mark's use of the story in two different versions.[95]
One might ask if Mark himself could have reintroduced the fish
in Stage 3, but he himself has no interest in the fish, since
he fails to include them in 6:38, 44 and 8:17-21.[96]

5. Matthew and Luke use the story.[97] They, too, are not
interested in the fish and minimize their role in the story.[98]

We could discuss this proposal at some length but will be
content with a short appraisal. We must first express misgivings about the incredible, unnecessary multiplication of
layers of tradition in Van Cangh's proposal. We are especially
skeptical about his claim that one feature of the feeding
stories--the fish--was at first a prominent part of the story,
but then was diminished in importance, then was raised again
to its former prominence, and then finally retained untouched
by an evangelist who had no particular fondness for it. Such
suppositions can be multiplied ad infinitum--by their very
nature they can be neither proven nor disproven. Resorting to
a solution of such extreme complexity to explain the supposed
tensions in a single verse (6:41) does not inspire confidence
in the solution. Our own proposal that Mark 6:30-44 is a
Markan composition and that 8:7 is a Markan addition to a
traditional story is a simpler and, we believe, a more persuasive proposal. The tension Van Cangh claims to find between
loaves and fish in 6:30-44 is greatly exaggerated. As we
pointed out above in Chapter 2, every time the five loaves are
mentioned the two fish are mentioned also, a careful balance
between the two elements. The argument that the presence of
fish in 6:30-44 is not due to the evangelist because, if the
evangelist were concerned to include fish in his story, he
would have mentioned them in 6:38, 44 and 8:17-21,[99] is
fallacious reasoning. As we demonstrated, the author is
concerned enough about the fish to add them to the traditional
story in 8:7 and to balance them with loaves in his own
composition in 6:30-44. The absence of fish in any one spot
elsewhere in the gospel is irrelevant to the question of who
is responsible for their presence in 6:30-44 and 8:7.

Besides providing an overly complex and unpersuasive
analysis of the development of the feeding stories, Van Cangh's

proposal founders, as do many, on the perennial problem of
the doublet. It is clear, as he proceeds with his analysis of
the five stages of the tradition, that the primary focus of
attention is the one dominant feeding story, the Feeding of the
Five Thousand, and especially the important verse 6:41.
Several times in the discussion of the stages he explicitly
refers to "story" in the singular: "Le récit. . . . ce récit. . . .
un récit. . . .le miracle. . . ."[100] However, when he
discusses Stage 4, where Mark takes up two different versions
of "le récit," he suddenly begins to speak of "une double
tradition pré-marcienne à l'origine des deux récits."[101]
Somehow the one story now becomes two; exactly how this happens
is not explained. The question of how the doublet arose remains
the unresolved crux of the matter. Van Cangh would have us
believe that the feeding stories are independent, pre-Markan
stories first brought together by Mark, but not before they
underwent identical *and* parallel modifications at the hands of
pre-Markan tradents. In other words, be would have us believe
that the stories have independent origins but identical
histories. Of course, added to this most remarkable coincidence
is the further coincidence that these utterly independent
stories with absolutely identical histories first appear, in
the extant literature at least, in the same composition. We
must insist, on the other hand, that this overdrawn series of
coincidences can only collapse under its own weight. This series
of coincidences is unlikely and incredible; we are well advised
to retrace our steps to the original presupposition of
"independent origins" and retract it. This is in fact what we
have done in the course of our own study; we have found good
reason to argue that one story is directly dependent on the
other. Our proposal solves the doublet problem, something that
Van Cangh's proposal does not do. Perhaps Van Cangh is not led
to reconsider his presuppositions because there are two major
ones--"independent origins" and "eucharistic interpretation"--
and they tend to buttress each other. As long as he is equally
loyal to both of them there is scarcely any way that they can
lead him into an inescapable contradiction and thereby betray
their falsehood. These two presuppositions form a formidable

combination and can lead to an infinite number of remarkably
imaginative proposals, as can be seen from Van Cangh's
elaborate five-stage reconstruction. Their fault is that they
ride roughshod over the text, encouraging the interpreter to
seek modifications in tradition that never took place and
meanings that were never intended.

Another advocate of the eucharistic interpretation is
Quentin Quesnell.[102] The focus of Quesnell's study is Mark
6:52, the important statement following the feeding story and
the water-walking episode that the disciples "did not understand about the loaves, but their hearts were hardened." After
examining this verse in its immediate context, Quesnell
embarks on a detailed study of the other passages in Mark where
it is said that the disciples failed to "understand" (συνίημι):
4:1-34, 7:1-23, and 8:14-21. This study is in general quite
perceptive and goes far in elucidating the recurrent theme
of the disciples' failure to understand Jesus and his actions.
Quesnell is particularly adept at pointing out how the
evangelist informs and guides the reader through the text;
comments on what the reader knows to be true at any one place
in the story or on how the reader is inclined to respond to a
certain element in the story are scattered throughout his
study.[103] In the early stages of Quesnell's study, many of
these comments concern the intrinsic information and guidance
for the reader provided in the text itself. In the latter
stages of his work, though, he feels compelled to go outside
of the text to "the Context of the Christian Thought-world"[104]
in order to see what kind of understanding of "the loaves"
Mark could have expected his Christian readers to bring to the
text. Openly and knowingly, Quesnell abandons the gospel
momentarily. The question is, when he returns to the gospel,[105]
is he once again exegeting the gospel or eisegeting "the
Context of the Christian Thought-world" into the gospel?
Quesnell's own conclusion to his study is most revealing:

> What did the disciples not understand about the
> breads? . . . The answer here proposed is that
> the evangelist meant to convey what he thought
> his readers would get from his statement: what
> he had a right to expect that normal Christian

> readers or hearers of that day were likely to get
> from the words he used in the frame of reference
> he used them; namely, a comment on the eucharistic
> implications of the story of the feedings in the
> wilderness. The same is true of 8,14-21.106

Was there ever a writer who did *not* wish "to convey what he
thought his readers would get from his statement"? Apparently
Quesnell is attempting to say that Mark tells his readers what
they already know, that being some vague notion about Jesus
and the Eucharist. In other words, having doggedly pursued the
nuances, subtleties, and surprises of the disciples' failure
to understand "the loaves" through most of the gospel, Quesnell
concludes his study by suggesting that the reader is only
supposed to see in these passages what he is already familiar
with: "eucharistic implications." Surely the gospel is not
so marvelously trivial a work as to communicate to the reader
only what the reader is already familiar with, without even
throwing new light on the familiar. Quesnell's unfortunate
recourse to the standard extrinsic eucharistic interpretation
is unworthy of the gospel and of Quesnell's own work. He
would have fared much better if he had pursued the disciples'
failure to understand through 4:1-34, 7:1-23, 8:14-21, and on
through the rest of the gospel up to the climactic meal scene
in Mark 14.[107] The misunderstanding of the loaves in Mark 4-8
must lead the reader to the total abandonment of Jesus predicted
in the context of the Passover meal in Mark 14 and not to vague
but comfortable notions of the Eucharist borrowed from
extrinsic sources.

Having urged that it is illegitimate to read the feeding
stories in Mark in the light of the Markan Last Supper
narrative, we now wish to qualify our adamant statement. It
is illegitimate to read the feeding stories in light of the
Last Supper, as we were careful to note above, *upon the first
reading of the gospel*. On a second or later reading of the
gospel we can scarcely deny to the reader his knowledge of what
lies ahead in the story as he reads it. The simple fact of
the matter is that a first reading of a literary work is often
a radically different experience than the second reading. By
virtue of the experience of the first reading itself, when a

reader re-reads a work he is not the same person with the same
insights that he was in the first reading. In the second
reading the reader is able to keep in mind a clearer image of
the work as a whole and is able to organize and understand
the elements of the story in relation to the whole in a way
impossible for a first-time reader. New associations are made
within the text; the sequence of events may be understood
somewhat differently. Literary critics concerned primarily with
the process involved in the reading of a literary work have
commented on the difference between first and second readings.
One of them has observed:

> When we have finished the text,and read it again,
> clearly our extra knowledge will result in a
> different time-sequence; we shall tend to
> establish connections by referring to our
> awareness of what is to come, and so certain
> aspects of the text will assume a significance
> we did not attach to them on a first reading,
> while others will recede into the background.
> . . . The time sequence that [the reader]
> realized on his first reading cannot possibly
> be repeated on a second reading, and this
> unrepeatability is bound to result in modifica-
> tions of his reading experience.[108]

Regarding the gospel of Mark, the reader engaged in a
second reading of the gospel has every right (duty?) to read
the feeding stories in the light of what lies ahead. It would
be a rare person who could avoid doing this. Of course, this
still does not justify the wholesale import of extrinsic cargo
into the text. We are talking instead about re-reading the text
in light of the text. If we have grasped correctly the
significance of the feeding stories and Last Supper upon our
first reading, then we can fully expect the second reading to
deepen and broaden our insight into how these narratives
function together in the story without fear of having to
experience a severe upheaval in the way we perceive the text.

We have not intended to claim that Mark's particular use
of the feeding stories and Last Supper has no bearing on the
early Christian Eucharist. The author may in fact have intended
to communicate something about the Eucharist to his first
readers, but he hardly intended to provide a simple reiteration
of what the readers already knew about the Eucharist. Granted

for the moment that the Last Supper narrative is a major
Christian tradition, what is the significance of Mark's
particular use of it in his gospel? The primary observation to
be made, as stated above, is the observation that Mark places
the Last Supper narrative under the domination of the theme
of discipleship failure. Previously the disciples had misunderstood Jesus; hereafter they will deliver him up, abandon him,
and deny him. The author's unique use of the feeding stories
and Last Supper effectively divorces Jesus' original disciples
from the idea of discerning, faithful discipleship. If other
Christian writers understood the disciples as the faithful
custodians of the Last Supper tradition, not so Mark. Mark
preserves the apostolic tradition of the Last Supper but severs
the apostles from it, preserving a Christian tradition without
acknowledging those by whom it was supposedly preserved. The
Last Supper and its context is not, in Mark's gospel, the
institution of the Christian Eucharist, but the last great meal
confrontation between Jesus and the Twelve wherein their
ultimate abandonment and betrayal is predicted. Nevertheless, it
is fascinating to observe that, in spite of Mark's elimination
of faithful apostles from this apostolic tradition, they are
still the bearers of the tradition insofar as they are the
characters present in the story when the meal is conducted.
They are unfaithful disciples, in Mark's opinion, but as foils
for the faithfulness of Jesus they still serve the useful
purpose of furnishing the reader with a vivid, memorable, and
instructive antithesis to faithful discipleship. As the
characters in Mark's story, they are the pawns through which the
Markan drama is played out, thereby handing on to the reader
the tradition they misunderstood and rejected (in the story!).
In Mark's story they fail, but if Mark's portrayal of their
failure achieves its objective, the reader will be more faithful
than they and their failure will not have been utterly in
vain.[109]

Conclusions

The major result arising from this chapter is the recognition that the doublets in Mark 4-8, especially the feeding stories, function quite well as integral components of the gospel as a whole. To rearrange or untangle these stories in an attempt to find pre-gospel cycles is, as we have repeatedly claimed, a vain effort to recover something that probably never existed; but even more seriously, it does violence to the text the author has given us. The repetition in Mark 4-8 has been intentionally cultivated or sometimes created *in toto* by the author, and when this fact is recognized, the critic must explore the author's purpose for the use of doublets. As we have noted, the function of the doublets may vary from instance to instance, but in each case our concern has been the same: what is the author attempting to communicate to the reader by the use of doublets? We will continue to address this interaction between author and reader in the following chapter.

CHAPTER IV

AUTHORS AND READERS: READER-RESPONSE
CRITICISM AND THE GOSPEL OF MARK

The Implied Reader of the Gospel of Mark

Thus far in our study we have made numerous observations
about the ways in which the author of the gospel has undertaken
to direct and control the reader's experience of reading the
gospel. In particular, we have discussed in detail the way in
which the experience of reading the Feeding of the Five
Thousand controls how the reader perceives the Feeding of the
Four Thousand. Such observations are typical of the general
interpretative strategy called by some literary critics "reader-
response criticism,"[1] a strategy which has as its focus of
attention the reader's experience of reading the text. According
to M. H. Abrams's convenient schema of critical theories, which
is organized in terms of the primacy given variously to the
artist (expressive theories), the work (objective theories),
the universe of the work (mimetic theories), and the audience
(pragmatic theories), reader-response criticism is a pragmatic
theory, oriented as it is to the reader of the literary work.[2]
As Abrams notes, "although any reasonably adequate theory takes
some account of all four elements, almost all theories, as
we shall see, exhibit a discernible orientation toward one
only."[3]

In our study of the feeding stories and the other doublets
in Mark, we have found that special attention given to how the
reader perceives the text is most crucial. Furthermore, we assert
that the entire gospel is especially amenable to this kind of
critical approach. The justification for this broad assertion
lies scattered throughout the literature of Mark, literature
which is full of random, fortuitous, and, for the most part,
accurate observations on how the reader of the gospel experiences
the text. In other words, countless interpreters with no special
interest in the reader's experience of the literary work have
casually made numerous perceptive and astute observations along
these lines. We may refer to the recently published works of
Howard Clark Kee and Norman R. Petersen to illustrate our point.[4]

149

Kee's methodology is "social-cultural-historical";[5]
explicitly literary critical concerns, such as the reader's
perception of the Markan narrative, are far outside the intended
focus of Kee's work. Petersen's approach, on the other hand, is
explicitly literary critical, but even he is not particularly
interested in the experience of the reader of Mark. In the
chapter on Mark in his book, his stated concern is to map out
the function of "story time" and "plotted time" in the Markan
narrative.[6] Nevertheless, both critics time and again make
astute though fortuitous comments on the reader's perception of
the Markan narrative. The comments of each may be gleaned from
the pages of their works and gathered into a catena:

> This literary technique . . . serves here to occupy
> the attention of the reader. . . . already disclosed
> to the reader. . . . Mark recalls for the reader. .
> . . Mark is addressing (or portrays Jesus as
> addressing) his readers. . . . only the "reader"
> who "understands" will perceive. . . . gives only
> tantalizing hints to his reader of the real
> meaning. . . . he puts the responsibility on
> the reader to provide the answer. . . . using
> the device of a rhetorical question, or one that
> only the discerning reader is prepared to answer
> accurately. . . . Mark intends the reader to
> discern the hidden meaning of the incident behind
> the outward phenomenon. . . . the reader of Mark
> has already been alerted. . . . there is for the
> reader no surprise, therefore, when the plot to
> have Jesus killed is actually put into action. . . .
> Mark gives the reader the impression. . . . the
> rhetorical questions place the responsibility on
> the reader to decide. . . . the reader can see in
> them the signs of the gospel.[7]

> The unfulfilled prediction about the kingdom
> introduces to the reader an element of *suspense*. .
> . . the reader is supplied with both information
> and expectations that give the reader a point of
> view--the narrator's--from which to construe what
> follows. . . . they have a retarding effect on the
> reader's progress through the narrative. . . . the
> reader then rethinks and perhaps rereads. . . . the
> same reading process is involved in 4:10-11, where
> we learn. . . . Mark unquestionably and self-
> consciously plots his narrative in such a way as to
> require the reader to do what we have just done. . . .
> the reader is required to reflect back on previously
> plotted incidents in order to understand both them
> and what has transpired between them and the
> incidents in which the backward reference occurs. . . .
> serve to involve the reader in a developing plot. . . .

> before the reader can fully assimilate this new
> information. . . . require the reader to revise
> further his previous understanding. . . . the
> reader learns. . . . inclining the reader to
> emphasize the question. . . . this incident
> functions for the reader, not for the actors, who
> do not understand it. . . . leads the reader to
> expect. . . . thus the discourse functions princi-
> pally in relation to the reader, supplying him
> with information the narrator wants him to have.
> This information must be examined accordingly,
> that is, as much in relation to the reader as to
> the disciples. . . . confirm the reader's narrator-
> controlled expectation. . . . lead the reader to
> believe. . . . the reader knows. . . . it answers
> the reader's potential question. . . . the reader
> is compelled to balance in his mind *two* questions. .
> . . the reader is explicitly reminded. . . .
> directed the reader. . . . the reader cannot
> doubt. . . . all but Jesus, the narrator, and the
> reader stand under a cloud of ignorance until
> Galilee.[8]

We could hardly ask for better examples of the kinds of
observations commonly made by reader-response critics, and this
from two biblical scholars who do not have the reader of the
gospel as their primary concern.[9] We could easily add to these
catenae the fortuitous comments of many other scholars;[10] the
comments we have gathered from the works of Kee and Petersen
are sufficient, we trust, to demonstrate that, regardless of
one's methodology, when one reads the gospel of Mark one is
naturally inclined to observe how the text directs and controls
one's reading experience. The gospel seems to elicit spontaneous-
ly such observations, and this justifies focusing on the
experience of the reader of Mark's gospel *as a primary concern*.

Coincidentally, reader-response criticism is currently a
topic of intense discussion among literary critics. This is
not the place, however, for an exhaustive review of this
discussion.[11] Rather, we will only sketch briefly some of the
major principles with which most reader-response critics work.
Fundamental are the notions of the implied author and the
implied reader of a literary work. The use of the former term
arises out of the recognition that when we read a literary work
we do not directly encounter a flesh-and-blood author; instead,
we encounter the author in the particular manifestation or guise
that he has chosen to adopt for the purposes of the work at

hand. A number of terms have been used to describe this
phenomenon; some critics refer to the flesh-and-blood author's
"second self," while others speak of his wearing a "mask" or
assuming a "persona." Following Wayne Booth we will use the
term "implied author," referring to the author implied in a
literary work as opposed to the flesh-and-blood author.[12]
Corresponding to the term "implied author" is the term "implied
reader,"[13] for just as the author dons a mask or assumes a persona to present the literary work to the reader, he also casts
the reader in a particular role, creating a mask or persona
for the reader as well. For the reader to participate fully in
the work, he must be willing to become, at least for the
moment, the reader envisioned by the author in the process of
composing the work. As Booth states, "the author creates, in
short, an image of himself and another image of his reader; he
makes his reader, as he makes his second self, and the most
successful reading is one in which the created selves, author
and reader, can find complete agreement."[14] Walter Ong goes so
far as to say that "the writer's audience is always a fiction":

> What do we mean by saying the audience is a
> fiction? . . . First, . . . the writer must
> construct in his imagination, clearly or vaguely,
> an audience cast in some sort of role--. . . .
> Second, . . . the audience must correspondingly
> fictionalize itself. A reader has to play the role
> in which the author has cast him, which seldom
> coincides with his role in the rest of actual
> life. . . .
>   The writer's audience is always a fiction. The
> historian, the scholar or scientist, and the
> simple letter writer all fictionalize their
> audiences, casting them in a made-up role and
> calling on them to play the role assigned.[15]

Again, just as our reading of a work does not bring us into
direct contact with a flesh-and-blood author but rather with his
second self, so also the reader implied in a work is always a
fiction, an invention of the author's imagination, and not a
flesh-and-blood reader.[16]

Having defined these two important concepts, we may outline
briefly the strategy generally adopted by reader-response
critics. Stated most succinctly, their work is characterized by
rigorous attention to the reader's experience of the text. This

is often a matter of noting how and where a reader gathers
insights from the text, how a reader forms expectations based
on the text, revises them, and experiences either their
fulfillment or nonfulfillment, and how a reader reappraises in
retrospect the portion of the text he has already read. Often
the sequential aspect of reading is emphasized, with special
attention to the experience of anticipation and retrospection
that may accompany it. Stanley Fish describes his methodology as
follows:

> The concept is simply the rigorous and disinterested
> asking of the question, what does this word, phrase,
> sentence, paragraph, chapter, novel, play, poem,
> *do*?; and the execution involves *an analysis of the*
> *developing responses of the reader in relation to*
> *the words as they succeed one another in time*. Every
> word in this statement bears a special emphasis.
> The analysis must be of the developing responses
> to distinguish it from the atomism of much stylistic
> criticism. A reader's response to the fifth word
> in a line or sentence is to a large extent the
> product of his responses to words one, two, three,
> and four. And by response, I intend more than the
> range of feelings (what Wimsatt and Beardslev call
> "the purely affective reports"). The category of
> response includes any and all of the activities
> provoked by a string of words: the projection
> of syntactical and/or lexical probabilities;
> their subsequent occurrence or non-occurrence;
> attitudes toward persons, or things, or ideas
> referred to; the reversal or questioning of those
> attitudes; and much more. . . .
>   Whatever the size of the unit, the focus of the
> method remains the reader's experience of it, and
> the mechanism of the method is the magic question,
> "what does this ------ do?"[17]

One can find similar methodological statements by other reader-
response critics. Wolfgang Iser, for example, describes the act
of reading as an act of recreating the text comparable to its
original creation: "We look forward, we look back, we decide,
we change our decisions, we form expectations, we are shocked
by their nonfulfillment, we question, we muse, we accept, we
reject; this is the dynamic process of recreation."[18] It is not
difficult to hear in these words an echo of the fortuitous
comments regarding the experience of the reader of Mark made
by Kee and Petersen. It is quite natural, we reiterate, for the
interpreter of Mark to comment upon the experience of reading

Mark's gospel, which encourages us to devote special attention
to that experience in this chapter.

In our study of the feeding stories in Mark, we took care
to observe how the author positioned his own composition in
6:30-44 as a backdrop for the story of 8:1-10, thereby controlling how the reader perceives the latter story. Especially
significant is the way in which 6:30-44 controls how we perceive
the disciples' question in 8:4. What was once an innocent
rhetorical question has been transformed by virtue of the backdrop against which it is now read. Moreover, we noted that 8:4
fits the criteria proposed by Booth for the detection of irony
in a narrative. The reader shares with the author the insight
that the disciples' question is an unwitting self-condemnation;
the disciples are the incognizant victims of their own words.
We further suggested that the study of the irony in Mark might
help considerably to explain the elusive phenomenon of the
Messianic Secret. Booth himself points out the vivid irony of
the passion narrative in Mark, where Jesus is mocked as the
Messiah, the King of Israel (15:32). The temptation that
confronts us at this point is the temptation to embark on a
thorough examination of all the places in Mark where the author
employs irony. There is certainly a longstanding precedent for
such an enterprise: Wrede long ago attempted to pinpoint the
exact locations in Mark where injunctions to keep the Messianic
Secret occur.[19] To attempt to do the same for instances of
irony in Mark, however, would not be advisable at this point.
Without the proper preparation, such an endeavor would be
chasing after a will-o'-the-wisp, just as the study of the
Messianic Secret has turned out to be. Before we can fully
grasp the degree to which Mark employs irony, we must first
explore the ways in which he has equipped his readers with the
proper insights and tools necessary to perceive and comprehend
his ironies. The successful ironist must see that his reader is
endowed with knowledge sufficient to allow the reader to realize
when the author is being ironic. In the remainder of this
chapter we will note the ways in which the author furnishes a
stable, reliable store of knowledge for the reader, just the
kind of knowledge over against which an author may construct
stable, covert ironies.

Guidance for our enterprise is provided by Booth, who has already shown us what to look for. In Booth's study on irony he notes that if an author wishes a reader to perceive his ironies, he must provide his reader with sufficient "clues to irony":

1. "Straightforward warnings in the author's own voice"
    a. "In titles"
    b. "In epigraphs"
    c. "Other direct clues" (direct statements by the author)

2. "Known Error Proclaimed" ("If a speaker betrays ignorance or foolishness that is 'simply incredible,' the odds are comparatively high that the author, in contrast, knows what he is doing.")
    a. "Popular expressions" ('incredible' distortion of popular expressions)
    b. "Historical fact" ('incredible' violation of historical fact)
    c. "Conventional judgment" ('incredible' violation of conventional judgment)

3. "Conflicts of Facts within the Work" ("All the examples in the previous section led us to rely on knowledge or conventional judgments brought to the work, knowledge on which we base our guesses about whether the author shares his speaker's ignorance. But many works of stable irony provide within themselves the knowledge necessary for establishing that a speaker's ignorance is not shared by the author.")

    "Dramatic irony" ("Drama has always been especially given to effects depending on the author's providing, early in the play, information that will point to an ironic effect later on.")

4. "Clashes of Style" ("If a speaker's style departs notably from whatever the reader considers the normal way of saying a thing, or the way normal for this speaker, the reader may suspect irony.")

5. "Conflicts of Belief" ("We are alerted whenever we notice an unmistakable conflict between the beliefs expressed and the beliefs we hold *and suspect the author of holding*.")

    "Illogicality" ("Every reader knows, or thinks he knows, what is 'logical.' Violations of normal reasoning processes will be subject to exactly the same manipulation as violations of other beliefs or knowledge.")[20]

Much of this outline has to do with what Booth called
"reliable commentary" in his earlier *The Rhetoric of Fiction*.
In this work, Booth demonstrates how an author may use the
rhetorical resources of fictional narrative to control his
reader, "as he tries, consciously or unconsciously, to impose
his fictional world upon the reader."[21] One way an implied
author may control his reader is by providing trustworthy,
dependable commentary for the reader as the narrative progresses. Among the many purposes for which it may be used,
reliable commentary may be used to furnish the reader with
exactly the kind of stable, dependable store of knowledge
necessary to be able to detect when the author is being ironic.
Booth outlines various means by which an implied author may
furnish his reader with reliable commentary as follows:

1. "Providing the Facts, 'Picture,' or Summary" ("The
   most obvious task for a commentator is to tell the
   reader about facts that he could not easily learn
   otherwise.")

2. "Molding Beliefs" (the shaping of norms or values for
   the reader's use in reading the text; "evaluative
   commentary")

3. "Relating Particulars to the Established Norms" ("If
   novelists must work hard to establish their norms,
   they often must work even harder to make us judge their
   characters accurately in the light of these norms.")

4. "Heightening the Significance of Events"

5. "Generalizing the Significance of the Whole Work"
   (". . . we turn to the task of generalizing the effect
   of the entire work, making it seem to have a universal
   or at least representative quality beyond the literal
   facts of the case. . . .")

6. "Manipulating Mood" (". . . when an author intrudes to
   address the reader's moods and emotions directly.")

7. "Commenting Directly on the Work Itself" ("Intrusions
   discussing the book itself"--either to praise or to
   confess shortcomings)[22]

Making use of these helpful guidelines, we will attempt to
outline a rudimentary catalog of reliable commentary in Mark in
the following pages.[23] Booth's guidelines have informed our work
but have not dominated it; the categories we have used are drawn
largely from the gospel itself. We have cast our net widely in
this venture; future work will no doubt demonstrate the need
for expansion in some parts of the catalog and for pruning in

others, but we offer the catalog here as an overture to the
future study of the implied author and implied reader of the
gospel of Mark.

A Catalog of Reliable Commentary
in the Gospel of Mark

I.   *Direct Comments to the Reader*

The preeminent example of the author addressing the reader
directly out of the text is in Mark 13:14: "But when you see the
desolating sacrilege set up where it ought not to be (let the
reader understand), then let those who are in Judea flee to the
mountains; . . ." Here is an awkward, obtrusive signal to the
reader that the author is saying something to which the reader
should pay particular attention. Unfortunately, exactly what
the author wishes the reader to understand is not entirely clear
to the modern reader (what the "desolating sacrilege" refers to
has always been a matter of intense debate), but the author's
comment encourages the reader to consider the passage with extra
care. It may well be that the comment was intended to have
special significance for the original flesh-and-blood readers
of the gospel who would have known what the "desolating
sacrilege" referred to--for them 13:14 may have been quite
clear. Although we no longer have the key to this cipher, it
does function to alert us to the fact that Mark 13 as a whole
functions as a message for the reader. Several verses in the
chapter employ second person plural pronouns which, although
these verses are ostensibly directed at Peter, James, John, and
Andrew, serves the purpose of directing Jesus' words directly
at Mark's readers: 13:5, 9, 23, 29, 37.[24] Indeed, the last verse
of the chapter (13:37) explicitly directs Jesus' words beyond
the bounds of the small group of four disciples: "And what I
say to you I say to all: Watch." Regarding Mark 13 as a message
for Mark's readers, Petersen states: ". . . the discourse
functions principally in relation to the reader, supplying him
with information the narrator wants him to have. This information
must be examined accordingly, that is, as much in relation to
the reader as to the disciples."[25]

A. *The Title and Epigraph*

A major piece of reliable commentary is provided for the
reader in the title ("The Beginning of the Gospel of Jesus
Christ, the Son of God"--Mark 1:1) and the epigraph (1:2-3) of
the gospel. The title informs the reader that the work he is
about to read is "the gospel" and that it concerns a certain
Jesus who is Christ and Son of God. Of course, at this stage
the reader has no idea what these titles mean to the author of
the work, but the reader has every right to expect to be told
what they mean as the story unfolds. Inasmuch as the reader
knows from the very beginning that Jesus is the Christ, the
Son of God, there is never any question of a Messianic Secret
for the reader of the gospel.[26] The datum provided for the
reader in 1:1 is bare and unadorned, and it requires the full
explication furnished by the author in the form of his gospel.
Mark's gospel will teach the reader what it means (in Mark's
opinion) to call Jesus "Christ" and "Son of God."

The epigraph of the gospel, a miniature collage of Old
Testament texts, places the gospel under the shadow of the
Jewish scriptures. Even before the gospel narrative begins,
the reader is alerted to the possibility that the events
narrated in the gospel may have some relation to the Old
Testament. Mark 1:2-3 is fair warning to the reader to be on
guard for Old Testament allusions; the author will not always
give an explicit introduction to his scriptural quotations
(e.g., 4:12, 11:9, 13:26, 14:62, 15:34). As for the content of
1:2-3, this epigraph introduces "the messenger" into the
Markan narrative. Mark 1:2-3 lies between the introduction of
Jesus in 1:1 and the introduction of John in 1:4, so it is not
instantly clear who prepares the way for whom, but the statement
in 1:4 that John is in the wilderness preaching leads one to
hypothesize that John is the "voice crying in the wilderness."
This supposition is confirmed in the verses that follow and in
the course of the entire gospel. The close association between
Jesus and John already suggested in 1:1-4 is maintained
throughout the gospel even though John is arrested and removed
from an active role in the narrative quite early (1:14). Although
bodily removed from the story, as it were, John's spirit haunts

the gospel. He and Jesus are *Doppelgänger*: they are similar in
demeanor, they are easily confused for one another (6:14-16,
8:28), and their fates are similar and even intertwined (9:11-
13). As Mark tells his story it becomes clear that the reader
who understands the role of Jesus (Son of Man) will also
understand the role of John (Elijah).

The title and epigraph provide the reader with reliable
but as of yet undeveloped insights. It is not too extravagant
to say that the entire gospel grows out of these few verses. To
put it another way, the opening verses of the gospel function
as the backdrop against which the entire gospel is read. These
verses play a crucial role, for example, in much of Mark's
irony. Against the backdrop of 1:1 the author is able to
devise a wealth of ironies for his reader: Jesus' suppression
of the seemingly correct statements of demoniacs, the disciples'
persistent inability to perceive who Jesus is, the idle and
inaccurate speculation about the identity of Jesus (6:14-16,
8:28), and the total abandonment of Jesus by his friends,
relatives, countrymen, and even his God. Mark 1:1-3 is the
cornerstone of the irony in Mark.[27]

II. *Linking Statements*

There are certain clear, unequivocal comments made in the
gospel that induce the reader to associate two different stories
with one another. Mark 6:52, for example, which occurs
immediately after the Walking on the Water, is a comment by the
narrator that the disciples were bewildered and frightened in
the water-walking episode because "they did not understand
about the loaves," a reference to the earlier Feeding of the
Five Thousand. The disciples' fear and astonishment in one
episode is explicitly linked to their lack of understanding in
the preceding episode, thus forcing the reader to consider the
stories together. This observation is reinforced by the
additional observation that the author has constructed the two
stories (6:30-44 and 6:45-52) as one continuous story--there
is no break or discontinuity between the feeding story and the
episode on the lake.

The other notable example of a linking statement that
immediately comes to mind is the recollection of the two feeding

stories placed on the lips of Jesus in 8:19-21. Even if the
reader has not observed by this point that he has encountered
two very similar episodes concerning the feeding of a crowd
by Jesus, he now has the obvious pointed out to him most
vividly by Jesus himself. The recollection of the two stories
almost in the same breath requires the reader, if he has not
already done so, to regard the feeding stories together as a
doublet, a matched pair.

III. *Parenthetical Constructions*

Parenthetical constructions occur frequently in Mark.[28]
These range from simple parenthetical explanations of foreign
customs or terminology to parenthetical constructions involving
entire pericopes. Not only do these constructions vary in
scope, but they also vary in function from instance to instance.
We cannot always predict what the significance of a parenthetical
construction in Mark will be, but once we have learned that the
author has a fondness for such constructions, we approach them
with extra care, for our reading experience teaches us that
such constructions play a prominent role in the composition
of the gospel.

A. *Explanations of Foreign Customs and Concepts*: 3:22,
7:2, 3-4, 9:43, 12:18, 42, 14:12, 15:16, 32, 42.

B. *Translations of Foreign Words*: 3:17, 5:9, 41, 7:11, 34,
10:46, 14:36, 15:22, 34.

Both of the above categories of parenthetical comments
involve mostly Jewish customs and terminology, from which we
may infer two things. First, the author envisioned at least a
partially Gentile audience for his work for whom such
explanations would be necessary. Second, although the author's
grasp of Jewish customs is not terribly subtle or profound,[29]
the frequency with which references to Jewish customs and
terminology are preserved and explained demonstrates that for
the author the Jewish component of early Christianity was still
prominent and a force to be reckoned with.

For the most part the parenthetical comments in these two
categories are rather unremarkable and seldom of major significance; yet even a humble parenthetical translation may contribute

to a noteworthy literary purpose. We turn, for example, to
Jesus' cry on the cross in 15:34. The narrator places on Jesus'
lips the (to a Gentile reader) Semitic-sounding cry Ελωι Ελωι,
which he hastens to translate as "my God, my God." Thus
equipped with the exact sounds of Jesus' cry and the narrator's
presumably correct translation, the reader is immediately
challenged to put that knowledge to use when it is reported
that the bystanders who hear the dying man's babble think he
is calling to Elijah (ʾΗλίας), not to God (15:35-36). Their
error is understandable; the words sound alike whether in
Hebrew, Aramaic, or in Greek transliteration. The reader
unacquainted with Semitic languages, though, is only able to see
through their error because he is equipped with the narrator's
reliable translation in 15:34. Clearly the misunderstanding of
the bystanders is ironical; the reader knows what they do not:
the true meaning of Jesus' cry. Further, the irony of their
misunderstanding goes even deeper. To perceive this we need
only to recall the role played by Elijah in the narrative so
far. First, let us recall that Jesus was thought by some to
be Elijah (6:15, 8:28), hence the additional irony in 15:35
that Jesus is thought to cry to one who he himself was thought
to be. Second, let us recall that, for Mark, Elijah has
appeared once already in the person of John the Baptist (9:9-
13) and that his fate was no less ignoble than Jesus'. Hence
the further irony in 15:35 that Jesus is thought to call to one
who has already come and who himself, instead of rescuing those
in need, died a cruel and unjust death at the hands of a duped
tyrant. The irony in 15:35 is rich indeed, and our perception
of it is made possible by the parenthetical translation in
15:34.

    C. *Winks at the Reader*: 2:10, 28, 3:30, 7:19b, 8:32a,
9:41, 11:32, 14:49b, 62.

    The parenthetical comments discussed above are generally
well integrated into their contexts; for the most part they are
able to fulfill their informative function without causing a
major disruption in the narrative. In this category, however,
we point to parenthetical comments that often seem to be
foreign additions to the text. They are usually characterized

by a disruption of syntax (anacoluthon or asyndeton), often
being inserted in or appended to an episode in a most awkward
fashion. As some interpreters have from time to time noted,
these particular parenthetical comments are authorial comments
serving to summarize for the reader the significance of the
surrounding material, hence our description of them as "winks
at the reader." Other interpreters prefer the expression
"appositive comments,"[30] or "asides to the Christian reader."[31]

Two of the winks that have received special attention are
those in 2:10 and 2:28, both of which refer to the enigmatic
"Son of Man." In the blink of an eye the author communicates to
the reader the true significance of the stories in 2:1-12 and
2:23-28: first, the Son of Man has authority on earth to forgive
sins; and second, the Son of Man is Lord of the Sabbath. These
are the first two references in the gospel to the Son of Man;
their abrupt appearance in stories about Jesus presents the
reader with the inescapable conclusion that the Son of Man is
Jesus himself. Later Jesus will repeatedly speak of the Son of
Man in the third person (8:31, 8:38, 9:12, 9:31, 10:33, 10:45,
etc.), but even the dullest reader will perceive that these are
veiled self-references. Such insight on the part of the reader
in the later chapters of the gospel is heavily dependent on
the insight granted already in 2:10, 28 that Jesus is the
authority wielding Son of Man.

Norman Perrin has made the provocative suggestion that just
as 2:10 and 2:28, the first references in Mark to the Son of
Man, are authorial asides to the reader, so also Mark 14:62,
the last Son of Man reference in Mark, is an aside to the
reader. Perrin notes that the verse makes far better sense as
a comment to the reader than as a comment to the High Priest.
In view of Mark's proclivity for authorial winks at the
reader, this suggestion has much merit.[32]

D. *Explanatory* γάρ *Clauses*: 1:16, 22, 2:15, 3:10, 21, 5:8,
28, 42, 6:14, 17, 18, 20, 31, 48, 50, 52, 7:3, 9:6, 31, 34,
10:22, 45, 11:13, 18, 32, 12:12, 14:2, 40, 56, 15:10, 16:4, 8.

Ever since C. H. Bird's 1953 article on γάρ clauses in
Mark,[33] the explanatory γάρ clause has been a recognized element
of Mark's literary style.[34] Bird was particularly concerned to

argue that the evangelist constructs his γάρ clauses as
allusions to familiar Old Testament passages. As we stated
earlier,[35] this thesis asserts too much; often the "allusions"
refer simply to other locations within the gospel. Mark 6:31,
we have argued, "alludes" to earlier episodes in the gospel
where large numbers of people flock to Jesus (2:2, 15) and
even go hungry (3:20). In a similar fashion, Kelber argues that
the γάρ clause in 11:13c concerning the καιρός "alludes" to
Jesus' proclamation of the καιρός in 1:15: "Mark's mentioning
of *kairos* points outside the immediate fig tree plot to the
principal affirmation of the arrival of the *kairos* in 1:15."[36]

We may state even more broadly, however, that the explanatory γάρ clauses in Mark often have the appearance of an afterthought. Morton Smith, who suggests that the miracle stories in
the early chapters of Mark are derived from an aretalogy,
attributes this tendency to the pre-Markan aretalogy. Regarding
1:43 he observes: "Here, then, it [the aretalogy] has put its
note on the technique of the exorcism after the main moment,
just as it did in 5:8-12."[37] Although 1:43 does not involve a
γάρ clause, *every other example cited by Smith (including 5:8-
12) involves an explanatory* γάρ *clause*: "Other examples of the
same trait: 3:9f.; 5:27f.; 6:16-19, 31, 48, 49f., 51f. . . .
9:5f. . . ."[38] We would insist, in opposition to Smith, that
this is a particularly Markan trait appearing throughout the
gospel, and it should not be attributed to a pre-Markan source.[39]
To illustrate how this trait functions in Mark, we may look
briefly at the explanatory γάρ clauses which occur "after the
main moment" in one pericope in Mark: 6:14-29. In 6:14a it is
stated that King Herod has heard about Jesus; the γάρ clause in
6:14b explains why: his name had become well known. Next we
find consecutive γάρ clauses in 6:17 and 6:18. The γάρ clause in
6:17 stating that Herod had arrested John provides background
information for the preceding statement in 6:16 that Herod had
beheaded John. Then the comment in 6:18 that John had rebuked
Herod for his marriage explains the motivation for John's arrest
(6:17). Finally, the explanatory γάρ clause in 6:20 stating that
Herod feared John and kept him safe explains the situation behind
the previous statement that Herodias was unable to vent her

hostility toward John (6:19). These explanatory γάρ clauses, which always occur "after the main moment" in 6:14-19, may be diagrammed as follows:

6:14a◄──6:14b   6:16◄──6:17◄──6:18   6:19◄──6:20

In each case, the explanatory γάρ clause provides the background information needed if one is to understand the preceding statement. These few examples are illustrative of the explanatory γάρ clause in Mark.

E. *Markan Insertions*: 2:6//8b, 2:9b//11a, 3:7//8, 3:14//16, 4:31//32, 5:10//23, 5:29//34, 6:14//16, 6:31b//32b, 6:35//35, 7:1-2//5, 7:20//23, 8:1//2, 8:17//21, 8:29//9:5, 9:12//13b, 10:23b//24b, 11:11//15, 13:5a//9//23//33, 13:33b//35b, 13:35//37, 14:18//22, 14:56//59, 15:2//4, 15:24//25.[40]

We have discussed this parenthetical construction at length in our discussion of the introductory verses of the two feeding stories. The function of this technique varies from instance to instance; it has no single function. As one can easily see from the label he chose for this technique, John Donahue is especially concerned with the material inserted between the repeated elements by the author. His study of this material has proved to his satisfaction that the material inserted in a Markan insertion frequently displays familiar Markan themes, giving the reader insight into the author's concerns.[41] In other words, the inserted material frequently functions for the reader as reliable commentary supplied by the implied author.

In our earlier discussion of the insertions in 6:31//32, 6:35//35, and 8:1//2, we focused not so much on the inserted material as on the repeated elements of the insertions. As we noted, in each of these three instances one of the repeated elements is a statement in direct speech by one of the characters in the story, while the other is a comment in indirect speech by the omniscient narrator of the gospel. One of the achievements of this kind of repetition is confirmation for the reader of the reliability of the commentary provided by the narrator. In two of these three instances the narrator anticipates a statement by a character in the story, thereby proving his reliability. (In the other instance, the narrator echoes a

statement made first by Jesus, thereby affirming Jesus'
reliability.) Whether one wishes to concentrate on the inserted
material or the repeated elements, it is clear that the reader
can often learn much from an encounter with this kind of
parenthetical construction.

   F. *Intercalations:* 3:20-21/22-30/31-35, 5:21-24/25-34/35-
43, 6:7-13/14-29/30ff., 11:12-14/15-19/20-25, 14:1-2/3-9/10-11,
14:53-54/55-65/66-72, 15:6-15/16-20/21-32.[42]

   Intercalation is another parenthetical construction used
frequently by Mark, one that resembles the insertion technique
except it occurs on a much larger scale, involving the insertion
of an entire story within another story. We discussed this
compositional technique above in Chapter 3, observing how the
author compels the reader to interpret the inserted story in
light of the framing story and vice versa. Examples like the
intercalation of the temple incident (11:15-19) into the story
of the fig tree (11:12-14, 20-25) or the intercalation of
Jesus' Sanhedrin trial (14:55-65) into the story of Peter's
denial (14:53-54, 66-72) have never presented themselves as a
puzzle to interpreters of the gospel, but even such seemingly
mismatched stories as the banquet of Herod (6:14-29) and the
mission of the Twelve (6:7-13, 30ff.) are intelligible when
viewed together, as we have argued. The author's positioning
of the banquet of Herod between the commissioning and the return
of the disciples demands that the reader view these episodes
together as a whole. The reliable commentary communicated to the
reader in such a construction is the indication of the proper
context for the interpretation of both episodes--each is to be
interpreted in light of the other.

   G. *Doublets*

   One of the doublets in Mark 4-8, the doublet of healing
stories in 7:31-37 and 8:22-26, functions very much like a set
of parentheses bracketing the intervening material in 8:1-21.
In these two stories Jesus gives hearing, speech, and sight to
two men, which contrasts starkly with his apparent inability
to cause his own disciples to perceive and understand. The
disciples' abysmal failure to comprehend Jesus is the central
theme of 8:1-21, which stands as an antithesis to the portraits

of comprehension and perception that bracket this section. Other doublets in Mark may serve a similar bracketing function; our study of the doublets in Mark 4-8 has demonstrated that such is the function of at least this one pair of stories in Mark.

IV. *Inside Views:* 1:22, 27, 34, 41, 2:5, 6-7, 8, 12, 3:2, 5, 4:40, 41, 5:15, 20, 28, 29, 30, 33, 42, 6:2, 3, 6, 19, 20, 26, 33, 34, 48, 49, 50, 51-52, 54, 7:24, 37, 8:2, 11, 16-21, 33, 9:6, 15, 30, 32, 34, 10:2, 14, 21, 22, 24, 26, 32, 38, 41, 11:18, 21, 31-32a, 32, 12:12, 13, 15, 17, 24, 34, 14:1, 4, 10, 11, 18, 19, 27, 30, 33, 40, 56, 57, 72, 15:5, 10, 15, 43, 44, 16:5, 8.[43]

Perhaps the most prominent trait of an omniscient narrator (like the narrator of Mark's gospel) is his ability to provide the reader with inside views. Constantly the narrator makes his readers privy to the inner-most workings of his characters' hearts and souls, revealing to the reader his characters' feelings, emotions (astonishment, amazement, awe, fear, anger, pity, etc.), desires, thoughts, intuitions, motivations, intentions, moods, knowledge, insights, perceptions and recollections--secrets of the heart and soul to which one is seldom if ever privy in everyday life. The steady stream of such insights furnished by the narrator compels the reader to use these insights to form attitudes and opinions about characters and events in the story. Most instructive are those passages which, in their telling, hang upon an inside view given to the reader. For example, in 2:6-7 scribes "question in their hearts" Jesus' "blasphemy." Jesus, in turn, perceives "in his spirit" their hostile thoughts and responds appropriately (2:8ff.). These two inside views--the revelation of the thoughts of the scribes and the revelation of Jesus' extraordinary awareness of their thoughts--make the telling of the story possible. Similarly in the story of the woman with a hemorrhage (5:25-34), at the heart of the story is the woman's realization ("she felt in her body that she was healed") of her healing and Jesus' instantaneous realization ("perceiving in himself that power had gone forth") that someone had availed herself of his power. Both realizations are subjective, internal feelings, but thanks to the omniscient narrator the reader is able to glimpse

into the souls of both characters and discern these feelings.
Thus the narrator puts the reader in a privileged position,
allowing the reader to have a full grasp of what is transpir-
ing in the story. The disciples, on the other hand, are
oblivious to what has happened, so when Jesus stops in the
middle of a pushing, shoving crowd and asks who touched him,
they think he is joking. Finally, we may look at the unit in
9:33-37 which immediately follows the second passion prediction
(9:31-32). In 9:33 Jesus asks the disciples what they were
talking about while traveling on the way. The disciples,
however, do not answer--they remain silent. Nevertheless, the
narrator does inform the reader of what they were discussing
("who was the greatest"), and then Jesus begins to instruct
them on the requirements for being first in the kingdom, which
demonstrates that he too has pierced the disciples' silence
and understands the ambition in their hearts. It is important
for the narrator, in this case, to relate both the disciples'
silence and the reason why they were silent. The reader must
be presented with both in order to appreciate the discernment
and wisdom displayed by Jesus in the following verses.

We could, of course, discuss at great length the use of
inside views as reliable commentary in the gospel, but we will
be content with these few examples. The numerous instances of
inside views uncovered by a rapid reading of the gospel (see the
list above) and the central importance of inside views in the
few examples we have discussed is an indication of the importance
of inside views as a source of reliable commentary for the
reader of Mark.

V. *Unanswered Questions*: 1:24, 27, 4:41, 6:2, 37, 8:4, 17-21,
9:19, 11:28.

There are a number of places in the gospel where a question
is raised that receives no explicit answer. Although in a sense
unanswered or rhetorical questions do not provide reliable
commentary per se for the reader, they do serve to guide the
reader's thoughts into the proper channels. Even if they do not
furnish the reader with the correct answers, as it were, they
at least furnish the correct questions; that is, the questions
the implied author deems important. Confronting the reader with

unanswered questions is without doubt a shrewd rhetorical ploy,
for it encourages the reader to seek out the answers. As
Stanley Fish states: "A question, after all, implies the
availability of an answer; and to ask it is always to create a
psychological need for its completing half."[44] In short, the
implied author poses the question for the reader; if the reader
wishes to have an answer, he must supply his own. We may turn
now to some examples of this device in Mark.

If, by the end of four chapters of the gospel, the reader
has not wondered exactly who Jesus is, the implied author poses
the question for him: "Who then is this, that even the wind
and the sea obey him?" (4:41). No answer is given; if the reader
desires an answer he must formulate his own.[45] Later the
question is raised regarding the source of Jesus' wisdom and
power: "Where did this man get all this? What is the wisdom
given to him?" (6:2). The implication of the question is that
the recognition of Jesus as "the carpenter, the son of Mary"
(6:3) is simply inadequate to explain the wisdom he has
displayed or the mighty deeds he has done. The questions remain
unanswered, however, which forces the reader to draw his own
conclusions as to the source of Jesus' wisdom and power.[46]
A similar situation arises in 11:28, where the question of who
gave Jesus his authority is asked but is never answered in the
text. Instead, Jesus thwarts his adversaries by posing a counter-
question about his *Doppelgänger*, John the Baptist: "Was the
baptism of John from heaven or from men? Answer me" (11:30).
Question and counter-question both remain unanswered; the
religious leaders refuse to answer Jesus' question so he refuses
to answer theirs. Nonetheless, the reader who has followed the
careers of John and Jesus to this point will have ample resources
with which to answer both questions correctly.[47]

VI. *Reliable Characters*

Certain characters in the story may be trusted to provide
the reader with reliable commentary:

A. *Jesus*

As the protagonist of the story, *Jesus is the predominant
source of reliable commentary for the reader*. As Tannehill
observes: "In the Gospel of Mark it is obvious that Jesus wears
the badge of reliability and authority. The most important
commentary in Mark is given by Jesus."[48] Jesus is the channel

through which the implied author's norms and values are most
often communicated to the reader: "The viewpoint of the
implied author merges with that of Jesus in Mark, since the
author has given him the role of chief commentator."[49]

    B. *The Voice from Heaven/the Cloud*: 1:11, 9:7.

The function of the heavenly voice is to vouch for the
authority and reliability of Jesus. Indeed, the function of
characters B. through E. is to vouch for the authority and
reliability of character A.: Jesus. Simply as an extra-
terrestrial phenomenon the voice commands attention, but even
more significant is the fact that it echoes the title of the
gospel by calling Jesus "the Son" (1:11, 9:7) and that it
demands that Jesus be heeded above Moses and Elijah (9:7). Such
a clear sign of heaven's favor is not to be scorned.

    C. *The Demons*: 1:24, 34, 3:11-12, 5:7.

Although the demons are odious "characters," as supernatural agents they can be expected to know who Jesus is. In
fact, the demons say they know who Jesus is (1:24, 5:7), the
narrator says they know who Jesus is (1:34), and Jesus certainly
acts like they know who he is (3:11-12). Of course, the demons
know him to be the Son of God, which agrees with both the
statement in the title and the acclamation by the heavenly
voice.

    D. *The Centurion at the Cross*: 15:39.

This is perhaps the only human character in the story,
other than Jesus himself, to make an acceptable confession of
who Jesus is. His confession of Jesus as the Son of God aligns
him with the heavenly voice and the demons, but his acclamation
of Jesus as the Son of God is particularly striking since he is
acclaiming the person he has just executed.

    E. *The Young Man*: 14:51-52, 16:5-7.

The νεανίσκος at Gethsemane and at the tomb, presumably
the same person, is an enigmatic character whose presence and
function in the gospel is extremely difficult to explain. His
appearance is sudden and mysterious; about all we know about him
is what he wears or does not wear. It is his important function
at the end of the gospel to inform the women (and the reader) of
the fulfillment of the one remaining unfulfilled component of
the passion predictions: "after three days he will rise" (8:31,

9:31, 10:34). In view of this thrice repeated prediction, the
young man's announcement in 16:6 comes as no real surprise to
the reader; inasmuch as the other components of the passion
predictions have been fulfilled, the reader naturally expects
the last component to be fulfilled also. The fulfillment of
Jesus' passion predictions in Mark 14-16, along with the fulfillment of other predictions made by Jesus in the course of
the story, confirms Jesus as a reliable source of knowledge to
the reader. Consequently, the reader is disposed to trust the
message he has been made to anticipate by Jesus' predictions--
even though the reader has absolutely no basis upon which to
trust the *messenger* himself. Since we know nothing about the
young man, we cannot automatically regard him as a reliable
commentator, yet his message is what we have anticipated and so
we are inclined to trust him because of that fact. Just as the
heavenly voice, the demons, and the centurion prove themselves
reliable commentators by virtue of the harmony between what
they claim about Jesus and what the implied author himself
claims in Mark 1:1 and elsewhere, the correspondence between
what the young man proclaims to the women and what the reader
has been led to expect by Jesus' words confirms the young
man as a reliable commentator. The message legitimates the
messenger.

VII. *Prospective Passages: Backdrops and Introductions*
        In this last section we turn to a kind of reliable
commentary that is far less obvious than that in preceding
sections. Here we are concerned about blocks of material that
emerge as sources of reliable commentary only as the reader
looks back upon them from a vantage point later in the gospel.
To discuss material that provides the reader with reliable
commentary in retrospect is, perhaps, to stretch the definition
of reliable commentary with which we have been working, but
nevertheless this is material that must be examined in any
thorough discussion of how an author informs and controls the
perceptions and expectations of his reader. The simple fact of
the matter is that there are places in the gospel where the
author takes extra care to put the reader in possession of
significant, reliable insights which may not be recognized as

such immediately, but can only be fully appreciated when viewed in retrospect. A variety of adjectives could be used to describe this material in the gospel--prospective, anticipatory, preparatory--but there are essentially two functions for which it is used. First, some sections of the gospel emerge in retrospect as backdrops for later sections, serving *to control* how the reader perceives the later material by establishing the background against which the later material is read. Second, other sections have an introductory function, serving *to introduce* to the reader details of the story--themes, characters, locales--which the author will employ and develop as the narrative progresses. Introductory sections do not control the reader's perception of later sections as much as they simply introduce into the story the elements from which the later sections will be fashioned. Some sections, in addition, mix these two functions, serving both as a backdrop to later parts of the story and as an introduction for new components of the story intended for future development.

The role played by prospection and retrospection in the reader's experience of a text is a familiar topic of discussion among reader-response critics. Iser, for example, who prefers the term "anticipation" to "prospection," observes that "during the process of reading, there is an active interweaving of anticipation and retrospection. . . ."[50] Reading a text is seldom if ever a rigidly sequential encounter with a string of words, but is instead a dynamic process rich with guesses as to what is to come and reflection over what is past. That certain passages in Mark serve a prospective or retrospective function (or both) has already been observed by Norman Perrin.[51] We are, of course, here concerned particularly with passages that serve a prospective function, either as a backdrop or as an introduction, and may now discuss several representative examples.

Our reader is by now quite familiar with our claim that the first feeding story in Mark has been composed by the evangelist himself and positioned in his gospel in such a way as to function as a backdrop for the traditional feeding story. That is to say, the first feeding story provides the crucial background

against which the reader views the second feeding story. The
first feeding story controls how the reader perceives the
second feeding story and, more particularly, how the reader
understands the disciples' question in 8:4. We attributed a
similar backdrop function to the first sea story in 4:35-41,
which provides the decisive background for the reading of the
second sea story in 6:45-52. Once again, a very understandable
reaction by the disciples in the face of a perplexing experience
(6:49-50) is given a totally different complexion thanks to the
backdrop against which it is read. Having once witnessed Jesus
control wind and wave, they should have no difficulty recognizing
one who comes to them on the water, through the wind. Both
6:30-44 and 4:35-41 function as stable, reliable backdrops
against which the author is free to compose his surprises and
ironies. Surprises and ironies do indeed come later, but in no
way is the stability or reliability of these passages ever
shaken.

For an example of a passage that serves to introduce
new features into the story, we may turn to Mark 3:1-19,
a passage that introduces into the gospel an amazing profusion of
new themes, new motifs, new characters, new geographical
locales, and new vocabulary. These new features may be listed
as follows:

3:4--Introduction of the verb "to kill" (ἀποκτείνω; cf.
6:19, 8:31, 9:31, 10:34, 12:5, 7, 8, 14:1)

3:5--First mention of "hardness of heart" (cf. 6:52, 8:17,
10:5)

3:6--Introduction of the Herodians, and the first mention of
the Pharisees and Herodians as a coalition (cf. 8:15,
12:13)

--Introduction of the plot against Jesus (cf. 11:18, 12:12,
14:1, 10)

3:8--Introduction of the cities of Tyre and Sidon (cf. 7:24,
7:31)

3:9--Introduction of the boat motif (cf. 4:1, 36-37, 5:2, 18,
21, 6:32, 45, 47, 51, 54, 8:10, 14)

--First mention of the crowd "pressing" (θλίβω) upon Jesus
(cf. the use of συνθλίβω in 5:24, 31)

3:10--Introduction of the motif of touching Jesus (cf. 5:27-28,
30, 31, 6:56)

3:13--Introduction of the mountain motif (cf. 5:5, 11, 6:46,
9:2, 9, 11:1, 23, 13:3, 14, 14:26)

--Introduction of the important term "to call, to summon"
(προσκαλέομαι; cf. 3:23, 6:7, 7:14, 8:1, 34, 10:42,
12:43, 15:44)

3:14--Introduction of the expression "the Twelve" (cf. 3:16,
4:10, 6:7, 9:35, 10:32, 11:11, 14:10, 17, 20, 43)

--First use of verb ἀποστέλλω ("to send forth, dispatch")
excluding its use in 1:2 (cf. 3:31, 4:29, 5:10, 6:7,
17, 27, [30], 8:26, 9:37, 11:1, 3, 12:2, 3, 4, 5, 6,
13, 13:27, 14:13)

3:16--Introduction of the name "Peter" for Simon; Peter is
never called Simon again in the gospel *except in 14:37*
(cf. 5:37, 8:29, 32, 33, 9:2, 5, 10:28, 11:21, 13:3,
14:29, 33, 37, 54, 66, 67, 70, 72, 16:7)

3:17--Introduction and sole use of the name Boanerges for the
brothers James and John

3:18-19--Introduction of the names of the rest of the Twelve;
the only time they are all named in the gospel

3:19--Introduction of Judas Iscariot, "who delivered him up"
(cf. 14:10, 43)

--First use of the verb παραδίδωμι ("to hand over, to
deliver up") with regard to *Jesus*; the only previous
use of the verb in Mark is with regard to *John the
Baptist*, who has already been delivered up (1:14, cf.
9:31, 10:33, 14:10, 11, 18, 21, 41, 42, 44, 15:1, 10,
15)

All these elements make their first appearances in the gospel
in 3:1-19. Some are mundane: the boat that will transport Jesus
across the lake several times in Mark 4-8 or the mountain that
will provide the setting for several episodes. Others are
foreboding and ominous: the talk about killing, the mention of
the plot against Jesus' life, and the introduction of a disciple
"who delivered him up." We can scarcely overemphasize the
importance of the revelation to the reader so early in the story
that a plot against Jesus has begun and that one of the Twelve,
one chosen to be his companion, will deliver him up. When
surveyed in retrospect, 3:1-19 is seen as having supplied the
reader with a considerable amount of information about what lies
ahead in the story, thus familiarizing the reader with what will
prove to be important features of the story before they are
fully developed by the author. This passage does not control
the reader's perception of later pericopes, but serves primarily
to introduce elements into the story for future development.

Finally we wish to look briefly at a passage that functions
both as a backdrop and an introduction: 8:27-9:1. Located

exactly at the halfway point of the gospel, 8:27-9:1 introduces
elements into the story that will be developed in the last
eight chapters of the gospel, while also serving as a backdrop
for some of the episodes in those last eight chapters. As for
the introductory function of this passage, the new elements may
be listed as follows:

8:27--Introduction of the motif of "the way" (ἐν τῇ ὁδῷ; cf.
9:33-34, 10:17, 32, 46, 52, 11:8)

8:29--First appearance of the title "Christ," excluding the
first verse of the gospel (cf. 9:41, 12:35, 13:21,
14:61, 15:32)

8:31--First passion prediction, introducing the notion that
the Son of Man must be rejected by the Jewish leaders,
killed, and rise after three days (cf. 9:31, 10:33-34)

8:34-37--Introduction of the notion that the disciple of
Jesus must renounce himself, take up his cross, and
follow Jesus (cf. 14:30, 31, 72)

8:34--First mention of the means of Jesus' execution: the
cross (cf. 15:13, 14, 15, 20, 21, 24, 25, 27, 30,
32, 16:6)

8:38-9:1--First mention of the coming of the Son of Man in
glory and power with the angels (cf. 13:26-27, 14:62)

The motif of the journey to Jerusalem and the passion, the true
nature of discipleship as self denial, the coming of the Son
of Man--all of these are new elements that receive considerable
attention in the second half of the gospel.

Just as 8:27-9:1 serves to introduce new elements into
the story, it also provides the crucial backdrop for several
passages in Mark 9-16. We note first that 8:27-9:1 contains the
first of three passion predictions in Mark 8-10 (8:31, 9:31,
10:33-34). As the first passion prediction, 8:31 is often
removed from its context and examined with 9:31 and 10:33-34
as a triplet of sayings of Jesus. Once we recognize, however,
that 8:31 is firmly embedded in 8:27-9:1 and is not a free-
floating saying of Jesus, then we recognize additionally that
9:31 and 10:33-34 must be read in the light of 8:27-9:1 and not
of 8:31 alone. Moreover, the disciples' persistent inability
to comprehend the passion predictions, especially notable in
the passages which follow the second prediction in 9:33-37 and
the third prediction in 10:35-45,[52] must be read in light of
Peter's strong objection to the first prediction *and* Jesus'

insistence that faithful discipleship requires denying oneself, taking up the cross, and forfeiting one's life. Long before the second and third passion predictions, Jesus has already spoken his mind on the matter of authentic discipleship, which makes the disciples' recurrent concern with status and glory (9:33-37, 10:35-45) all the more lamentable and ironic. We suspect, in fact, that a careful study of the function of 8:27-9:1 as a backdrop for 9:33-37 would uncover a use of irony similar to that found in the two feeding stories earlier in the gospel, but we must postpone such a study for now.

One particularly vivid instance of a later passage whose significance is controlled by 8:27-9:1 is Jesus' prediction of Peter's denial in 14:29-31 and the fulfillment of that prediction in 14:66-72. That Peter, the first disciple, denies Jesus is in itself a serious enough matter, but when it is perceived in light of 8:27-9:1 the gravity of the denial is greatly intensified. We should note here that the verb ἀπαρνέομαι ("to deny, renounce") is used four times in the gospel, three times with reference to Peter's denial of Jesus (14: 30, 31, 72) and once earlier in 8:27-9:1: "If any man would come after me, *let him deny himself* and take up his cross and follow me" (8:34; emphasis added). Connected to this admonition to deny oneself is the solemn woe pronounced on the one who fails to keep this charge: "For whoever is ashamed of me and of my words in this adulterous and sinful generation, of him will the Son of Man also be ashamed, when he comes in the glory of his Father with the holy Angels" (8:38). Already Peter has demonstrated in 8:32 that he is "ashamed" of the Son of Man's words; later he will demonstrate that he is ashamed of the Son of Man himself when he denies Jesus in order to "save his life" (8:35). As Dewey states: "Thus it is clear that by his opposition to and denial of Jesus Peter must come under the jurisdiction of 8:35-38: having been ashamed of Jesus, Peter is and will be excluded from the present and future communities; in saving his life he loses it. Peter fails in the proper role of discipleship, self-denial (8:34)."[53] The key that makes this observation possible, indeed, necessitates it, is the backdrop of 8:27-9:1 against which 14:29-31, 66-72 is read, thereby controlling the reader's perception of Peter's denial of his master.[54]

Conclusions

This completes our brief catalog of the means by which the gospel's implied author provides the reader with reliable commentary. We must acknowledge that this is a preliminary study; much remains to be said about what the implied author says in his reliable commentary and how he uses it as a foundation for irony. Still, we were able to demonstrate the practical value of this kind of reader-response criticism earlier in our study of the function of the doublets in Chapter 3, and we have attempted throughout this chapter to give indications of how the evangelist uses reliable commentary for his intended purposes, irony being among them.

In such a preliminary study it is always reassuring to discover a relatively objective, internal indication of the validity of one's work. Such in fact occurs in our catalog of reliable commentary when we begin to discover instances of reliable commentary recurring under more than one category. Three prominent examples are 6:31-32, 6:51-52, and 7:1-5. Already in Chapter 2 we noted the Markan insertion in 6:31-32, two of the introductory verses of the Feeding of the Five Thousand. Furthermore, we noted that the material lying between the repeated elements of the insertion is an explanatory γάρ clause alluding to earlier passages in the gospel where a crowd gathers around Jesus. In this chapter we have observed how both techniques--the Markan insertion and the explanatory γάρ clause--are used by the author to supply reliable commentary for the reader. In 6:31-32 these two techniques are used hand in glove. Mark 6:51-52, our second example, also involves an explanatory γάρ clause, as well as two other kinds of reliable commentary. First, 6:52 functions as a linking statement, explicitly linking the disciples' lack of perception and their astonishment in the sea story to their failure to understand the previous episode--one verse linking two episodes. Second, 6:51-52 gives us a threefold inside view into the disciples by telling us that they were utterly astonished, they did not understand (the loaves), and their hearts were hardened. The last of our three examples, Mark 7:1-5, is a complex piece of authorial commentary. First, we note that 7:1-2, 5 involves a

considerable amount of repetition; it is a Markan insertion
framing an extensive parenthetical comment in 7:3-4. The
parenthesis in 7:3-4 is both an explanatory γάρ clause and an
explanation of a foreign (Jewish) custom. An additional but
much shorter parenthetical explanation of a foreign custom is
found in v. 2, within the repeated material of the insertion,
where it is explained what it means to eat with hands that are
κοινός ("common, profane, impure")--all in all 7:1-5 is a
parenthetical construction with four different tokens of
reliable commentary.

Besides observing these internal conjunctions of different
categories of reliable commentary, which tends to support the
validity of our literary critical observations, we may be
allowed to observe where the results of our work coincide or
intersect with the results produced by a different methodology;
i.e., redaction criticism. As it turns out, many of the instances
of reliable commentary that we have pointed out in our catalog
are instances of Markan redaction, according to redaction
critics. We need go no further than the three examples cited
above of places in Mark where there are multiple signs of
reliable commentary: 6:31-32, 6:51-52, and 7:1-5. Coincidentally,
each of these passages is widely held to be redactional material
by redaction critics. Does this mean that the literary critic's
reliable commentary is the same as the redaction critic's
redactional material?

To a certain extent the literary critic who looks for the
implied author's reliable commentary and the redaction critic
who looks for clear signs of the evangelist's redactional
activity are both looking for the same thing: the authentic,
trustworthy guidance provided for the reader by the author of
the gospel. The literary critic is willing to look for this
guidance wherever it is to be found, but the redaction critic
has a very specific idea of where it should occur: seams,
summaries, and insertions. Unfortunately, the latter presupposition tends to impose severe restrictions upon the author,
restrictions that he may not have felt obliged to observe. In
our own work we have discovered that the author of Mark's
gospel commonly uses *entire pericopes* to relay reliable

commentary to the reader; for example, in the use of doublets
or the technique of intercalation. Once we realize that the
author manipulates his material on such a large scale as a
matter of course, then the narrow attention customarily given
to seams, summaries, and insertions by redaction critics simply
will not suffice. Time and again we discover that careful,
serious attention to doublets and intercalations bears rich
dividends; their significance is not difficult to perceive if
one is first willing to grant the possibility that they may
indeed have significance.

We would like to suggest that redaction critics have been
observing and discussing the author's reliable commentary all
along, but have been limited by the lack of a critical method
that would allow them to acknowledge manifestations of the
author beyond the bounds of seams, summaries, and insertions;
that is, wherever the author chooses to manifest himself.
Redaction critics have often perceived reliable commentary in
Mark and have made the correct conclusion--"here we have the
reliable voice of the author"--but for the wrong reason--"it
is redactional." The only justification for concluding that a
passage provides us with a reliable manifestation of the author
is the recognition that it fits the previously established
literary critical criteria for reliable commentary. The fact
that an author redacts material has nothing to do with whether
the redactional material functions as reliable commentary for
the reader. An author may use redaction to insert ambiguity,
paradox, or even falsehood into his story, none of which is
reliable. On the other hand, an author may adopt traditional
material as his own and use it to provide reliable commentary
for the reader. In short, redaction may not be reliable, and
reliability may not be redactional. Only a self-consciously
literary critical method is adequate to deal with redactional
unreliability and reliable tradition.[55]

Fortunately for redactional critics, the author of Mark
does often provide reliable commentary that is also redactional
material, so the recognition of a manifestation of the author
is often accurately characterized as a discovery of Markan

redaction. Even more fortunate for the redaction critic is the
fact that reliable commentary shapes his reading experience
regardless of whether it is consciously acknowledged or not.
All readers of the gospel, redaction critics and literary
critics alike, encounter all of the implied author's commentary
and have their reading experience shaped by it whether they
recognize it or not. The text exerts a sovereignty over
different methodologies that tends to bring their different
interpretations closer together than the practitioners of those
methodologies often suspect is possible. Thus our literary
critical reading of Mark is not substantially different from
many redaction critical readings. We only hope that our study
has brought greater clarity and awareness to the endeavor in
which we all engage, the reading of the gospel of Mark.

Redaction critics, like all readers of Mark, read all of
his commentary, but because of the categories with which they
work they are only free to acknowledge the manifestation of the
evangelist in certain places. Once we begin to speak of the
evangelist as an author, though, we become willing to hear the
implied author from whatever location in the text he chooses to
speak; the distinction between tradition and redaction is no
longer relevant as a way of sorting out those special places
in the gospel (redaction) where the author speaks to us, for the
author may manifest himself anywhere, in tradition or redaction.
When an author adopts the tradition of his forebears it becomes
wholly his own, and when he shares it with us we must regard it
as if it all came from him originally, for indeed, as far as
we are concerned, it does. Thus in this chapter we have sought
out the implied author's reliable commentary *wherever* it is
to be found. We have danced to the tune composed by the author.

CHAPTER V

CONCLUSIONS

We may state briefly some general observations arising out of our study. First, there is no need to continue to explain the repetitions, both real and imagined, in Mark 4-8 on the basis of multiple pre-Markan traditions. The theories proposing pre-Markan cycles behind these chapters either fail to solve the very problem they are supposed to solve, the doublet problem, or they assume what they are supposed to prove, the pre-Markan connections between these stories. After a detailed examination of the preeminent doublet in Mark, the feeding stories, we found no reason to conclude that they are variant, traditional stories. Rather, one story is traditional (8:1-10) and the other a Markan composition (6:30-44). The evangelist has composed his own story as a backdrop for the traditional story, thereby controlling how the reader perceives the traditional story.

The second observation to be made is the recognition of the impetus toward the literary critical examination of the feeding stories provided by our redaction critical study. As it developed, our study of the feeding stories was conducted in two stages, the first redaction critical and the second literary critical. The second stage completed and cohered with the first but was in no way dependent on the first. Indeed, the literary critical analysis of the function of the feeding stories in the text as a whole could have been conducted quite independently of our redactional study. Our observation of how the feeding stories function in the text as a whole would be valid even if we were utterly mistaken in our claim that one of the stories is traditional and one Markan. Even if both are traditional, as so many claim, our observation of how they function now in the text would still be valid.

Our redaction critical study, however, would have been incomplete without the additional literary critical study. Redaction criticism could show us what the author did but it could not tell us why, because redaction criticism, as commonly practiced, is simply not used to interpret the

"redactional" creation or manipulation of entire pericopes.
To answer the question of why an author would rewrite a traditional story, place his new composition two chapters before the
old story, and allow a certain problematic tension to exist
between these stories, we found it necessary to consult
literary critics. Especially helpful were the insights provided
by reader-response critics and critics like Wayne Booth who
have given careful study to the phenomenon of irony in
literature. In the case of the feeding stories, in short,
redaction criticism is extremely valuable, but it eventually
reveals its own inadequacies and points us toward a fuller,
more adequate approach in the form of literary criticism.

One last observation concerns the audience for which the
gospel was presumably written. After a long tradition of
scholarly guesses as to the historical milieu in which the
gospel was written, we have found it most refreshing to engage
in a discussion of the implied community of the gospel; i.e.,
the community of those who read aright Mark's gospel. This
particular community is one about which a critic may speak
quite intelligibly; it is far more difficult to speak intelligibly about the supposed historical Christian community out of
which the gospel came or to which it was addressed (the distinction is often blurred). Nevertheless, we may be allowed to
hazard our own guess regarding its historical setting.

The gospel seems to be written almost as a writ of
divorce between certain segments of Judaism and Christianity.
Jesus, the protagonist, although himself a Jew, is repeatedly
opposed by every Jewish group he encounters: his disciples fail
to understand him and eventually abandon him, his family thinks
he is crazy, his neighbors think him an upstart, the crowd is
enthralled but ultimately fickle, the religious leaders despise
him and orchestrate his death.[1] It is as if nothing good can
come out of Judea. We suspect that such an attitude reflects
the period *circa* the Jewish War of the 60s C.E., when Christians
had little to gain and everything to lose by maintaining ties
with Judaism. Like a seaman jettisoning cargo in a storm, Mark
undertook a thorough and severe critique of all things Jewish

in his Christian heritage. That the Jewish component is still
prominent in his segment of Christianity is evident from his
preservation of many bits of Jewish lore; that the Jewish
component has been considerably weakened is evident from the
need to explain or translate those bits of Jewish lore.

Exactly where the gospel was written is impossible to tell.
The language of the gospel, although expressive and vigorous,
is unpolished and shows no great learning. Consequently, the
gospel could have been written almost anywhere in the Roman
Empire where a writer could have received a grade school
education in Greek (almost anywhere) and where Christians and
Jews, through the exigencies of history, were compelled to
part company and travel their separate ways.

CHAPTER I

NOTES

[1]See, e.g., Rudolf Bultmann, *The Gospel of John*, trans.
G. R. Beasley-Murray et al. (Philadelphia: Westminster Press,
1971), pp. 210-11.

[2]E.g., Ernst Haenchen, *Der Weg Jesu: Eine Erklärung des
Markus Evangeliums und der kanonischen Parallelen*, 2d ed.
(Berlin: Walter de Gruyter, 1968), p. 283 (includes a comparison
with John 6); Vincent Taylor, *The Gospel According to St. Mark*,
2d ed. (New York: St. Martin's Press, 1966), pp. 628-32; D. E.
Nineham, *Saint Mark* (Baltimore: Penguin Books, The Pelican
New Testament Commentaries, 1963), p. 206; Norman Perrin, *The
New Testament: An Introduction. Proclamation and Parenesis,
Myth and History* (New York: Harcourt Brace Jovanovich, 1974),
p. 146. For references to the older literature, see Taylor,
Mark, p. 628; and Frans Neirynck, *Duality in Mark: Contributions
to the Study of the Markan Redaction*, BETL, no. 31 (Leuven:
Leuven University Press, 1972), p. 26, n. 50.

[3]Luke H. Jenkins, "A Marcan Doublet," in *Studies in History
and Religion: Presented to Dr. H. Wheeler Robinson*, ed. Ernest
A. Payne (London: Lutterworth, 1942), pp. 87-111.

[4]Ibid., p. 91.

[5]Ibid., pp. 95-96; the stories have in common: *"Jesus,
disciples* and *crowd* in *desert place: crowd excites Jesus' pity:
Jesus and disciples* discuss *how to feed crowd: bread and fish*
produced, *blessed, broken, distributed: baskets filled with
surplus pieces: thousands of people"* (ibid., p. 91; Jenkins's
italics).

[6]For the former, one may look at Jenkins's explanation for
the absence of a second boat trip in cycle A corresponding to
the one mentioned in cycle B in 8:13; ibid., p. 105. For the
latter, see Jenkins's omission of Mark 6:31-33 from his synoptic
comparison of the two feeding stories: "Mk. vi. 31-33 is omitted
from this comparison because it shows no connection with [8:1-
9a]" (ibid., p. 95).

[7]Ibid., p. 100.

[8]Taylor, *Mark*, p. 628.

[9]Ibid., p. 629.

[10]Ibid., p. 630.

[11]Ibid., p. 631.

[12]Ibid.

[13]Ibid., p. 318, where all of this is stated explicitly.

[14]There are other problems with Taylor's analysis. In his
discussion of Mark 6:30-7:37 and 8:1-26 Taylor has too quickly
dismissed the extensive agreements between 7:31-37 and 8:22-26,
which many scholars believe are sufficient to suggest that these
stories also form a doublet (ibid., pp. 631, 368). Earlier in
his commentary he discusses this matter in detail (pp. 368-70),
providing a helpful synoptic comparison of the Greek texts and
clearly showing the numerous verbal agreements between the two
stories. In spite of these agreements, which have led many to
argue that the stories are variations of one story produced by
the same hand, he suggests that they are actually two distinct
stories, the language of which has been assimilated by a
redactor: "Mark, therefore, or a predecessor, deliberately uses
the framework supplied by vii. 32-7, but fits into it a new
story suitable to his didactic purpose" (p. 370). We will
return to these two stories later to consider carefully the
possibility that Mark intends for these stories to be read as
a matched pair no less than the two feeding stories, regardless
of the fact that the stories narrate two different episodes,
the healing of a deaf-mute and the healing of a blind man.
In order to do this we will require a methodology appropriate
for the doublets we find in Mark, which we hope to develop
first with the two feeding stories. For the present, it suffices
to realize that Taylor's own presuppositions and methodology
do not allow him to match up 6:45-56 with 8:10 as a doublet.

[15]E.g., Mark 6:52 and 8:17, but especially 7:31-37 and 8:22-
26.

[16]*JBL* 84 (1965): 341-58.

[17]Ibid., p. 344.

[18]Ibid., pp. 350-51.

[19]". . . Mark's own understanding of the Son of God category
is sufficiently different from these stories to enable us to
infer that he took them into his gospel partly because they
allowed him to present the divine sonship during Jesus' life-
time and partly because he wanted to check and counterbalance
this way of understanding Jesus' life and work" (ibid., p. 358).
". . .he has taken up the θεῖος ἀνήρ materials and
restricted their significance by interpreting the life of Jesus
as a whole in light of the cross, both that borne by Jesus and
that borne by the disciples--Mark's theology is indeed in
tension with the θεῖος ἀνήρ materials" (ibid., p. 357).
Keck's claim that Mark has taken up material dominated by
a θεῖος ἀνήρ theology in order to correct it has wide currency
in Markan studies, due in large part perhaps to the provocative
pursuit of this idea by T. J. Weeden in "The Heresy that
Necessitated Mark's Gospel," *ZNW* 59 (1968): 145-58; and in
Mark--Traditions in Conflict (Philadelphia: Fortress Press,
1971).

[20]"Mark 3:7-12," pp. 343-44.

[21]Taylor is typical: "The summary looks forward. By mentioning the crowds, the boat, and the demoniacs it prepares the way for iv. 1ff., the account of the lakeside teaching, and the miracle-stories of iv. 35-v. 43, especially the Gerasene Demoniac. The reference to the desire of the crowds to touch Jesus (iii. 10) anticipates v. 28-31 and vi. 56, and the mastery over the daemons described in iii. 11f. is a foil to the claim of Jesus, implicit in iii. 27, to have bound Satan, the Strong Man" (*Mark*, p. 225).

[22]Perrin, *Introduction*, p. 152; idem, "The High Priest's Question and Jesus' Answer," in *The Passion in Mark*, ed. Werner H. Kelber (Philadelphia: Fortress Press, 1976), p. 80.

[23]For references to the literature see p. 75 of Thierry Snoy's lengthy article, "Les miracles dans l'évangile de Marc," *RTL* 3 (1972): 449-66, 4 (1973): 58-101. Snoy devotes pp. 73-95 to Mark 3:7-12, providing a detailed critique of Keck's article and thoroughly demonstrating the Markan character of the entire unit. Snoy takes up and develops the criticisms of Keck by T. A. Burkill ("Mark 3:7-12 and the Alleged Dualism in the Evangelist's Miracle Material," *JBL* 87 [1968]: 409-17) and Wilhelm Egger ("Die Verborgenheit Jesu in Mk 3,7-12," *Bib* 50 [1969]: 466-90; and now also *Frohbotschaft und Lehre: Die Sammelberichte des Wirkens Jesu im Markusevangelium*, Frankfurter theologische Studien, no. 19 [Frankfurt am Main: Josef Knecht, 1976], pp. 85-111), enhancing their criticisms by his own meticulous study of Mark's language, grammar, thematic concerns, and literary style.

[24]Neirynck, *Duality*, p. 77.

[25]Ibid., pp. 49-50.

[26]Ibid., p. 29.

[27]This is perhaps easier to see in the specially arranged Greek text constructed by Neirynck, *Duality*, p. 145; Egger adopts Neirynck's typographical arrangement of the text in his book, *Frohbotschaft*, pp. 92-93.
The point we are making here about these examples of Markan duality in 3:7-8, 10-11 has already been made by Snoy: "La répétition πολὺ πλῆθος--πλῆθος πολύ, aux. v. 7 et 8, et de ἐπιπίπτειν--προσέπιπτον, aux v. 10 et 11, est typique du style de Marc en général. Impossible de s'en servir pour départager dans le texte éléments traditionnels et rédactionnels" ("Les miracles," p. 79).

[28]For example, the use of εἶπεν (3:9) in the sense of "to command" is Markan; so Snoy, "Les miracles," p. 84, n. 95. The use of γάρ (3:10) in explanatory comments is a well known Markan feature; so Taylor, *Mark*, pp. 308, 335; and C. H. Bird, "Some γαρ clauses in St. Mark's Gospel," *JTS* 4 (1953): 171-87. Observations of this kind, coupled with the realization that the boat motif and the motif of touching Jesus are borrowed by Mark himself from the later stories in which these motifs actually play a part, provide ample evidence of Mark's composition of 3:7-12.

[29]It is a crucial point that the only story in the complex involving touching Jesus is at the heart of an intercalation; the story of the woman with a hemorrhage has been placed in the framework of the story of Jairus' daughter (5:21-24a/24b-34/35-43). Keck offers only an unsupported assertion that "this was probably done before Mark" ("Mark 3:7-12," p. 349), in spite of the fact that the technique of intercalation is widely recognized as a Markan characteristic; see John R. Donahue, *Are You the Christ? The Trial Narrative in the Gospel of Mark*, SBLDS, no. 10 (Missoula: Society of Biblical Literature, 1973), pp. 42-43, 58-59, and the literature cited there. We are inclined to argue, against Keck, that Mark himself brought these two stories together in a typical manner, and repeated the touching motif in the authorial summaries he composed in 3:7-12 and 6:53-56.

[30]Snoy, "Les miracles," pp. 96-98; idem, "La rédaction marcienne de la marche sur les eaux (Mc., VI, 45-52)," *ETL* 44 (1968): 234-42. Keck also overlooks another redactional *Sammelbericht* in 6:30-34.

[31]Keck, "Mark 3:7-12," pp. 348, 349.

[32]Snoy, "Les miracles," p. 81.

[33]Ibid.

[34]Rudolf Pesch, *Das Markusevangelium*, HTKNT, no. 2, 2 vols. (Freiburg, Basel, and Vienna: Herder, 1976-77), 1:277-81.

[35]Ibid., 1:279.

[36]Frans Neirynck, "L'Évangile de Marc. À propos d'un nouveau commentaire," *ETL* 53 (1977): 153-81.

[37]Rudolf Pesch, *Naherwartungen. Tradition und Redaktion in Mk 13* (Dusseldorf: Patmos Verlag, 1968).

[38]Idem, *Markusevangelium*, 1:24 and passim; Neirynck, "L'Évangile de Marc," pp. 176-79.

[39]Ibid., pp. 161-62.

[40]Ibid., pp. 162, 177.

[41]Pesch, *Markusevangelium*, 1:16, 21.

[42]Neirynck, "L'Évangile de Marc," p. 159.

[43]Pesch, *Markusevangelium*, 1:278.

[44]For Pesch, in 8:10, 13; ibid., 1:405-6.

[45]Neirynck, "L'Évangile de Marc," p. 167.

[46]Ibid., pp. 171-72.

[47]Ibid., pp. 177-78.

[48]Heinz-Wolfgang Kuhn, *Ältere Sammlungen im Markusevangelium*, SUNT, no. 8 (Göttingen: Vandenhoeck & Ruprecht, 1971), pp. 191-213.

[49]Ibid., pp. 29-32.

[50]Ibid., p. 31.

[51]Ibid., pp. 191-92; see also pp. 27-28.

[52]Ibid., pp. 204, 208, 210-211. Kuhn follows Martin Dibelius closely here. For the *Novellen* see Martin Dibelius, *From Tradition to Gospel*, trans. Bertram Lee Woolf (New York: Charles Scribner's Sons, n.d.), pp. 70-103: "Whoever wished to spread the cult of Serapis told such stories, and thus miracle-stories became instruments of the mission. The New Testament Tales are to be understood as stories of this kind, useful in spreading the new cult" (ibid., p. 96).

[53]Kuhn, *Sammlungen*, pp. 193-200, 204-6, 211-13. Here Kuhn is largely dependent upon Ferdinand Hahn, *Christologische Hoheitstitel: Ihre Geschichte im frühen Christentum*, FRLANT, no. 83 (Göttingen: Vandenhoeck & Ruprecht, 1963) and Dieter Georgi, *Die Gegner des Paulus im 2 Korintherbrief: Studien zur religiösen Propaganda in der Spätantike*, WMANT, no. 11 (Neukirchen-Vluyn: Neukirchener Verlag, 1964).

[54]Kuhn, *Sammlungen*, pp. 208-9.

[55]This section also contains the story of John the Baptist's death.

[56]Ibid., p. 209.

[57]Ibid.

[58]In this and other criticisms to follow we have been preceded by Jean-Marie Van Cangh, "Les sources de l'Evangile: les collections prémarciennes de miracles," *RTL* 3 (1972): 76-85, a superb critique of the hypotheses advanced by Kuhn and Paul J. Achtemeier (see below).

[59]Ibid., p. 79.

[60]Kuhn, *Sammlungen*, p. 204; Dibelius, *Tradition*, pp. 71-72.

[61]Kuhn, *Sammlungen*, p. 204.

[62]On this matter see our discussion of Paul J. Achtemeier's work below.

[63]Emil Wendling, *Ur-Marcus: Versuch einer Wiederherstellung der ältesten Mitteilungen über das Leben Jesu* (Tübingen: J. C. B. Mohr [Paul Siebeck], 1905); idem, *Die Entstehung des Marcus-Evangeliums* (Tübingen: J. C. B. Mohr [Paul Siebeck], 1908).

[64]Dibelius, *Tradition*, pp. 78-79, n. 1. The Feeding of the Five Thousand *is* a *Novelle*, according to Dibelius: ibid., pp. 71, 75, 77, 80, 90, 92, 95.

[65]Van Cangh has stated this quite clearly and has called for a thorough redaction critical examination of the material thought to belong to pre-gospel collections:
"Nous pensons, pour notre part, que la détermination des collections pré-marciennes dépend immédiatement du progres des études de la *Redaktionsgeschichte* de Marc. . . . La présente note voudrait être un appel à des études *redaktions-geschichtlich* plus nombreuses,--condition préalable à la détermination des collections pré-marciennes" ("Les collections," p. 85).

[66]*JBL* 89 (1970): 265-91.

[67]*JBL* 91 (1972): 198-221.

[68]Achtemeier, "Isolation," p. 291.

[69]Ibid., p. 278. See also p. 188, n. 29, above.

[70]Snoy, "Mc., VI, 45-52."

[71]Achtemeier, "Isolation," pp. 282-84; Snoy, "Mc., VI, 45-52," p. 234. Snoy's claim that Mark first joined 6:30-44 and 6:45-52 is, we believe, correct, but his claim that 6:53 was the original conclusion to the feeding story is tenuous, as we hope to show later.

[72]Achtemeier, "Origin and Function," pp. 208-9.

[73]Ibid., pp. 210-12, 218. Achtemeier provides a convenient summary of his thesis:
"The most likely background out of which the catenae were formed is to be found in (hellenistic-) Jewish traditions about Moses; the groups which formed the catenae drew from these traditions in ways similar to those in which Paul's opponents in Corinth drew upon them; the catenae were formed as a part of a liturgy which celebrated an epiphantic Eucharist based on bread broken with the θεῖος ἀνήρ, Jesus, during his career and after his resurrection; and Mark sought to overcome that view of Jesus and of the Eucharist by the way in which he used the catenae in his own narrative" (ibid., p. 198).

[74]Achtemeier, "Isolation," pp. 286, 291.

[75]Ibid., p. 275.

[76]A recent study of this type on 5:1-20 finds considerable indication of Markan redaction: Franz Annen, *Heil für die Heiden: Zur Bedeutung und Geschichte der Tradition vom besessenen Gerasener (Mk. 5, 1-20 parr.)*, Frankfurter theologische Studien, no. 20 (Frankfurt am Main: Josef Knecht, 1976).

[77]Achtemeier, "Isolation," p. 278.

[78]Our comments here about Achtemeier's treatment of the connections in the catenae have been stated previously by J.-M. Van Cangh, "Les collections," pp. 80-84. With regard to 5:21, to cite just one example, Van Cangh asserts that its language indicates that it is Markan in origin (ibid., pp. 81-82), citing the work of Snoy ("Mc., VI, 45-52," pp. 216-17, n. 41). Having followed Snoy in his analysis of 6:45-52 and 6:53, Achtemeier has apparently chosen to ignore him here.
In general, Van Cangh has observed that it is precisely this detailed examination of style and vocabulary that is missing in the work of Achtemeier and H. W. Kuhn: "Les critères employés par H. W. Kuhn et P. J. Achtemeier doivent être complétés par une étude minutieuse des caractéristiques stylistiques et du vocabulaire marciens" ("Les collections," p. 85; also see p. 190, n. 65, above).

[79]One such example is 8:22: "And they came to Bethsaida. . . ." The fact that this verse mentions Bethsaida is the justification for placing 8:22-26 after 6:45-51, another story mentioning Bethsaida, in the second catena. Van Cangh urges that this is far too slender a thread with which to tie these stories together. If one were to apply this principle consistently then, e.g., all stories located in Capernaum would have to be brought together into a Capernaum catena ("Les collections," p. 83), a suggestion that few would find acceptable. In addition, we are surprised to note that Achtemeier admits that the phrase with which 8:22 begins, καὶ ἔρχονται εἰς βηθσαϊδάν, "may be Markan" ("Isolation," p. 285, n. 76). Although the wording of the phrase may be Markan, he argues, the association of Bethsaida with the following story is traditional. The method by which this traditional datum is distilled from what may be a Markan phrase is not revealed.

[80]A notable exception is Emil Wendling in *Ur-Markus* and *Entstehung*.

[81]The late Norman Perrin was a leading proponent of this development, as can be seen in the shift in his own thinking from an orientation towards redaction criticism to an emphasis on literary criticism. Typical of literary critical concerns are attention to the genre of a work, plot, characters, thematic concerns, and narrative structure. See Norman Perrin, "The Christology of Mark: A Study in Methodology," *JR* 51 (1971): 173-87 (later reprinted in *L'Evangile selon Marc: Tradition et rédaction*, ed. M. Sabbe, BETL, no. 34 [Leuven: Leuven University Press, 1974], pp. 471-85); idem, "The Evangelist as Author: Reflections on Method in the Study and Interpretation of the Synoptic Gospels and Acts," *BR* 17 (1972): 5-18; idem, "The Interpretation of the Gospel of Mark," *Int* 30 (1976): 115-24.

[82]Van Cangh, "Les collections," p. 85: "La part d'hypothèse dans ce genre de reconstruction est trop grande encore. . . ."

[83]Frans Neirynck, "Mark in Greek," *ETL* 47 (1971): 144-98;
idem, "Duality in Mark," *ETL* 47 (1971): 394-463; idem,
"Duplicate Expressions in the Gospel of Mark," *ETL* 48 (1972):
150-209; idem, *Duality in Mark: Contributions to the Study of
the Markan Redaction*, BETL, no. 31 (Leuven: Leuven University
Press, 1971). All of our references will use the pagination
of the book.

[84]Part III in the book, ibid.

[85]See ibid., pp. 193-94, for explanation.

[86]Part II in the book, ibid.

[87]Part I in the book, ibid.

[88]Ibid., pp. 9, 14.

[89]Ibid., p. 19.

[90]Ibid., pp. 49-50.

[91]". . . pure redundancy is extremely rare in Mark" (ibid.,
p. 46).

[92]Ibid., pp. 46, 50, 55, 62-63, 71-72.

[93]Ibid., p. 63; "The survey of temporal and local statements,
double questions, antithetic parallelism and the use of
oratio recta and *oratio obliqua* has shown that the progressive
double-step expression is a more general Markan characteristic.
This does not exclude indebtedness to tradition and sources, but
in each particular case the source critic has to reckon with the
possibility that the composite expression reflects the author's
own manner of writing" (ibid., pp. 71-72).

[94]Ibid., p. 37.

[95]Ibid., pp. 25-26.

[96]See Chapter 5 of *Die Entstehung des Marcus-Evangeliums*:
"Die grosse Einschaltung 6:45-8:26," pp. 68-97. See also *Ur-
Marcus*, pp. 15-16.

[97]Neirynck, *Duality*, p. 25, n. 48.

[98]Karl Ludwig Schmidt, *Der Rahmen der Geschichte Jesu:
Literarkritische Untersuchungen zur ältesten Jesusüberlieferung*
(Berlin: Trowitzsch & Sohn, 1919; reprint ed., Darmstadt:
Wissenschaftliche Buchgesellschaft, 1964), p. 194, n. 2.

[99]Wendling, *Entstehung*, pp. 68-75.

[100]Actually 6:32-34 is from the M^1 stratum and 6:35-44 is
from the M^2 stratum (6:30-31 is from "Ev"--the evangelist).

Wendling describes the strata of the gospel as follows:
"M[1] = Apophthegmata Jesu in knappem, aber anschaulichem
Erzählungsrahmen.
M[2] = Erzählungen von Wundertaten Jesu in ausführlicher, zum
Teil poetisch gehobener Darstellung. . . .
Die Kombination M[1] + M[2], . . . bildete die Vorlage des
Evangelisten" (Wendling, *Ur-Marcus*, p. 13).
See the charts, ibid., pp. 29-33, for the material assigned to
M[1], M[2] and Ev.

[101]Wendling, *Entstehung*, pp. 66-67.

[102] Ibid., pp. 69-72.

[103]Ibid., p. 69.

[104] Ibid., p. 71.

[105]Ezra P. Gould, *The Gospel According to St. Mark*, ICC,
no. 7 (New York: Charles Scribner's Sons, 1896), p. 142. For
references to this and other similar judgments see V. Taylor,
Mark, pp. 358-59.

[106]Robert H. Stein, "The Proper Methodology for Ascertaining
a Marcan Redaktionsgeschichte" (Ph.D. dissertation, Princeton
Theological Seminary, 1968); idem, "What is *Redaktionsgeschichte?*"
JBL 88 (1969): 45-56; idem, "The 'Redaktionsgeschichtlich'
Investigation of a Markan Seam (Mc. 1:21f.),"*ZNW* 61 (1970):
70-94; idem, "The Proper Methodology for Ascertaining a Markan
Redaction History," *NovT* 13 (1971): 181-98; Thierry Snoy, "Les
miracles"; idem, "Mc., VI, 45-52"; idem, "Marc 6,48: '. . .et il
voulait les dépasser.' Proposition pour la solution d'une
énigme," in *L'Evangile selon Marc: Tradition et rédaction*, ed.
M. Sabbe, BETL, no. 34 (Leuven: Leuven University Press, 1974),
pp. 347-63--we have been unable to examine Snoy's dissertation,
"La Marche de Jésus sur les eaux: Étude de rédaction marcienne"
(Ph.D. dissertation, Leuven University, 1967); Donahue, *Trial
Narrative*; Annen, *Heil für die Heiden*.

[107]John C. Hawkins, *Horae Synopticae: Contributions to the
Study of the Synoptic Problem*, 2d ed. (Oxford: Clarendon
Press, 1909; reprint ed., Grand Rapids, Mich.: Baker Book House,
1968); in conjunction with Hawkins's work one should now consult
Frans Neirynck, "Hawkins's Additional Notes to his 'Horae
Synopticae,'" *ETL* 46 (1970): 78-111; also see the more precise
statistical analysis by Lloyd Gaston, *Horae Synopticae
Electronicae: Word Statistics of the Synoptic Gospels*, SBLSBS,
no. 3 (Missoula, Mont.: Society of Biblical Literature, 1973);
Henry B. Swete, *The Gospel According to St. Mark*, 3d ed. (London:
Macmillan & Co., 1909); Marie-Joseph Lagrange, *Evangile selon
Saint Marc*, EBib, 3d ed. (Paris: Librairie Victor Lecoffre,
1920); Taylor, *Mark*.

[108]C. H. Turner, "Marcan Usage: Notes, Critical and Exegetical
on the Second Gospel," *JTS* 25 (1924): 377-86; 26 (1925): 12-20,
145-56, 225-40; 27 (1926): 58-62; 28 (1927): 9-30, 349-62; 29

(1928): 275-89, 346-61; Ernst von Dobschütz, "Zur Erzählerkunst des Markus," *ZNW* 27 (1928): 193-98; Max Zerwick, *Untersuchungen zum Markus-Stil: Ein Beitrag zur stilistischen Durcharbeitung des Neuen Testaments*, Scripta Instituti Pontificii Biblici, no. 5 (Rome: Pontifical Biblical Institute, 1937); C. H. Bird, "Γαρ clauses"; G. D. Kilpatrick, "Some Notes on Marcan Usage," *BT* 7 (1956):2-9, 51-56, 146; John C. Doudna, *The Greek of the Gospel of Mark*, SBLMS, no. 12 (Philadelphia: Society of Biblical Literature, 1961).

[109] Eduard Schweizer, "Anmerkungen zur Theologie des Markus," in *Neotestamentica et Patristica: Eine Freundsgabe, Herrn Professor Dr. Oscar Cullmann zu seinem 60. Geburtstag überreicht*, NovTSup. no. 6 (Leiden: E. J. Brill, 1962), pp. 35-46; idem, "Die theologische Leistung des Markus," *EvT* 24 (1964): 337-55; Ernest Best, *The Temptation and the Passion: The Marcan Soteriology*, SNTSMS, no. 2 (Cambridge: Cambridge University Press, 1965); Béda Rigaux, *The Testimony of St. Mark*, trans. Malachy Carroll (Chicago: Franciscan Herald Press, 1966); Jan Lambrecht, *Die Redaktion der Markus-Apokalypse: Literarische Analyse und Strukturuntersuchung*, AnBib, no. 28 (Rome: Pontifical Biblical Institute, 1967); idem, "Redaction and Theology in Mk., IV," in *L'Évangile selon Marc*, pp. 269-307; idem, "Jesus and the Law. An Investigation of Mk 7, 1-23," *ETL* 53 (1977): 24-82; Van Cangh, "Les collections"; idem, "Le thème des poissons dans les récits évangéliques de la multiplication des pains," *RB* 78 (1971): 71-83; idem, "La multiplication des pains dans l'évangile de Marc: Essai d'exégèse globale," in *L'Évangile selon Marc*, pp. 309-46--we have been unable to examine Van Cangh's doctoral dissertation, "Les récits de la multiplication des pains dans la tradition synoptique: Problèmes de méthode et exégèse d'ensemble," 2 vols. (Ph.D. dissertation, Leuven University, 1974), but a condensation of it has been published as *La multiplication des pains et l'eucharistie*, LD, no. 86 (Paris: Cerf, 1975); Neirynck, "L'Evangile de Marc"; idem, *Duality*; idem, ed., in collaboration with Theo Hansen and Frans Van Segbroeck, *The Minor Agreements of Matthew and Luke against Mark with a Consultative List*, BETL, no. 37 (Leuven: Leuven University Press, 1974); Werner H. Kelber, *The Kingdom in Mark: A New Place and a New Time* (Philadelphia: Fortress Press, 1974); Howard Clark Kee, *Community of the New Age: Studies in Mark's Gospel* (Philadelphia: Westminster Press, 1977).

[110] New Testament scholars who have begun to apply the insights of literary critics to the study of the gospels include Amos N. Wilder, *Early Christian Rhetoric: The Language of the Gospel* (Cambridge: Harvard University Press, 1964); Robert W. Funk, *Language, Hermeneutic and Word of God: The Problem of Language in the New Testament and Contemporary Theology* (New York: Harper & Row, 1966); idem, *Jesus as Precursor*, Semeia Supplements, no. 2 (Missoula, Mont.: Scholars Press, 1975); Dan O. Via, *The Parables: Their Literary and Existential Dimension* (Philadelphia: Fortress Press, 1975); Perrin, "Christology of Mark"; idem, *Jesus and the Language of the Kingdom: Symbol and Metaphor in New Testament Interpretation* (Philadelphia: Fortress Press, 1976);

John Dominic Crossan, *In Parables: The Challenge of the Historical Jesus* (New York: Harper & Row, 1973); Robert C. Tannehill, *The Sword of His Mouth*, Semeia Supplements, no. 1 (Missoula, Mont.: Scholars Press, 1975); idem, "The Disciples in Mark: The Function of a Narrative Role," *JR* 57 (1977): 386-405; Norman R. Petersen, *Literary Criticism for New Testament Critics*, Guides to Biblical Scholarship, New Testament Series (Philadelphia: Fortress Press, 1978). One may also consult the various issues of the journal *Semeia*, among which are entire issues devoted to the work of Paul Ricoeur and Erhardt Güttgemanns.

[111]The plea to regard the gospels as wholes have been ably made by Roland M. Frye and Erhardt Güttgemanns; Roland M. Frye, "A Literary Perspective for the Criticism of the Gospels," in *Jesus and Man's Hope: Essays from the Pittsburgh Festival on the Gospels*, ed. D. G. Miller and D. Y. Hadidian, 2 vols. (Pittsburgh: Pittsburgh Theological Seminary, 1970-71), 2:214 (see also the response to Frye by Paul J. Achtemeier, "On the Historical-Critical Method in New Testament Studies: Apologia pro Vita Sua," *Perspective* 11 [1970]: 289-304; to which Frye responded in "On the Historical Critical Method in New Testament Studies: A Reply to Professor Achtemeier," *Perspective* 14 [1973]: 28-33); Erhardt Güttgemanns, *Offene Frage zur Formgeschichte des Evangeliums: Eine methodologische Skizze zu Grundlagenproblematik der Form- und Redaktionsgeschichte*, BEvT, no. 54 (Munich: Chr. Kaiser, 1970), pp. 184-88, 256-61.

CHAPTER II

NOTES

[1]Stated long ago by Alfred Loisy: "Le récit de la
multiplication des pains qui vient maintenant le second n'est
pas necessairement moins ancien que le premier, et celui-ci,
au contraire, peut être le dernier venu dans la relation
évangélique" ("Le Second Evangile," *Revue d'Histoire et de
Littérature Religieuses* 8 [1903]: 524).
    Some exegetes have apparently understood Loisy to be
claiming that the second feeding story is in fact the earlier
account (see, e.g., Wendling, *Entstehung*, p. 69, n. 3), but
Loisy actually seems to stop short of making such a claim.

[2]There are several important works that we were unable to
examine, most of them dissertations. Besides the dissertations
of T. Snoy (see p. 193, n. 106, above) and J. M. Van Cangh (see p.
194, n. 109, above), these include the works of Georg Kronthaler,
"Die Dublettenfrage bei Mk 6,34-44 und 8,1-9" (Ph.D. dissertation, Salzburg University, 1967); G. Theunis, "Le récit de la
multiplication des pains (Marc 6,30-44) et les accords mineurs
de Matthieu 14,13-21 et de Luc 9,10-17. Contribution à la
théorie des deux sources" (Mémoire de licence, Leuven University,
1970); Thierry Snoy, "Analyse philologique et littéraire de
Marc 6,30-44" (Travail polycopié, Séminaire de Nouveau Testament, Leuven University, 1969-70); M. Fitzpatrick, "The Structure
of St. Mark's Gospel: With a Reconsideration of the Hypothesis
of Pre-Markan Collections in Mark 1-10" (Ph.D. dissertation,
Leuven University, 1975).
    When the writing of this dissertation was substantially
completed, there appeared in print a study of the Markan
literary style by E. J. Pryke, *Redactional Style in the Marcan
Gospel: A Study of Syntax and Vocabulary as guides to Redaction
in Mark*, SNTSMS, no. 33 (Cambridge: Cambridge University Press,
1978). We were gratified to see an entire volume devoted to
"a study of syntax and vocabulary as guides to redaction in
Mark," for that is exactly the approach adopted in the present
chapter. Pryke operates with an acknowledged form critical
perspective on the gospel, and he is intent on sorting out
redactional material from source material. He begins his study
by providing a lengthy catalog of virtually every verse in the
gospel that has at one time been regarded as redactional by
twentieth-century exegetes along with references to the comments
of those exegetes. The aim of his study is to analyze this
material in light of the observations regarding Markan syntax
and vocabulary made by Hawkins, Turner, Taylor, and many others,
to see if the occurrences of Markan syntax and vocabulary
coincide with the observations of Markan redaction made on the
basis of source or form criticism. The main body of his study
is a discussion of fourteen commonly recognized Markan syntactical features and their presence in both redactional and source
material. The results of Pryke's study of these syntactical
features, along with his compilation and study of the favorite
Markan vocabulary, tend to cohere with the earlier source and
form critical observations of Markan redaction--Markan

197

redaction tends to display prominently the syntax and
vocabulary generally regarded as characteristic of the evangelist. In fact, Pryke repeatedly uses the insights into Markan
syntax and vocabulary to claim as 'redactional' many verses
that are often thought to be source material. This is one aspect
of his work with which we are particularly sympathetic, as will
become clear when we demonstrate the Markan syntax and
vocabulary present in Mark 6:30-44 below. We will offer a more
detailed critique of Pryke's work in a future book review to
be published in the journal *Dialog* (18 [1979]: 151-52), but for
the present it suffices to say that Pryke has provided us with
a convenient compendium of insights into Markan syntax and
vocabulary, and he has demonstrated that such insights largely
confirm past observations of Markan redaction while at the
same time pointing beyond the boundaries of these observations
toward an even larger amount of redactional material in Mark.

[4]See, e.g., Neirynck, *Agreements*.

[5]As Robert H. Stein has correctly observed in his dissertation, "The Proper Methodology of Ascertaining a Marcan
Redaktionsgeschichte"; see also idem, "What is *Redaktionsgeschichte?*"; idem, "Markan Seam"; idem, "Markan Redaction
History."

[6]Idem, "Mark Redaction History," p. 182; Van Cangh, "Les
collections," p. 85; Annen, *Heil für die Heiden*, pp. 39-40.
See also the similar comments by Donahue, *Trial Narrative*, p.
39; Lambrecht, *Markus-Apokalypse*, p. 89; and William G.
Thompson, *Matthew's Advice to a Divided Community: Mt. 17,22-18,
35*, AnBib, no. 44 (Rome: Biblical Institute Press, 1970), p.9.

[7]Annen, *Heil für die Heiden*, p. 41.

[8]A few exegetes have commented on this: Zerwick, *Untersuchungen*, pp. 7-10; Snoy, "Mc., VI, 45-52," p. 446, n. 212.

[9]Donahue, *Trial Narrative*, pp. 77-84, 241-43.

[10]Ibid., p. 79. The last criterion assures that at least two
early readers of Mark found the phrases in question sufficiently
repetitive that they could modify or eliminate the repetition
without rendering the surrounding material incomprehensible.

[11]Ibid., p. 81.

[12]Neirynck, *Duality in Mark*.

[13]Ibid., p. 117.

[14]*Genitive absolute* (especially at the beginning of a
sentence): Taylor, *Mark*, p. 333; Doudna, *Greek of Mark*, pp.
57-59; Béda Rigaux, *The Testimony of St. Mark*, trans. Malachy
Carroll (Chicago: Franciscan Herald Press, 1966), p. 64; Snoy,
"Les miracles," p. 61; Neirynck, *Agreements*, pp. 244-46; Annen,
Heil für die Heiden, p. 43; Pryke, *Redactional Style*, pp. 62-67;

Stein, "Marcan Redaktionsgeschichte," p. 115, n. 15: "Certainly
the use of the genitive absolute is a Markan stylistic
characteristic."

[15]Taylor, *Mark*, p. 357.

[16]πάλιν: Hawkins, *Horae Synopticae*, p. 13; Turner, "Marcan
Usage," *JTS* 29 (1928): 283-87; Schmid, *Matthäus und Lukas*, p.
42; Taylor, *Mark*, p. 192; Schweizer, "Leistung," p. 341, n. 14;
Snoy, "Mc., VI, 45-52," p. 446, n. 213, and p. 457; Neirynck,
Agreements, pp. 276-77; Pryke, *Redactional Style*, pp. 96-99.
  Bultmann claims that Mark uses πάλιν merely as a connective; Rudolf Bultmann, *Die Geschichte der synoptischen Tradition*,
8th ed. (Göttingen: Vandenhoeck & Ruprecht, 1970), p. 364;
but Lagrange observes correctly, to the contrary, that "πάλιν
a toujours dans Mc. le sens itératif" (*Marc*, p. xcii). In
numerous cases, πάλιν marks the second time an action or
episode occurs, as can be seen in Neirynck's convenient chart
of all the occurrences of πάλιν in Mark with the antecedents
to which they allude; *Agreements*, pp. 276-77.

[17]See, e.g., Kelber, *Kingdom*, p. 56. Besides 6:34 and 8:1,
ὄχλος πολύς appears in 5:21, 24, 9:14, and 12:37. Cf. also
ὄχλος πλεῖστος in 4:1, ὄχλου ἱκανοῦ in 10:46, πολὺ πλῆθος in
3:7, 8, and numerous occurrences of ὁ ὄχλος and οἱ πολλοί.

[18]ἔχω: Turner, "Marcan Usage," *JTS* 28 (1927): 357-60;
Turner's claim that ἔχω occurs in Mark with unusual frequency
is substantiated by the statistical study of Lloyd Gaston,
Horae Synopticae Electronicae, p. 19.

[19]προσκαλέομαι: Swete, *Mark*, p. xlix; Taylor, *Mark*, p. 343; Kee,
Community, pp. 52-53; Pryke, *Redactional Style*, pp. 51, 137. Snoy
is particularly aware of the important role of this verb in the
evangelist's composition: "Mc. utilise 9 fois προσκαλέομαι,
presque toujours au participe aoriste et à propos de Jésus,
soit au début d'une péricope ou entre deux séries de logia dans
une phrase rédactionnelle qui fait à la fois transition et
liaison avec ce qui précède" ("Mc., VI, 45-52," p. 457).

[20]*Historical present*: Hawkins, *Horae Synopticae*, pp. 14,
143-49; Schmid, *Matthäus und Lukas*, p. 38; Taylor, *Mark*, pp.
46-47; Donahue, *Trial Narrative*, pp. 54-55 (and see the
literature cited there); Annen, *Heil für die Heiden*, p. 48
(and see the literature cited there); Neirynck, *Agreements*,
pp. 223-29 (and see the literature cited there).
  λέγω *in introductory phrases*: Hawkins, *Horae Synopticae*,
p. 12; Zerwick, *Untersuchungen*, pp. 60-62; Snoy, "Mc., VI, 45-
52," p. 457; Annen, *Heil für die Heiden*, p. 48; Neirynck,
Agreements, pp. 224-25; Kee, *Community*, pp. 51-52.

[21]Doudna, *Greek of Mark*, pp. 31-32, 81. Doudna claims that
such a use of ἐπί with the accusative has no parallel in Attic
Greek, nor is it found in the papyri. Other occurrences in the
gospel are found in 9:22 and in 9:12, 13 (with γράφω).

[22]Mark 6:35 (N.B.--twice), 8:2, 11:11, 15:42. Pryke places ἤδη in his list of Markan redactional vocabulary (*Redactional Style*, p. 136).

[23]"πλοῖον ist ein mk Vorzugswort," according to Annen, *Heil für die Heiden*, p. 212; see also Gaston, *Horae Synopticae Electronicae*, p. 21; and Pryke, *Redactional Style*, p. 137. For a fuller discussion see our excursus on the boat motif in Mark, below.

[24]As Neirynck has noted, of course, two-step actions in Mark are quite common.

[25]See above, p. 199, n. 16.

[26]Against the weight of the Alexandrian witnesses, we are inclined to read εἰς τὸ πλοῖον in 8:13. See the other occurrences of this phrase with ἐμβαίνω in 5:18, 6:45, 8:10; cf. also 4:1.

[27]εὐθύς: Hawkins, *Horae Synopticae*, p. 12; Swete, *Mark*, p. xlviii; Lagrange, *Marc*, p. lxv; Schmid, *Matthäus und Lukas*, pp. 41-42; Taylor, *Mark*, p. 44; Gaston, *Horae Synopticae Electronicae*, p. 19; Neirynck, *Agreements*, pp. 274-76; Pryke, *Redactional Style*, pp. 87-96.

[28]Although he regards the occurrences of the boat motif in Mark 3-6 as part of "die vormarkinische Wundergeschichten-sammlung," Pesch is willing to admit the redactional nature of 8:10, 13; *Markusevangelium*, 1:405-6. See above, Chap. 1. Pesch also claims that 8:9b is redactional, which may be correct; ibid., 1:404-5.

[29]Snoy, "Les miracles," pp. 456-64.

[30]See, e.g., Dibelius, *Tradition*, p. 229; Taylor, *Mark*, p. 363; Quentin Quesnell, *The Mind of Mark: Interpretation and Method through the Exegesis of Mark 6,52*, AnBib, no. 38. (Rome: Pontifical Biblical Institute, 1969), pp. 105-6; Kelber, *Kingdom*, p. 61.

[31]Taylor, *Mark*, p. 360; Nineham, *Saint Mark*, p. 209; Van Cangh, "Le thème des poissons," pp. 72-73, 81; idem, *La multiplication des pains*, pp. 106, 165.

[32]Van Cangh, "Le thème des poissons," p. 73, n. 5.
    Diminutives: C. H. Turner, "Marcan Usage," *JTS* 28 (1928): 349-52; Schmid, *Matthäus und Lukas*, p. 55; F. Blass, A. Debrunner, and Robert W. Funk, *A Greek Grammar of the New Testament and Other Early Christian Literature* (Chicago: University of Chicago Press, 1961), p. 60, sec. III, pt. 3; Taylor, *Mark*, p. 45.
    εἶπεν *with an infinitive with the sense of "to command"*: Taylor, *Mark*, pp. 62, 298, 360 (regarding 8:7); Snoy, "Les miracles," p. 84, n. 95.
    In the article cited above, Van Cangh argues on the basis of the Markan literary characteristics found in 8:7 that the verse is a Markan composition ("Le thème des poissons," pp.

72-73, 81). Later, however, he withdrew this assertion in *La multiplication des pains*, pp. 85, 106, 165-66. Nevertheless, he still maintains that 8:7 is a redactional interjection into the story, only now he claims that this redactional activity took place at a pre-Markan stage of the tradition. Unfortunately, he has not offered a satisfactory reassessment of the Markan features he previously pointed out in 8:7. He does claim now that the use of εἶπεν may betray Semitic influence, implying that it was already in Mark's *Vorlage* (ibid., p. 106), but he does not actually deny that it is a common, characteristic feature in Mark. On the Markan fondness for diminutives he is totally silent. We will discuss Van Cangh's position in greater detail below in this study, but for now we will suggest that his earlier suspicion that 8:7 was added to the story by Mark himself was correct.

[33] Cf. 8:1-2, and see above, p. 199, n. 18.

[34] Although the *hapax legomena* in 8:1-10 are prominent and often commented upon, the *hapax legomena* and other characteristics in 6:30-44 that could be construed as non-Markan are so scarce that they are virtually nonexistent. Taylor and Van Cangh have made comments on the prominence of *hapax legomena* in 8:1-10:

"A comparison of vi. 35-44 and viii. 1-9 leaves the impression that in many respects the second is an abbreviated version of the first, and the words peculiar to it, προσμένω, νῆστις, ἐκλύω, περίσσευμα, ἐρημία, and σφυρίς, and the forms εἶχαν and ἤκασιν suggest independent compilation" (Taylor, *Mark*, p. 360).

"La différence entre les chiffres et les nombres des deux récits et les nombreux *hapax legomena* du deuxième favorisent plutôt la thèse d'une double tradition pré-marcienne à l'origine des deux récits du même miracle" (Van Cangh, *La multiplication des pains*, p. 169).

We fail to see how the prominence of *hapax legomena* in *one* of the two feeding stories leads to the conclusion that both stories are "independent," "pré-marcienne" stories. The emphasis placed by both Taylor and Van Cangh on the unusual vocabulary in 8:1-10 is a tacit recognition of the familiar, characteristic vocabulary of 6:30-44. Rather than indicating the independent, pre-Markan origin of both stories, the language of the stories suggests that only one of them is pre-Markan--the one with the unusual vocabulary (8:1-10)--and the other is a Markan composition displaying Mark's familiar compositional tendencies.

[35] The use of the diminutive of ἰχθύς in 8:7 is analogous to the use of the diminutive of πλοῖον in 3:9, which is also a *hapax* and redactional.

[36] The conjectures about the proper geography of 8:10 began with Matthew, who substituted Magadan for Dalmanutha (Matt. 15:39), they persisted among the scribes, who substituted Magadan or Magdala in their copies of Mark, and they thrive to this day; Taylor, *Mark*, pp. 360-61.

[37] See our excursus on the boat motif, below.

[38] Snoy, "Mc., VI, 45-52," p. 239, n. 143. Pryke places both ἔρημος and τόπος in the Markan redactional vocabulary (*Redactional Style*, pp. 136, 137).

[39] Cf. 9:17, 12:29. C. H. Turner studied the phenomenon of the absence of λέγω after various verbs of saying used to introduce direct speech; "Marcan Usage," *JTS* 29 (1928): 359-61. In his study, he made reference to these three cases (8:4, 9:17, 12:29) where ἀποκρίνομαι is used without λέγω to introduce direct speech. Later, Schmid mistakenly took this to mean that Mark *regularly* uses ἀποκρίνομαι without λέγω; *Matthäus und Lukas*, pp. 77-78. However, this is not the conclusion that Turner reached. At the end of his study he observed: "It is not meant to be suggested that Mark's normal usage is to employ [verbs of saying] without λέγω" ("Marcan Usage," p. 361). On the contrary, Mark's customary practice, at least in the case of ἀποκρίνομαι, is to use the verb with λέγω. This has been recognized by Doudna: "In the bulk of the examples [ἀποκρίνομαι] appears participially with λέγειν in the form ἀποκριθεὶς λέγει"; this construction has "extensive use" in Mark (*Greek of Mark*, p. 57). See also Neirynck, *Agreements*, pp. 249-51.

[40] Gaston's statistical study demonstrates the relative frequency of ἐσθίω in Mark in comparison to Matthew and Luke; *Horae Synopticae Electronicae*, p. 19.

[41] ἐπερωτάω: Hawkins, *Horae Synopticae*, p. 14; Taylor, *Mark*, p. 44; Donahue, *Trial Narrative*, p. 85; Snoy, "Mc., VI, 45-52," pp. 458, 463; Gaston, *Horae Synopticae Electronicae*, p. 19; Annen, *Heil für die Heiden*, p. 52; Pryke, *Redactional Style*, p. 136.

[42] The dominance of non-Markan language in 8:3-6, 8-9 is clear. However, there are a few sparse instances of language that conceivably could be regarded as Markan: ἐν τῇ ὁδῷ, ἀπὸ μακρόθεν (v. 3); ὅτι recitative (v. 4); ἔχω (v. 5); and the use of the historical present (v. 6). For the most part these are minor examples with little cumulative weight. They are completely overshadowed by the predominant non-Markan language in which they are enveloped.

Some exegetes regard ἐν τῇ ὁδῷ as a Markan phrase (Hawkins, *Horae Synopticae*, p. 12) but usually in connection with the journey from Galilee to Jerusalem in Mark 8:22-10:52. Werner Kelber, for example, argues that this section of the gospel is "structured by the motif of the way" (*Kingdom*, p. 67), but he regards most of the occurrences outside of this section as traditional (p. 69, n. 4; 8:3 is not, however, mentioned explicitly). Clearly the use of ἐν τῇ ὁδῷ in 8:3 bears no relation whatsoever to the common motif in Mark 8-10 of Jesus and his disciples traveling "on the way." Appearing as it does in 8:3 it is far from being an impressive indicator of Markan composition.

Ἀπὸ μακρόθεν is a familiar pleonastic expression in Mark and may well have been inserted by the evangelist into the traditional story. See Hawkins, *Horae Synopticae*, p. 12; Schmid, *Matthäus und Lukas*, p. 57; Taylor, *Mark*, pp. 50-52; Donahue, *Trial Narrative*, p. 56; Neirynck, *Duality*, pp. 75-76.

῞Οτι *recitative* is also a common Markan feature: Turner, "Marcan Usage," *JTS* (1927): 9-15; Schmid, *Matthäus und Lukas*, p. 53; Zerwick, *Untersuchungen*, pp. 39-48; Doudna, *Greek of Mark*, pp. 61-62; Neirynck, *Agreements*, pp. 213-16; Pryke, *Redactional Style*, pp. 73-79. However, since it occurs in a verse that contains the notably non-Markan uses of ἀποκρίνομαι, χορτάζω, and ἐρημία, this isolated, minor feature pales to insignificance.

Such is also the case with the use of ἔχω in 8:5. This verse is introduced by the distinctively non-Markan ἠρώτα, and the use of ἔχω is followed immediately by the relatively infrequent connective δέ. If we may take the liberty of comparing this verse with the corresponding verse in the other feeding story, we will see that 6:38 is far more typical of Mark. There the use of ἔχω is followed by the asyndetic juxtaposition of two imperatives, ὑπάγετε and ἴδετε--asyndeton is a favorite Markan construction. One of these verbs (ὑπάγω) is a Markan favorite. Furthermore, the next phrase is not attached with δέ, as it is in 8:5, but with the familiar καί parataxis followed by an instance of the historical present. Mark 8:5 cannot even begin to match the wealth of Markan characteristics found in 6:38.

The last of these possible Markan features is the use of the *historical present* in 8:6 (see above, p. 199, n. 20). The use of the historical present is one of the more prominent characteristics of the Markan literary style and may have been introduced into the story here by the evangelist. Nevertheless, the use of the verb itself (παραγγέλλω) is extremely rare in Mark, occurring elsewhere only in 6:8, thereby creating room for the suspicion that Mark found the verb already in his source and preserved it but in the historical present. This suspicion is corroborated in a most decisive manner when one observes which verbs of saying Mark habitually employs when he is using the historical present. Seventy-five times Mark uses a verb of saying in the historical present. In seventy-two cases the verb is λέγω, leaving only three exceptions, one of which is 8:6 (Neirynck, *Agreements*, pp. 224-25). The scarcity of παραγγέλλω in Mark, coupled with the fact that Mark has an overwhelming preference for λέγω when using the historical present, gives us a clear indication that the verb was present in Mark's source and was preserved by the evangelist in the historical present.

It is fair to say that these supposed instances of Markan language in 8:3-6, 8-9 are unimpressive and inconsequential. They in no way detract from the conclusion that a story from Mark's *Vorlage* lies beneath the present text of 8:1-10; in some cases they actually furnish valuable additional evidence for the fundamentally non-Markan character of 8:3-6, 8-9.

[43]*Kingdom*, pp. 48-65.

[44]Ibid., pp. 51-53.

[45]Ibid., p. 48.

[46]Ibid.

[47]For example, two consecutive boat excursions in 5:1 and 5:21 proceed "to the other side," which would be impossible if the author were carefully using the phrase to refer to only one shore of the lake. Some interpreters also point out John's use of πέραν in John 6:25 to refer to Capernaum on the western shore of the Sea of Galilee.

[48]Going back at least to Augustine; see Nineham, *Saint Mark*, p. 207.

[49]*Kingdom*, pp. 56-57, 59-60.

[50]*Heil für die Heiden*, pp. 40-44, 64, 70, 211-14. Logically, Annen dismisses theories of pre-Markan cycles: "Ein vormk Komplex 4,1-5,43 oder 4,35-5,43 in Form eines itinerarartigen Ablaufs erscheint also vom Rahmen her höchst unwahrscheinlich. Vielmehr hat wohl erst Mk die verschiedenen Perikopen durch die See-Szenerie redaktionell zusammengefügt" (ibid., p. 214).

[51]"Mc., VI, 45-52," pp. 238, 232-34, 234-36.

[52]Wendling recognized that there are three boat trips in Mark and that their movement is "zu . . . und zurück" (*Entstehung*, p. 97).

[53]Interestingly, the privacy and boat motifs which were in conflict in Mark 4 coalesce in 6:32. The boat trip is conducted here with the express purpose of withdrawing from the crowd. Note also that the description of the withdrawal employs the progressive double-step expression analyzed by Neirynck (*Duality*, pp. 45-53, 95): εἰς ἔρημον τόπον/κατ'ἰδίαν.

[54]Cf. 6:31 where the coming and going of the crowd (πολλοί) drives Jesus and his followers into the boat to seek privacy and rest.

[55]See the literature cited and discussed by Taylor, *Mark*, pp. 278-79.

[56]Should we consider a third possibility that the name is purely the invention of the author's fertile imagination?

[57]Snoy believes that 6:53 was the original conclusion to the feeding story: "Mc., VI, 45-52," pp. 234-36.

[58]ἄρχομαι *auxiliary*: Turner, "Marcan Usage," *JTS* 28 (1927): 352-53; Lagrange, *Marc*, p. lxvi; Schmid, *Matthäus und Lukas*, p. 40; Taylor, *Mark*, pp. 44, 48; Doudna, *Greek of Mark*, pp. 53, 111; Donahue, *Trial Narrative*, p. 56; Neirynck, *Agreements*, pp. 242-44; Annen, *Heil für die Heiden*, p. 211; Kee, *Community*, pp.

51, 53-54; Pryke, *Redactional Style*, pp. 79-87.
    Adverbial πολλά: Hawkins, *Horae Synopticae*, p. 13;
Lagrange, *Marc*, p. lxv; Schmid, *Matthäus und Lukas*, p. 48;
Taylor, *Mark*, pp. 313, 320; Kelber, *Kingdom*, p. 56, Neirynck,
Agreements, p. 278; Annen, *Heil für die Heiden*, p. 54.

[59] διδάσκω, διδαχή: Snoy, "Mc., VI, 45-52," p. 239; Best,
Temptation and Passion, pp. 71-72; Taylor, *Mark*, p. 318; Kee,
Community, p. 53; Pryke, *Redactional Style*, p. 136; Schweizer,
"Anmerkungen," pp. 37-38; idem, "Leistung," p. 340:" . . .
typisch markinischen termini διδάσκειν und διδαχή . . . ."

[60] See Pryke, *Redactional Style*, pp. 15, 142.

[61] *6:32*: Eduard Schweizer, *The Good News According to Mark*,
trans. Donald H. Madvig (Atlanta: John Knox Press, 1970),
pp. 135-36; Pesch, *Markusevangelium*, 1:345.
    6:33: A. E. J. Rawlinson, *St. Mark* (London: Methuen,
1925), pp. 83-84; Karl Kertelge, *Die Wunder Jesu im
Markusevangelium*, SANT, no. 23 (Munich: Kösel, 1970), p. 130.
    6:34: Schmidt, *Rahmen*, pp. 186-90; Bultmann, *Geschichte*,
pp. 231, 259, 365; Nineham, *Saint Mark*, p. 182.
    6:35: Taylor, *Mark*, p. 318; Best, *Temptation and Passion*,
p. 76.
    A larger sampling would, no doubt, produce an even broader
range of opinions.

[62] Most would regard Mark 6:6b-13 as a Markan construction
based on traditional sayings of Jesus:
    "This narrative appears to have been put together by the
    Evangelist himself; it is little more than a framework for
    the Mission Charge to the Twelve. The sayings are the his-
    torical kernel. . . . The narrative itself is redactional"
    (Taylor, *Mark*, p. 302).

[63] *Duality*, p. 95.

[64] See our discussion of 8:1-2, above.

[65] Appearing in Mark only in 6:36, 8:1,2, the expression
τί φάγωσιν is an indirect question employing the deliberative
subjunctive; Taylor, *Mark*, p. 322; Blass, Debrunner, and Funk,
Grammar, p. 186, sec. 368; Walter Bauer, William F. Arndt, and
F. Wilbur Gingrich, *A Greek-English Lexicon of the New Testament
and Other Early Christian Literature* (Chicago: University of
Chicago, 1957), s.v. "τίς," p. 827.

[66] Schmidt, *Rahmen*, pp. 194-96; Bultmann, *Geschichte*, p. 366;
Taylor, *Mark*, p. 331; Snoy, "Mc., VI, 45-52," pp. 235, 240
(and see the literature cited there).

[67] "Les miracles," p. 98. Also noted by Nineham, *Saint Mark*,
p. 177.

[68] Taken from Wendling, *Entstehung*, p. 87.

[69] πᾶς/ὅλος: Schweizer, "Leistung," p. 340; see also idem, "Anmerkungen," p. 39; Wendling, *Entstehung*, p. 79; Donahue, *Trial Narrative*, pp. 66-70.

[70] We observe that the town of Gennesaret itself plays no role in 6:53-56; as we noted in our discussion of the boat trips in Mark, many such place names in Mark 4-8 are little more than ornamentation in the narrative. The action in 6:54-56—such as there is—is played out in the arena of "the whole region" and in the "villages, cities, and farms."

[71] Also, both compositions use the Markan ἄρχομαι auxiliary to describe Jesus' teaching or healing:

> *6:34*: ἤρξατο διδάσκειν αὐτούς. . . .
> *6:55*: ἤρξαντο . . . τοὺς κακῶς ἔχοντας περιφέρειν. . . .

For the literature discussing this Markan characteristic, see above, p. 204, n. 58.

[72] We should make clear that the "hardness of heart" in 6:52 is not really equivalent to the hardness of heart commonly expressed by the familiar English adjective "hardhearted" which has the sense of "unfeeling" or "pitiless." Rather, the hardness of heart here has to do more with a lack of perception or understanding; i.e., dullness, obtuseness, insensibility, or blindness. This can be readily seen in the verbs associated with the hardness of heart in Mark 6:52 and 8:17-19: συνίημι, νοέω, βλέπω, ἀκούω, μνημονεύω, etc. The full range of the disciples' blindness will become evident later as we discuss in greater detail the failure of their mission in 6:30ff. and the confrontation between them and Jesus in 6:36-37. For "hardness of heart" see Bauer, Arndt, and Gingrich, *Lexicon*, s.v. "πωρόω," "πώρωσις"; Quesnell, *Mind of Mark*, pp. 180-83, 262-63.

[73] *Mark*, p. 318.

[74] συνάγω: Concerning 6:30 Snoy states: "À propos de συνάγονται, remarquons que ce verbe est employé à cinq reprises, en *Mc.*, II, 2; IV, 1; V, 21; VI, 30; VII, 1, chaque fois dans l'introduction sans doute rédactionnelle de péricopes; sauf en V, 21, le verbe est précédé de καί et au début d'une phrase; en IV, 1; VI, 30 et VII, 1, il est au présent historique que *Mc.* affectionne" ("Mc.", VI, 45-52," p. 238). See also Hawkins, *Horae Synopticae*, p. 14; Taylor, *Mark*, p. 318; Pryke, *Redactional Style*, p. 137.

[75] *Naming Jesus in introductory phrases*: Donahue, *Trial Narrative*, p. 64.

πρὸς τὸν Ἰησοῦν/πρὸς αὐτόν: Annen states: "Mk hat den Ausdruck πρὸς τὸν Ἰησοῦν 4 mal, dazu 16 mal πρὸς αὐτόν. Die klare Vorliebe des Mk ergibt sich aus der Tatsache, das πρὸς αὐτόν/πρὸς τὸν Ἰησοῦν öfters in Summarien (Mk 1, 32.45; 3, 8) und Perikopen-Einleitungen (1, 40; 2, 3.13; 3, 13.31; 4, 1; 6, 30; 7, 1; 10, 1; 11, 27; 12, 13.18) steht. Immer wieder wird bei Mk berichtet, dass Volk bei Jesus zusammenläuft (mit πρὸς αὐτόν/πρὸς τὸν Ἰησοῦν in 1, 45; 2, 13; 3, 8; 4, 1; 5, 15; 10, 1)" (*Heil für die Heiden*, p. 59).

[76] ἀπαγγέλλω: Taylor, *Mark*, p. 318.
ὅσος with ποιέω: Taylor, *Mark*, pp. 284, 318; Snoy, "Les miracles," pp. 83-84; idem, "Mc., VI, 45-52," pp. 238-39; Annen, *Heil für die Heiden*, pp. 64-67. Cf. Mark 3:8, 5:19, 20, 9:13.

[77] For the theme of teaching in Mark, see above, p. 205, n. 59.

[78] For the use of πᾶς and ὅλος, see above, p. 206, n. 69. Cf. also the use of πᾶς in 6:50; the use of ὅλος in 6:55.

[79] See above, p. 199, n. 20, for the historical present and the use of λέγω.
δεῦτε: Taylor, *Mark*, p. 319.

[80] Ibid., pp. 319, 322, 376; Bauer, Arndt, and Gingrich, *Lexicon*, s.v. "σύ," p. 779.

[81] κατ' ἰδίαν: Taylor, *Mark*, p. 319; Kee, *Community*, p. 53; Pryke, *Redactional Style*, p. 137; Schweizer, "Leistung," p. 341: "ἴδιος kommt nur in dieser Formel und nur in redaktionnellen Abschnitten vor."
ἔρημος τόπος: Taylor, *Mark*, p. 319; Snoy, "Mc., VI, 45-52," p. 239, n. 143. See also our comments on Mark 8:4 above, pp. 55-56.

[82] *Parenthetical statement introduced with* γάρ: Taylor, *Mark*, pp. 308, 335; Stein, "Markan Seam," pp. 84-85; Snoy, "Mc., VI, 45-52," p. 448, n. 218; Annen, *Heil für die Heiden*, p. 51; Pryke, *Redactional Style*, pp. 40, 45, 110, 126-35.

[83] *JTS* 4 (1953): 171-87.

[84] "Mc., VI, 45-52," p. 448, n. 218.

[85] Bird, "Γαρ Clauses," p. 183.

[86] Another is 2:2, where the result of the crowding is not a lack of food but a lack of space.

[87] ἔρχομαι *and compounds*: Hawkins, *Horae Synopticae*, pp. 12, 34; Taylor, *Mark*, p. 235; Donahue, *Trial Narrative*, pp. 57, 66: ". . .the Marcan fondness for compounds of *erchesthai*"; Annen, *Heil für die Heiden*, pp. 41, 43, 63; Pryke, *Redactional Style*, p. 136.

[88] ὑπάγω: Swete, *Mark*, p. xlix; Taylor, *Mark*, p. 319; Pryke, *Redactional Style*, p. 137.
For ἐσθίω, see above, p. 56.

[89] *Impersonal plural*: Lagrange, *Marc*, p. 159; Bultmann, *Geschichte*, pp. 368-69; Turner, "Marcan Usage," *JTS* 25 (1924): 381; Schmid, *Matthäus und Lukas*, p. 43; Taylor, *Mark*, pp. 47-48; Doudna, *Greek of Mark*, pp. 6-8; Stein, "Markan Seam," p. 75; Snoy, "Mc., VI, 45-52," p. 240; Neirynck, *Agreements*, pp. 261-66; Annen, *Heil für die Heiden*, pp. 41-42; Pryke, *Redactional Style*, pp. 107-115.

[90]See above, p. 49.

[91]"Marcan Usage," *JTS* 28 (1927): 359. Also, see above, p. 199, n. 18.

[92]For teaching, ἄρχομαι auxiliary, and adverbial πολλά, see above, p. 67.

[93]For λέγω, see above, p. 199, n. 20; for ὅτι recitative, see above, p. 203, n. 42; for ἔρημος τόπος, see above, p. 55, and cf. 6:31-32.

[94]Taylor, *Mark*, p. 321; Taylor also notes "the tone of astonishment, amounting to reproof, in the question. . . ." (ibid., p. 323). Wendling has also described the disciples' acrimony with clarity:
"Die Frage der Jünger 6:37, durch welch sie den Befehl δότε φαγεῖν ad absurdum führen wollen, steht auf der gleichen Linie wie ihr Vorwurf 4:38, ihre Bestürzung 4:41, ihr Befremden über Jesu Worte 5:31: überall das gleiche Mittel, die Erhabenheit des Meisters durch die menschliche Kurzsichtigkeit der Jünger zu steigern, also eine ausgezeichnete Handhabung der indirekten Charakteristik" (*Entstehung*, p. 66).

[95]See above, p. 54, for our discussion of the same trait in 8:7.

[96]*Adversative* δέ: Zerwick, *Untersuchungen*, p. 12 (see also ibid., pp. 7-10); Snoy, "Mc., VI, 45-52," p. 446, n. 212.

[97]Note that the two instances of δέ in 8:1-10 (vv. 5, 9) are *not* adversative but copulative; moreover, Mark abandons them for καί parataxis in 6:38, 44.

[98]κύκλῳ: Hawkins, *Horae Synopticae*, p. 13; within the gospels κύκλῳ appears in Mark 3:34, 6:6, 36 and in the Lukan parallel to Mark 6:36 (Luke 9:12), and then it appears in only four other places in the entire New Testament.

[99]"Marcan Usage," *JTS* 26 (1925): 337-46. Regarding the *use of numbers* in Mark, see also Schmid, *Matthäus und Lukas*, pp. 59-62; Rigaux, *Testimony*, p. 60.

[100]"Marcan Usage," *JTS* 26 (1925): 338.

[101]Rigaux, *Testimony*, p. 60.

[102]An important insight arising out of our discovery that the two hundred denarii is a Markan embellishment added to the traditional story is the realization that the evangelist John preserves this detail in his version of the feeding story, thereby betraying his knowledge of and dependence on the Markan composition in Mark 6:30-44. Matthew and Luke omit the reference to two hundred denarii; John's preservation of it reveals his dependence on Mark's gospel at this point (John 6:7).

Furthermore, when one discerns the echo of the two
hundred denarii (Mark 6:37) in the reference to the three
hundred denarii (Mark 14:5), some fascinating observations may
be made concerning John's modification of both of these
references to money in Mark. Stated succinctly, John redeems
the disciples. To begin with, in both instances he places the
words about the money on the lips of individual disciples. In
the feeding story, it is Philip who mentions the sum of two
hundred denarii (John 6:7) but only after being prompted by
Jesus. In John it is Jesus who broaches the topic of buying
food, and he does so to test the disciples. Rather than
responding defensively and peevishly in the Markan manner,
Philip laments that even two hundred denarii worth of bread
would be inadequate to feed the crowd. Philip, and Andrew too
(John 6:8-9), displays a humane sensitivity to the gravity
of the situation, unlike the tightfisted disciples in Mark.

In the anointing scene, John redeems the disciples
(Matthew too has understood this scene to involve the disciples--
Matt. 26:8) by placing the callous remark on the lips of a
scapegoat: Judas Iscariot (John 12:4-6). For good measure he
adds that Judas was the betrayer, he did not really care for
the poor, and he stole from the disciples' treasury. If our
reading of Mark 6:37 and 14:5 is correct, viz., that the
disciples in Mark have an extraordinary, unhealthy concern for
the cost of feeding the crowd and anointing their teacher,
could John have perceived this negative portrayal of the
disciples in Mark and transferred their faults to Judas? At
the very least, John has taken the disciples' treasury, which
is only mentioned implicitly in Mark when the disciples worry
about their two hundred denarii, he has referred to it
explicitly in his own gospel, and he has placed the traitor
Judas in charge of it (John 13:19).

^{103}The reading of τοὺς ἄρτους in v. 44 is doubtful and
probably should not be accepted, especially in view of the
author's effort to keep bread and fish together.

^{104}Taylor, *Mark*, p. 359.

^{105}Taylor, *Mark*, p. 323: "The asyndetic construction in
Πόσους ἔχετε ἄρτους; ὑπάγετε ἴδετε is a common feature of Mark's
style." Regarding *asyndeton* in Mark, see also Turner, "Marcan
Usage," *JTS* 28 (1927): 15-18; Lagrange, *Marc*, pp. lxvii-lxviii;
Taylor, *Mark*, pp. 49-50, 58; Donahue, *Trial Narrative*, p. 56.

^{106}Schweizer believes that the use of γινώσκω in Mark is
often redactional:
"γινώσκειν ist das besondere Erkennen der Jünger 4, (11.) 13,
Jesu 5,29; 8, 17, das Wissen der Welt, das Jesus vermeiden
will 5, 43; 7, 24; 9, 30 (anders dann erst 12, 12 . . .);
doch findet sich das Wort auch traditionell 6, 38 [!]; 13,
28f.; 15, 10. 15. Vgl. ferner νοεῖν, αγνοεῖν; ἐπιγινώσκειν
ist nicht eindeutig" ("Leistung," p. 341).
Pryke also places γινώσκω with the Markan redactional vocabulary
(*Redactional Style*, p. 136).

[107]Reading ἀνακλῖναι, a transitive verb.

[108]ἐπιτάσσω: Swete, *Mark*, p. xlix. The verb only occurs ten times in the entire New Testament, four of which occurrences are in Mark. The same form of this verb is used earlier in Mark 6:27 where Herod orders the death of John the Baptist.

[109]Distributive doubling occurs frequently in Hebrew and also in the Septuagint; however, it is not unknown in Greek literature; Doudna, *Greek in Mark*, p. 35. See also Blass, Debrunner, and Funk, *Grammar*, p. 130, sec. 248, pt. 1; p. 261, sec. 493, pt. 2.

[110]See the lists of such series by Neirynck, *Duality*, pp. 110-12; and T. A. Burkill, *New Light on the Earliest Gospel: Seven Markan Studies* (Ithaca and London: Cornell University Press, 1972), pp. 256-58.

[111]Matthew is careful to add "women and children" (Matt. 14:21).

[112]ἀναβλέπω: Swete, *Mark*, p. xlix. The identical phrase occurs also in 7:34: ἀναβλέψας εἰς τὸν οὐρανόν. Wendling has alertly linked 6:41 and 7:34 to other, comparable expressions in Mark 6-8, thereby uncovering a recurring Markan motif of "looking up":
   "6:41 ἀναβλέψας εἰς τὸν οὐρανὸν εὐλόγησεν
   7:34 ἀναβλέψας εἰς τὸν οὐρανὸν ἐστέναξεν
   8:12 ἀναστενάξας (10 ἀπὸ τοῦ οὐρανοῦ)
   8:24 ἀναβλέψας" (*Entstehung*, p. 93).
For πᾶς, cf. 6:30 and see our discussion above.

[113]Other miracle stories in Mark have a similar dual arrangement. See, e.g., the calming of wind *and* sea in 4:35-41 and the healing of a man who is deaf *and* mute in 7:31-37. We will discuss these stories in greater detail later.

[114]Bauer, Arndt, and Gingrich, *Lexicon*, s. v."κλάω," p. 434; Johannes Behm,"κλάω κτλ," in *Theological Dictionary of the New Testament*, ed. G. Kittel and G. Friedrich, trans. G. Bromiley, 10 vols. (Grand Rapids: Eerdmans, 1964-76), 3:726-43.

[115]One wonders, nevertheless, if Mark has a preference for εὐλογέω, since this is the verb he uses both in his composition of 6:30-44 and in his editorial interjection in 8:7. Nothing can be learned about this matter from the Markan account of the Last Supper, where both εὐλογέω and εὐχαριστέω are used (14:22, 23).
The entire enterprise of distinguishing eucharistic traditions on the basis of these two terms is extremely problematical, since the terms are virtually synonymous in Christian literature; Herman W. Beyer,"εὐλογέω κτλ," *TDNT*, 2:762; Hans Conzelmann, "εὐχαριστέω κτλ," *TDNT*, 9:411; A. D. Nock, "Hellenistic Mysteries and Christian Sacraments," in *Arthur Darby Nock: Essays on Religion and the Ancient World*, ed. Zeph Stewart, 2 vols. (Oxford: Clarendon Press, 1972), pp. 810-11.

[116] πλήρωμα: Hawkins, *Horae Synopticae*, p. 13; Swete, *Mark*, p. xlix. Πλήρωμα is used again in the recollection of the feeding stories in 8:19-21, only it is used in the reference to the Feeding of the Four Thousand while πλήρης is used in the reference to the Feeding of the Five Thousand. Otherwise, Mark is extraordinarily careful there to preserve the terminology used previously in the two stories.

[117] Just as in the case of the verbs for blessing/giving thanks, it is often suggested that the two terms for "basket" indicate that the two stories came from different streams of tradition, perhaps Jewish and Hellenistic. Often the claim is made that the κόφινος was the kind of basket used especially among Jews: J. H. Moulton and G. Milligan, *The Vocabulary of the Greek Testament Illustrated from the Papyri and Other Non-Literary Sources* (London: Hodder & Stoughton, 1914-30), s. v. "κόφινος"; H. G. Liddell and R. Scott, *A Greek-English Lexicon*, ed. H. Stuart Jones and R. McKenzie, 9th ed. (Oxford: Clarendon Press, 1940), s. v. "κόφινος"; R. C. Horn, "The Use of the Greek New Testament," *LQ* 1 (1949): 301; Bauer, Arndt, and Gingrich, *Lexicon*, s. v. "κόφινος"; Taylor, *Mark*, p. 325. In every instance, the same meager evidence is offered to support this claim. This evidence consists of two references to Juvenal's *Satires* wherein Juvenal depicts a Jew using a κόφινος (*Satires*, 3:14, 6:542). How this can be regarded as sufficient evidence is difficult to understand. One need only offer a counterexample to show its weakness. For example, in Josephus' account of the *Jewish War* (3:95), the κόφινος is specified as part of the equipment of a Roman infantryman. One could just as easily cite the other "non-Jewish" users of the κόφινος which are discussed in the literature cited above. Rather than a sign that Mark 6:30-44 is a "Jewish" feeding story, the use of the term κόφινος is adequately explained as an alternate term introduced by the author for the sake of variety.

[118] Taylor's observation is on the mark: "ἀπὸ τῶν ἰχθύων, which Mt and Lk omit, is an inelegant pendant, which has almost the appearance of an afterthought" (*Mark*, p. 326).

CHAPTER III

NOTES

[1]Actually in 6:30-56; see especially 6:51-52.

[2]B. Harvie Branscomb, *The Gospel of Mark* (New York and London: Harper & Bros., n.d.), p. 136; Gould, *Mark*, p. 142. See also the literature cited by Taylor, *Mark*, p. 359.

[3]A few interpreters have generously given the author credit for this portrayal of the disciples:
"The historical critics' perpetually raised eyebrows over the fact that the disciples should have so soon forgotten the previous feeding if there really was one, rather miss the whole point of the role Mark has been giving the disciples from the first. They are not supposed to understand. They speak the reaction of the natural man in the face of the mysteries of God" (Quesnell, *Mind of Mark*, p. 164).
"The fact that after the experience described in 6:32-44 the disciples now (vs. 4) have no idea whatever about what can be done cannot be explained psychologically. This very impossibility is what is important to Mark, who was the first to put the two variant accounts side by side. He wants to use this means to show how absolutely and unimaginably blind man is to the activity of God" (Schweizer, *Good News*, p. 156). Neither Quesnell nor Schweizer suspect, however, the lengths to which Mark has gone to induce the reader to see blindness and obtuseness in 8:4.

[4]Wayne Booth, *A Rhetoric of Irony* (Chicago and London: University of Chicago Press, 1974).

[5]Ibid., pp. 5-6.

[6]Ibid., p. 10.

[7]In comparison to the traditional story, Mark's version involves fewer provisions, a larger crowd, and more leftover food, just the kind of enhancement of the miraculous that form critics have observed in secondary accounts. Bultmann calls this phenomenon the "Steigerung des wunderbaren" (*Geschichte*, p. 243).

[8]Booth, *Irony*, p. 11.

[9]Ibid.

[10]Ibid., p. 12.

[11]Notably the widely praised *The Rhetoric of Fiction* (Chicago and London: University of Chicago Press, 1961).

[12]Booth, *Irony*, p. 13.

[13]Ibid., pp. 28-29.

[14]Two exegetes who have made this important observation are Nils A. Dahl and his student, Donald Juel; Nils A. Dahl, "The Purpose of Mark's Gospel," in *Jesus in the Memory of the Early Church* (Minneapolis: Augsburg Publishing House, 1976), p. 56: "The Christ-mystery is a secret only for those persons who appear in the book. The readers know the point of the story from the very beginning: it is the Gospel of Jesus Christ"; Donald Juel, *Messiah and Temple: The Trial of Jesus in the Gospel of Mark*, SBLDS, no. 31 (Missoula, Mont.: Scholars Press, 1977), p. 46. Juel also is acutely aware of Mark's use of irony in the passion narrative (ibid., pp. 47-48).

[15]For example, we find Booth's comments on the fellowship or community of readers who share in common the accurate discernment of Mark's irony to be a refreshing literary critical alternative to the constant reference to the historical Christian community for which the author supposedly composed his work. The former "community" lives and thrives today and its characteristic feature (perception of irony) can be discussed with some precision and objectivity. The latter "community" is anonymous, probably extinct, and notoriously difficult to reconstruct.

Regarding the literature on irony, two general works on irony in the biblical literature are Edwin M. Good, *Irony in the Old Testament* (Philadelphia: Westminster Press, 1965); and Jakob Jónsson, *Humour and Irony in the New Testament. Illuminated by Parallels in Talmud and Midrash* (Reykjavík: Bókaútgáfa Menningarsjóds, 1965). In the gospels, irony has often been perceived in the teaching of Jesus and in the gospel of John: Henri Clavier, "La méthode ironique dans l'enseignement de Jésus," *ETR* 4 (1929): 224-41, 323-44; 5 (1930): 58-99; idem. "L'ironie dans l'enseignement de Jésus," *NovT* 1 (1956): 3-20; W. Harnisch, "Die Ironie als Stilmittel in Gleichnissen Jesu," *EvT* 32 (1972): 421-36; Henri Clavier, "L'ironie dans le quatrième Evangile," *SE* 1 (1959): 261-76; George W. MacRae, "Theology and Irony in the Fourth Gospel," in *The Word in the World: Essays in Honor of Frederick L. Moriarty*, ed. Richard J. Clifford and George W. MacRae (Cambridge, Mass.: Weston College Press, 1973), pp. 83-96; David W. Wead, *The Literary Devices in John's Gospel*, Theologischen Dissertationen, no. 4 (Basel: Friedrich Reinhardt Kommissionsverlag, 1970); idem, "Johannine Irony as a Key to the Author-Audience Relationship in John's Gospel," in *Biblical Literature: 1974 Proceedings. Preprinted for the Section on Biblical Literature, American Academy of Religion, Annual Meeting, 1974*, comp. Fred O. Francis (Tallahassee, Fla.: American Academy of Religion and Florida State University, 1974), pp. 33-44. Other helpful works are J. A. K. Thomson, *Irony: An Historical Introduction* (Cambridge: Harvard University Press, 1927); D. C. Muecke, *The Compass of Irony* (London: Methuen & Co., 1969); idem, *Irony*, Critical Idiom Series, no. 13 (London: Methuen & Co., 1970). Selected bibliographies of the vast literature on irony may be found in Booth, *Irony*, pp. 279-84; and Muecke, *Compass*, pp. 260-69.

[16]In a certain sense, we are still advocating that the feeding stories are variant accounts of the same story--we are simply claiming that the author of one of the variants is the evangelist himself, instead of attributing both variants to pre-gospel tradition and thereby absolving the evangelist of all responsibility for how they function in his story. Is this not exactly how variants arise, through a story teller handing down a story different from the one told to him, perhaps handing down the original version as well?

[17]Bultmann observes that this sea story is, as it stands now, a *Mischbildung* (*Geschichte*, p. 231). He suggests that the original motif of 6:45-52 was the *Seewandeln* to which the *Sturmmotiv* was added secondarily. This is intuitively an attractive proposal, especially in light of our discovery that Mark similarly adds the motif of the fish to 8:1-10 to endow it with a hint of duality. Apparently the evangelist is not reluctant to add new features to old stories.
    Other interpreters have made suggestions similar to Bultmann's. Ernst Lohmeyer suggests that the basis of 6:45-52 is an "Epiphanie Jesu auf dem Wasser," to which has been added the storm motif (*Das Evangelium des Markus*, MeyerK, 17th ed. [Göttingen: Vandenhoeck & Ruprecht, 1967], p. 131). In an interesting departure from the usual supposition, Lohmeyer further proposes that the material added to the sea epiphany was not derived from 4:35-41 but from a sea story that originally followed 8:1-9. That story is no longer there, of course, because Mark has merged it with the epiphany story to create 6:45-52. When Lohmeyer begins to make suggestions like this we are forced to agree with Snoy that "Lohmeyer fait une part trop large à la pure conjecture" ("Mc., VI, 45-52," p. 225).
    Others who follow the same general line of interpretation include Erich Klostermann, *Das Markusevangelium*, HNT, 4th ed. (Tübingen: J. C. B. Mohr [Paul Siebeck], 1950), pp. 64-65; and Nineham, *Saint Mark*, pp. 180-81. Also, as usual Wendling's comments are quite perceptive; *Entstehung*, pp. 82-87.

[18]So also Snoy, "Mc., VI, 45-52," p. 440.

[19]See, e.g., Bultmann, *Geschichte*, p. 231; Lohmeyer, *Markus*, pp. 131-32, 135; Snoy, "Mc., VI, 45-52," pp. 480-81.

[20]Ibid.

[21]*Entstehung*, pp. 84-85.

[22]This synopsis has been adapted from Taylor's synopsis; *Mark*, pp. 368-69. One may also compare the synoptic comparisons of the stories in Wendling, *Entstehung*, p. 77; and Lagrange, *Marc*, pp. lxxiii-lxxiv.

[23]Wendling, *Entstehung*, pp. 77-79; Taylor, *Mark*, pp. 368-70. Although he admits that a single author, either Mark or a predecessor, has used the same framework and vocabulary to compose the present stories, Taylor insists that two distinct traditional stories lie behind them. Wendling, of course, argues

that both stories are wholly Markan compositions, observing
perceptively the connections between these stories and other
parts of the gospel also composed by the evangelist.

[24]See our chart of the duality in the doublets above,
p. 100.

[25]Wendling's remarks are quite correct:
"Die beiden Heilungsgeschichten zeigen also durchgehends die
eigentümliche Auffassung und Arbeitsweise des Redaktors. . . .
Der Redaktor hat die zwei Wundererzählungen nach derselben
Schablone gearbeitet. . . . Der Ausgangspunkt für die
Konzeption liegt in dem Zitat 8:18 ὀφθαλμοὺς ἔχοντες οὐ
βλέπετε καὶ ὦτα ἔχοντες οὐκ ἀκούετε zutage, woraus sich
ergibt, dass die beiden Heilungsgeschichten für den Ev eine
symbolische Bedeutung gehabt haben müssen, ebenso wie die
beiden wunderbaren Speisungen, die er im gleichen Zusammenhang
(8:19f.) in Parallele stellt. Die Verdoppelung der Speisungs-
geschichte, . . . und die Zwillingsgeschichten 7:31ff. 8:22ff.
sind im Zusammenhang geplant und ausgeführt wordern"
(Entstehung, p. 79).

[26]Quesnell states: "To a certain extent, it must even be
said, it tends to pull together everything between 6,30 and 8,21
in the reader's mind" (Mind of Mark, p. 125).

[27]Neirynck has noted the double imperative and the double
group of persons here; Duality, pp. 84, 109.

[28]For example, see Nineham, Saint Mark, p. 215. It is
difficult to decide whether one should read ἔχουσιν or ἔχομεν
in 8:16. If one were to read the latter, thereby understanding
ὅτι to be recitative, then one would have in 8:14, 16 the kind
of shift from the indirect, narrative mode to direct, discourse
mode that we observed in the Markan insertions in 6:31-32,
6:35 and 8:1-2. The verbal agreement in these two verses
(ἄρτον οὐκ εἶχον/ἄρτους οὐκ ἔχομεν) is undeniable.

[29]Neither Matthew nor Luke was comfortable with the rich
unspecificity of this metaphor; they felt compelled to inform
the reader exactly what the term "leaven" referred to, turning
Mark's plurisignificant metaphor into a one-dimensional image.
Matthew (who exchanges "Herod" for "Sadducees") tells us that
Jesus warned the disciples, not "of the leaven of bread," but
of "the teaching of the Pharisees and Sadducees" (Matt. 16:12).
Similarly, Luke places on the lips of Jesus a warning about the
leaven of the Pharisees, "which is hypocrisy" (Luke 12:1).

[30]Noted by Quesnell, Mind of Mark, p. 240.

[31]Taylor states correctly: "The description is tautolo-
gous. . . ." (Mark, p. 372).

[32]Coincidentally, we have here another example of the overlapping of frameworks mentioned above. Mark 6:30-44, along with
6:6b-13, frames 6:14-29, while at the same time it functions
as a doublet with 8:1-10.

[33]*Saint Mark*, p. 172. A similar opinion is expressed by Achtemeier, who states that the author uses the story in 6:14-29 "to fill out the space between the sending forth of the twelve and their return" ("Isolation," p. 270). Schweizer states: "A considerable period of time elapsed between the sending of the disciples and their return. Consequently, Mark must fill in the interval" (*Good News*, p. 132). These comments echo the earlier statement by Bultmann: "Mk hat die Geschichte eingeschoben, um den Raum zwischen Aussendung und Rückkehr der Jünger auszufüllen" (*Geschichte*, p. 329).

[34]*Saint Mark*, pp. 300-1. Earlier we expressed our misgivings for the rubric so commonly used for the episode in 6:14-29: "The Death of John the Baptist." We have similar qualms about the common rubric of 11:15-19: "The Cleansing of the Temple." Where is "cleansing" even mentioned in this passage? Is "cleansing" an unconscious interpretation of the text imported from Mal. 3:1-4? One interpreter who has commented on this misleading label for 11:15-19 is Kelber, who states:
"Understood in a religious sense, the obstruction of the vessel's transport effects the cessation of the temple's cultic functions. In the view of Mark, therefore, Jesus not only puts an end to the temple's business operation, but he also suspends the practice of cult and ritual. At this point the temple no longer operates. It is shut down in all its functions. . . . Can this demonstration in the temple be properly classified as a "cleansing" at all? Mark himself never refers to the temple incident in terms of a purge or cleansing. . . . In the context of Mark's framing design the fig tree stands for the temple, and the disaster which befell the tree illustrates what occurred to the temple. Far from being "cleansed" in order to serve in a new and purified fashion, the temple is condemned and ruined beyond all hope of recovery (the tree is ravaged from the roots up, not merely from the leaves down!)" (*Kingdom in Mark*, pp. 101-2).

[35]Nineham, *Saint Mark*, p. 399. The same understanding of this intercalation has been restated recently by Kim Dewey:
"As a complement to the denial story, the Sanhedrin hearing (14:55-65) further focuses Mk's intentions. The synchronized contrast between a Jesus who confesses and Peter who denies is patent, as is the fact that Jesus is condemned while presumably Peter extracts himself from that same fate. Peter, too, functions as a false witness, failing to confess. Thus, the Peter-Jesus opposition is further emphasized here" ("Peter's Curse and Cursed Peter [Mark 14:53-54, 66-72]," in *The Passion in Mark: Studies on Mark 14-16*, ed. Werner H. Kelber [Philadelphia: Fortress Press, 1976], pp. 109-10).

[36]The incomprehension of the disciples in 6:30ff. is to be contrasted with the crowd's ability to "recognize" (ἐπιγινώσκω) Jesus in the opening and closing verses of 6:30-56 (6:33, 54).

[37]Against the opinion of Robert C. Tannehill, "The Disciples in Mark: The Function of a Narrative Role," *JR* 57 (1977): 397. This article is a penetrating discussion of Mark's narrative technique. Also to be recommended is Tannehill's *The Sword of*

His Mouth, Semeia Supplements, no. 1 (Missoula, Mont.: Scholars Press, 1975).

[38]*Mark*, p. 116.

[39]Schweizer, *Good News*, pp. 138-39: "Surely their counter-question is meant only to show the impossibility of Jesus' proposition, since the amount of money mentioned is far more than they had." Lohmeyer, *Markus*, p. 126: "Das ist nicht nur für die Jünger unerschwinglich, sondern auch für den Zweck zu wenig."

In Matt. 20:1-16 the denarius is the daily wage of a laborer. Consequently, two hundred denarii would constitute the better part of a year's wages for a laborer, not an insignificant sum for the disciples' treasury.

[40]See, e.g., 4:19, 10:17-31, and 12:41-44; cf. also 14:5 and our discussion of 6:37 in Chap. 2 above. The attention given to wealth and possessions in the gospel has been noted by Kee, *Community*, pp. 90, 153-55. Kee states:
"That confidence in possessions as evidence of personal achievement was indeed a problem in the Markan community is evident not only from the interpretation of the passage under discussion [10:17-31], but from the interpretation of the parable of the sower (4:19), where the thorns that sprang up and choked the seeds (4:7) are explained as 'concerns for this age, *the seduction of wealth*, and *lusting after other things*'" (ibid., pp. 154-55; Kee's italics).

[41]See the standard work by Ferdinand Hahn, *Christologische Hoheitstitel* (E. T.: *The Titles of Jesus in Christology: Their History in Early Christianity*, trans. Harold Knight and George Ogg [New York and Cleveland: The World Publishing Co., 1969]).

[42]Mark 6:14-15 and 8:28 are worthy candidates for the title "doublet." There can be little doubt that this pair was composed by the evangelist and functions to stress those personages to whom Jesus wishes to be compared.

Perhaps it is instructive here to see what Luke has done to Mark 6-8 (Luke 9:7-20). First, he eliminates Mark 6:17-29, the narrative of the banquet and John's death, retaining only the speculation about Jesus' identity from Mark 6:14-16. After the feeding story of Mark 6:30-44 comes Luke's "Great Omission," the omission of Mark 6:45-8:26. He takes up the Markan text again beginning with Mark 8:27, which introduces the companion to 6:14-16 in 8:28. Theories suggesting that Luke used a mutilated manuscript or even an Ur-Markus are unnecessary. Clearly he has preserved the dual tableaux of 6:14-16 and 8:28 while eliminating everything between them, with the exception of the Feeding of the Five Thousand. The final result is most interesting: the feeding story is framed by the dual tableaux of the personages for whom Jesus has been (mis)taken. Luke's text is sharply structured, compact, and focused on the identity of Jesus. If he is not John, Elijah, or a prophet of old, who is he? For Luke, unlike Mark, Peter's answer is allowed to stand as a valid, perceptive, and knowing confession: "The Christ of God" (Luke 9:20).

[43] Josephus, *Antiquities* 18:7:2.

[44] For the familial relationships of the Herodians and the apparent factual errors in 6:14-29, see Lohmeyer, *Markus*, p. 118; Taylor, *Mark*, pp. 310-12.

[45] See Donahue's article, "Temple, Trial, and Royal Christology (Mark 14:53-65)," in *The Passion in Mark: Studies on Mark 14-16*, ed. Werner H. Kelber (Philadelphia: Fortress Press, 1976), pp. 72-78.

[46] Other than in 13:9, the warning that Jesus' followers will be brought before governors and kings, the word βασιλεύς occurs only in Mark 6, where it refers to Herod, and in Mark 15, where it refers to Jesus.

[47] The awkward manner in which the reference to Herod is repeated in vv. 14 and 16 is often noted. Such repetition is typical, however, of Mark's insertion technique (Donahue, *Trial Narrative*, p. 241; Neirynck, *Duality*, p. 98). The verbal agreement is obvious:

> 6:14 καὶ ἤκουσεν ὁ βασιλεὺς Ἡρῴδης. . . .
> καὶ ἔλεγον ὅτι Ἰωάννης . . . ἐγήγερται
> 6:16 ἀκούσας δὲ ὁ Ἡρῴδης
> ἔλεγεν, . . . Ἰωάννην, οὗτος ἠγέρθη.

Note also the typically Markan use of γάρ to introduce the parenthesis in vv. 14b-15 and the consistent use of λέγω to introduce direct speech.

[48] Mark's comparison of Jesus with John, Elijah, and a prophet is transformed in John's gospel into a comparison of *John the Baptist* with "the Christ," Elijah, and "the prophet" (John 1:20-21, 25).

[49] Even if the imagery of the prophet and the king is already present in Mark 6, the portrayal of Jesus as Prophet-King is a wholly integral element of John's gospel; see Wayne Meek's superb study, *The Prophet-King: Moses Traditions and the Johannine Christology*, NovTSup, no. 14 (Leiden: E. J. Brill, 1967).

[50] Swete quotes the intriguing comment by Origen: "Origen (in *Jo.* t. vi. 30) suggests that the Baptist and our Lord were so like in personal appearance ὥστε διὰ τὸ κοινὸν τῆς μορφῆς Ἰωάννην τε Χριστὸν ὑπονοεῖσθαι τυγχάνειν καὶ Ἰησοῦν Ἰωάννην" (*Mark*, p. 120).

[51] Cf. 1 Kgs. 19:4-8. The "beasts" in Mark 1:13 may recall the ravens who on another occasion provided food for Elijah (1 Kgs. 17:2-7).

[52] In Mark's gospel, ἔρχεσθαι ὀπίσω μου (1:7, 17, 20, 8:33, 34) appears to be a synonym for ἀκολουθέω; both describe the

disciple's fundamental obligation to follow his master. This insight is especially crucial in 8:33 where Jesus' rebuke to Peter should be understood as "Get back into my following, Satan." That 8:33 refers to following Jesus as a disciple is confirmed by the following verse: εἴ τις θέλει ὀπίσω μου ἀκολουθεῖν . . . . (8:34). For a perceptive discussion of the expression ὀπίσω μου, see Morton Smith, *Tannaitic Parallels to the Gospels*, SBLMS, no. 6 (Philadelphia: Society of Biblical Literature, 1951), pp. 30-31.

[53]The recurrent Markan theme of "delivering up" has been emphasized by Norman Perrin: "We may represent Mark's fundamental conception as follows:
    a) John the Baptist 'preaches' and is 'delivered up.'
    b) Jesus 'preaches' and is 'delivered up.'
    c) The Christians 'preach' and are to be 'delivered up.'"
(*Introduction*, p. 144; see also idem, "The Use of [*Para*]*didonai* in Connection with the Passion of Jesus in the New Testament," in *Der Ruf Jesu und die Antwort der Gemeinde: Festschrift für Joachim Jeremias*, ed. Edward Lohse, Christoph Burchard, and Berndt Schaller [Göttingen: Vandenhoeck & Ruprecht, 1970], pp. 204-12.)

[54]The iterative πάλιν in 11:27a points back to the previous entry into Jerusalem in 11:15a; Neirynck, *Agreements*, p. 277.

[55]To be sure, Jesus is also identified as a John the Baptist *who has been raised from the dead*, which foreshadows the young man's announcement of Jesus' resurrection in 16:1-8.

[56]*St. Matthew and St. Mark* (London: Dacre Press, 1954), p. 14. Farrer can often be justly criticized for fanciful, overly speculative interpretations. Nevertheless, his consistently holistic approach to the gospels has enabled him to perceive the natural interconnections in the texts, such as the one between Mark 6 and Mark 15, missed by those who regard the texts as collections of disjointed fragments.
    In addition to the observations made above by Farrer, there is also an interesting comparison to be made between the burials of John (6:29) and Jesus (15:43-46). John is buried by his disciples; Jesus is buried by a stranger--his disciples have abandoned him. This was first pointed out to us by a fellow student, Gary W. Jacob, in a seminar paper presented to Norman Perrin's seminar in 1976. The same observation has been made recently by Tannehill, "The Disciples in Mark," pp. 404-5.

[57]See the discussions by Taylor, *Mark*, pp. 393-95; Nineham, *Saint Mark*, pp. 238-41.

[58]Mal. 4:5-6 (= 3:23-24 MT); Sir. 48:10; the controversy between Jews and Christians over whether Jesus had been preceded by Elijah continued into the second century; see Justin Martyr, *Dialogue with Trypho*, 49.

[59]*John the Baptist in the Gospel Tradition*, SNTSMS, no. 7 (Cambridge: Cambridge University Press, 1968), p. 16.

[60]*Der Aufbau des Markusevangeliums*, NTAbh, vol. 17, nos. 2-3 (Münster: Aschendorffschen Verlagsbuchhandlung, 1936), pp. 146-151. A chart of Hartmann's suggested comparison between 2 Kgs. and Mark may be conveniently found in Raymond Brown's article, "Jesus and Elisha," *Perspective* 12 (1971): 95.

[61]"Hartmann does show clearly what we have already found, namely, that between the miracles of Elisha and those of Jesus there are impressive parallels; but he has failed to show that the sequence in Mark is directly dependent on the sequence in the Elisha cycle" (Brown, "Jesus and Elisha," p. 96).

Besides the cautious acceptance of limited parallels between the miracles in Mark and those in the Elisha cycle, Brown admits the possibility that Jesus "was given an Elisha role" at an early stage of Christian tradition (ibid., p. 90).

[62]For a general discussion of the expectation of "the prophet," see the section in Hahn's *Titles of Jesus* entitled "The Eschatological Prophet," pp. 352-406. For a more exhaustive study of Jewish, Samaritan, and Christian speculation on the prophet like Moses, see Meeks, *Prophet-King*.

One place where the prophet like Moses is mentioned is the Qumran literature, where Deut. 18:18-19 is quoted in the Testamonia from Cave 4. Regarding Christian literature, Meeks has ably demonstrated that the prophet like Moses is the model behind the Johannine "prophet who is to come into the world." According to Meeks, Moses was traditionally regarded as "the prophet" and "first of the prophets"; moreover, "'prophet' is a designation for Moses familiar in more diverse circles than any other" (ibid., pp. 116, 156).

[63]The similarities between these episodes are often noted. Morton Smith suspects that these episodes mark the original boundaries of an aretalogy that Mark incorporated into the first nine chapters of his gospel. Interestingly, Smith regards this "doublet" as the boundary markers for a pre-Markan cycle of stories, thereby employing the same kind of argument used by those interpreters who regard the doublets in Mark 4-8 as boundary markers for similar, but shorter, pre-Markan cycles. In the minutes of the April 12, 1973 colloquy of the Center for Hermeneutical Studies in Hellenistic and Modern Culture, Berkeley, California, Smith is reported to have remarked:
"If there was an aretalogy, it began (so my hypothesis goes) with Jesus being made the son by the descent of the spirit. And it concluded with the revelation of the true nature by the voice in the Transfiguration. There is no question that the baptism story and the transfiguration story are parallels in this respect. In the baptism story according to Mark the voice is heard by Jesus; in the transfiguration story, the glory is revealed to the disciples and the voice is heard by the disciples as well. Between this time you have a series of miracles of which the significance is revealed by the confessions of the demons. . . ." (Morton Smith, *The Aretalogy Used by Mark*, Protocol of the Colloquy of the Center for Hermeneutical Studies in Hellenistic and Modern Culture, no. 6

[Berkeley, Cal,: The Center for Hermeneutical Studies in Hellenistic and Modern Culture, 1975], pp. 28-29).

[64]Among those commenting on the unusual order of these figures are Klostermann, *Markusevangelium*, p. 87; and Hahn, *Titles of Jesus*, p. 342, n. 16.

[65]Usually linked with Mal. 3:1.

[66]To insure that the reader perceives the inappropriateness of Peter's suggestion, the author inserts the parenthetical comment that Peter did not know what he was saying because of his fear (9:6). The matter of "speaking properly" has been discussed above in relation to 7:31-37.

[67]The command in Mark 9:7--ἀκούετε αὐτοῦ--alludes to the Septuagint's expression: αὐτοῦ ἀκούσεσθε (Deut. 18:15 LXX).

[68]Typical advocates of this position include Van Cangh, *La multiplication des pains*, pp. 24, 29-30, 36-37, 63-66, 162; and Alkiun Heising, "Exegese und Theologie der alt- und neutestamentlichen Speisewunder," *ZTK* 86 (1964): 80-94; idem, *Die Botschaft der Brotvermehrung*, SBS, no. 15 (Stuttgart: Verlag Katholisches Bibelwerk, 1966); idem, "Das Kerygma der wunderbaren Fischvermehrung (Mk 6, 34-44 parr)," *BibLeb* 10 (1969): 52-57.
  A notable opponent of this position is Bultmann, who asserts: "Dass etwa die Speisungsgeschichten aus der Geschichte von der Mannaspeisung Ex 16 entstanden seien, ist durchaus unwahrscheinlich." He is, however, willing to allow the possibility of the limited influence of 2 Kgs. 4:42-44: "Dagegen könnte für die Speisungsgeschichten wenigstens *ein* Ursprungsort in 4. Reg 4,42-44 (Speisung von hundert Mann mit zwanzig Gerstenbroten) vorliegen; die Geschichten vom Ölkrug 3. Reg 17,10-16; 4. Reg 4,1-7 kommen jedoch nicht in Betracht" (*Geschichte*, p. 245).

[69]Van Cangh (*La multiplication des pains*, pp. 63-64) quotes an extensive passage from Strauss's *Das Leben Jesu*, as indeed we shall.

[70]*The Life of Jesus Critically Examined*, ed. and with an introduction by Peter C. Hodgson, trans. George Eliot (Philadelphia: Fortress Press, 1972), pp. 517-18.

[71]Robert A. Hausman has written a perceptive dissertation on "The Function of Elijah as a Model in Luke-Acts" (Ph.D. dissertation, University of Chicago, 1975) in which he carefully explicates the use of the Elijah model in Luke-Acts. We suggest that many of the uses to which Luke puts the Elijah model are developments of ideas borrowed from Mark's use of the same model. Hausman does not discuss this possibility in sufficient detail; it is worthy of further study.

[72]*Geschichte*, pp. 245-46.

[73]To be sure, the author makes clear that Jesus is superior

to these worthies, but most of the details of *how* are left for
the reader to fill in.

[74]We have already commented on the similarities between
Herod and Pilate implied by the feast narratives in 6:14-29
and 15:6-15; Jesus, too, is called upon to grant a banquet-
related request in 10:35-40. The request to sit on the right
and left of Jesus (10:37) is a clear reference to the anticipated eschatological banquet; according to Mark's understanding
of Jewish meal customs, the references to the cup and to
"baptism" also are to be seen as banquet terminology (see Mark
7:4; cf. Luke 11:38, John 13:1-20). There is no indication
within 10:35-40 itself that this is figurative language referring to Jesus' passion and the disciples' martyrdom, but in
view of the material surrounding this passage in the gospel
(10:32-34, 41-45), these are valid inferences. The language of
the meal--cup, baptism, sitting at the right and left--is used
to describe the impending passion of Jesus. Conversely, in the
narrative of the Last Supper the language of the passion--body
and blood--is used to describe the meal. Unlike Herod and
Pilate, who are able to fulfill the requests made of them,
Jesus in 10:35-40 is *unable* to fulfill the brothers' unwitting
request. James and John, *if* they but understood what they were
asking, ask for death sentences just as the girl (6:25) and
the crowd (15:13) do. Although they may eventually drink the
same cup and be washed with the same ablution as Jesus, in the
drama of body and blood which is about to unfold the seats of
honor at the right and left of Jesus have been reserved for
others (10:40). When the reader arrives at Mark 15:17, he will
recall the remarkable prescience of this solemn statement.

[75]1:6, (1:13?), (1:31?), 2:15-17, 18-20, 23-28, 3:20, 5:43,
6:8, 14-29, 30-44, 52, 7:1-8, 14-23, 27-28, 8:1-10, 13-21, 9:41,
10:35-40, (10:45?), 11:12-14, 12:39-40, 14:1-2, 3-9, 12-16, 36,
15:6, 23, 36, (15:41?).

[76]Joanna Dewey has pointed out the importance of "eating"
and "fasting" in the controversy stories of 2:1-3:6; "The
Literary Structure of the Controversy Stories in Mark 2:1-3:6,"
JBL 92 (1973): 394-401.

[77]Recently, Vernon Robbins has stated correctly: "This final
meal completes the drama of the Feeding Stories (Mk 6:30-44;
8:1-10)" ("Last Meal: Preparation, Betrayal, and Absence [Mark
14:12-25]," in *The Passion in Mark*, ed. Werner H. Kelber
[Philadelphia: Fortress Press, 1976], p. 21). Unfortunately, he
seems to adopt Achtemeier's understanding of the function of
the feeding stories in Mark (ibid., pp. 27, 38), which we have
examined above in Chap. 1, so we are not satisfied that Robbins
has correctly grasped the full significance of his own observation.

[78]Mark goes out of his way to stress that the one who
delivered Jesus up was a disciple: ʼΙούδας ʼΙσκαριὼθ ὁ εἷς τῶν
δώδεκα (14:10; cf. 3:19).

Note also that the statement that Judas was promised money for his treachery is preceded by the controversial "waste" of three hundred denarii; in Mark, Jesus' disciples are constantly concerned about financial matters.

[79]Bauer, Arndt, and Gingrich, *Lexicon*, s.v. "παραδίδωμι."

[80]The English expression is paralleled in German by the use of *Verrat* and *verraten*; the French *livrer* is much closer to the Greek παραδίδωμι.

[81]The crucial text is, of course, 1 Cor. 11:23, with regard to which Bauer, Arndt, and Gingrich state: "To be sure, it is not certain that when Paul uses such terms as 'handing over,' 'delivering up,' 'arrest' . . . he is thinking of the betrayal by Judas" (*Lexicon*, s.v. "παραδίδωμι"). The passive παρεδίδετο could just as easily be taken as an oblique reference to being delivered up by God (Rom. 4:25, 8:32). Once Paul even states that Jesus delivered himself up (Gal. 2:20).

Moreover, Paul shows no knowledge of Judas' demise; in 1 Cor. 15:5 he states that the risen Christ appeared *to the Twelve*.

[82]With regard to Peter's renunciation and curse in 14:71, Kim Dewey has stated:
"Peter utters a series of curses designed to dissociate himself publicly from Jesus. The ambiguity over the object of the curse is perhaps best understood as intentional on the part of Mk who creates the highly ironic situation in which Peter either directly curses himself or indirectly does so by cursing Jesus, and by attempting to save himself in this situation in reality loses himself and is placed in even greater jeopardy. Peter, in denying Jesus, denies his own identity and becomes subject to the curse spoken by Jesus (8:38). In effect then Jesus and Peter have cursed each other" ("Peter's Curse," p. 101).

[83]The reader may consult our bibliography for the myriad variations on this theme; notable examples include: B. Van Iersel, "Die wunderbare Speisung und das Abendmahl in der synoptischen Tradition," *NovT* 7 (1964); 167-94; Heising, *Botschaft*, pp. 61-68; Van Cangh, *La multiplication des pains*, pp. 24-25, 30-31, 37-38, 67-109, 165-66.

[84]A notable example is the proposal by Achtemeier that pre-Markan miracle catenae now found in Mark 4-8 "were formed as part of a liturgy which celebrated an epiphantic Eucharist based on bread broken with the θεῖος ἀνήρ, Jesus, during his career and after his resurrection; and Mark sought to overcome that view of Jesus and of the Eucharist by the way in which he used the catenae in his own narrative" ("Origin and Function," p. 198).

[85]See Walter Ong, "The Writer's Audience Is Always a Fiction," *Publications of the Modern Language Association of America* 90 (1975): 9-21.

[86]Primarily in his book, *La multiplication des pains*, but also in his earlier article, "Le thème des poissons."

[87]"Die wunderbare Speisung."

[88]*La multiplication des pains*, pp. 171-72.

[89]"Le récit primitif de la multiplication des pains. . . ." (ibid., p. 171).

[90]"La réinterprétation eucharistique. . . ." (ibid., p. 104).

[91]Ibid., pp. 101, 104, 171.

[92]Ibid., pp. 105, 171-172.

[93]"Pour rétablir le parallélisme entre les éléments multipliés, un rédacteur antérieur à Marc a réintroduit les poissons. . . ." (ibid., p. 105).

[94]"Un rédacteur antérieur à Marc semble avoir réintroduit ce motif des poissons pour remettre l'accent sur le récit de miracle. . . ." (ibid.).

[95]Ibid., pp. 171-72.

[96]Ibid., pp. 105-9, 172.

[97]"Chaque évangéliste va réinterpreter *le miracle*, en lui donnant *une place* déterminée dans le structure générale de son évangile et en mettant en lumière certains aspects caractéristiques de sa théologie propre" (ibid., p. 172; our italics).

[98]Ibid., pp. 148, 155.

[99]Ibid., p. 172.

[100]Ibid., pp. 171-72.

[101]Ibid., p. 172.

[102]*The Mind of Mark.*

[103]Ibid., pp. 67, 75, 81-82, 95, 97, 99, 106, 113, 125, 140, 146-47, 157-59, 162, 167-73, 176-77, 206, 211, 213, 220, 232, 246, 256-57, 259, 275-76.

[104]Ibid., pp. 177-208 (his Chap. 6).

[105]After the excursion into "the Context of the Christian Thought-world," Quesnell returns to the gospel for "Rereading the Texts" (ibid., pp. 209-74; his Chap. 7).

[106]Ibid., pp. 275-76.

[107]Strangely, Quesnell gives scant attention to the Last Supper in Mark.

[108]Wolfgang Iser, "The Reading Process: A Phenomenological Approach," *New Literary History* 3 (1972); 286; This article has been reprinted as Chap. 11 of Iser's *The Implied Reader* (Baltimore: Johns Hopkins University Press, 1974); see p. 281. See also the comments by Stanley Fish on first and second readings in *Self-Consuming Artifacts: The Experience of Seventeenth-Century Literature* (Berkeley: University of California Press, 1972), pp. 14, 205-6. The comments by Walter J. Slatoff are also perceptive:

"A second reading is a quite different experience from the first. There are less mystification, groping, and tension and far more reverberation and illumination as one brings to bear on earlier sections information and awareness gleaned from later ones. And with each successive reading, of course, this process continues until it seems not too much to say that the form and structure have been radically transformed. The very same structures which had served to fragment experience now serve to pull it together" (*With Respect to Readers* [Ithaca: Cornell University Press, 1970], p. 20).

[109]Why Mark wishes to denigrate the disciples so consistently is a matter of speculation, but it may well have something to do with Mark's denigration of Jesus' relatives, the Jewish religious leaders, and, in general, all persons and things Jewish. As Samuel Sandmel has stated:

"Whatever the full range of the purpose of Mark, the denigration of Jews, especially the Jewish disciples, is a leading motif. So extreme is this denigration that it appears to suggest a disconnection between Christianity and the Judaism in which it was born" (*Judaism and Christian Beginnings* [New York: Oxford University Press, 1978], p. 351).

CHAPTER IV

NOTES

[1]For a discussion of the wide spectrum of critics for whom this label is apt, see Steven Mailloux, "Reader-Response Criticism?" *Genre* 10 (1977): 413-31.

[2]M. H. Abrams, *The Mirror and the Lamp: Romantic Theory and the Critical Tradition* (London, Oxford, and New York: Oxford University Press, 1953), pp. 3-29.

[3]Ibid., p. 6.

[4]Howard Clark Kee, *Community of the New Age: Studies in Mark's Gospel* (Philadelphia: Westminster Press, 1977); Norman R. Petersen, *Literary Criticism for New Testament Critics* (Philadelphia: Fortress Press, 1978).

[5]*Community*, p. ix.

[6]Petersen, *Literary Criticism*, pp. 49-80 (chap. 3: "Story Time and Plotted Time in Mark's Narrative").

[7]Kee, *Community*, pp. 55, 59, 61, 66, 67, 111, 117, 121, 127, 146, 150, 167, 167, 172.

[8]Petersen, *Literary Criticism*, pp. 52, 54, 56-57, 57, 57, 58, 58, 59, 61, 62, 64, 64, 65, 68, 70, 73, 73, 75, 75, 76, 76, 77, 77, 78.

[9]At the 1977 meeting of the Society of Biblical Literature in San Francisco, these works by Howard Clark Kee and Norman R. Petersen were discussed in the Seminar on the Gospel of Mark. In a critique of Petersen's work, Joanna Dewey observed, as we have, that Petersen makes numerous comments on the "implied reader" of Mark. This statement caught Petersen by surprise; he had not been aware of this recurrent feature of his work, and he promised to explore it in greater detail.

[10]See, for example, the numerous insights into the experience of Mark's reader furnished by Quesnell, which we have already noted above in chap. 3, p. 144. One recent attempt to address explicitly the experience of the reader (or hearer) of the gospel is the rhetorical critical study by Thomas E. Boomershine, "Mark, the Storyteller: A Rhetorical-Critical Investigation of Mark's Passion and Resurrection Narrative" (Ph.D. dissertation, Union Theological Seminary--New York, 1974).

[11]For a review of the current discussion see Mailloux, "Reader-Response Criticism?" Among the works we have found helpful are Booth, *Fiction*; idem, *Irony*; Stanley E. Fish, "Literature in the Reader: Affective Stylistics," *New Literary History* 2 (1970): 123-62; idem, *Self-Consuming Artifacts: The Experience of Seventeenth-Century Literature* (Berkeley: University of California Press, 1972); Wolfgang Iser, "The Reading

Process: A Phenomenological Approach," *New Literary History* 3 (1972): 272-99; idem, *The Implied Reader* (Baltimore: Johns Hopkins University Press, 1974); Ong, "The Writer's Audience"; Georges Poulet, "Phenomenology of Reading," *New Literary History* 1 (1969-70): 53-68; Walter J. Slatoff, *With Respect to Readers: Dimensions of Literary Response* (Ithaca, N.Y.: Cornell University Press, 1970). For a psychoanalytic approach to reader-response criticism one may consult Norman N. Holland, *The Dynamics of Literary Response* (New York: W.W. Norton & Co., 1968). A major portion of the Fall 1977 issue of *Genre* (The University of Oklahoma) was devoted to reader-response criticism; among the articles appearing there were Mailloux, "Reader-Response Criticism?"; Norman N. Holland, "Stanley Fish, Stanley Fish," *Genre* 10 (1977): 433-41; and Susan R. Horton, "The Experience of Stanley Fish's Prose or The Critic as Self-Creating, Self-Consuming Artificer," *Genre* 10 (1977): 443-53.

[12]Booth, *Fiction*, pp. 71-76 and passim. Interpreters of the gospels would do well to take to heart the distinction between the author and the implied author. Too often it is assumed that when reading the gospels we experience a direct, unmediated encounter with their flesh-and-blood authors. Insight into the implied author of Mark should not be regarded automatically as insight into the author of Mark, although everyone assumes, and probably correctly, that the implied author of Mark is a trustworthy reflection of the flesh-and-blood author.

[13]Booth himself does not use the term "implied reader" in *Fiction*, preferring instead "mock reader." However, Iser's book *The Implied Reader* has secured a place for the term in the vocabulary of literary criticism.

[14]*Fiction*, p. 138. Booth also quotes Henry James: "The author makes his readers, just as he makes his characters" (ibid., p. 302, and the epigraph to Part I).

[15]Ong, "The Writer's Audience," pp. 12, 17.

[16]Biblical scholars often refer to the historical Christian communities supposedly reflected dimly in the gospel narratives. However, what often passes for reflections of a palpable, historical, flesh-and-blood audience, is in fact an aspect of the fictionalized audience created in the evangelist's imagination. We must be careful not to mistake the implied reader of a gospel for a historical, flesh-and-blood reader. We may state with assurance that the "community" for which Mark writes is primarily the "community" of readers molded and shaped by the experience of reading his gospel. The literary critical examination of the "implied community" in Mark, if you will, must precede the posing of the historical question of the degree, if any, to which the implied community of Mark's gospel corresponds to a palpable, historical, Christian community.

[17]Fish, *Self-Consuming Artifacts*, pp. 387-88, 398. These quotations are from the "early" Stanley Fish; he has since become a structuralist, but still advocates this method of

criticism as one of many valid methods. See the discussion of Fish's work by Mailloux, "Reader-Response Criticism?" pp. 414-16.

[18]Iser, "The Reading Process," p. 293.

[19](1)Prohibitions addressed to the demons: 1:25, 34, 3:12; (2) prohibitions following (other) miracles: 1:43-45, 5:43, 7:36, 8:26; (3) prohibitions after Peter's confession: 8:30, 9:9; (4) intentional preservation of his incognito: 7:24, 9:30-31; (5) a prohibition to speak which did not originate with Jesus: 10:47-48; see William Wrede, *The Messianic Secret*, trans. J. C. G. Greig (Cambridge and London: James Clark & Co., 1971), pp. 34-36.

[20]Booth, *Irony*, pp. 53-76.

[21]See the preface to Booth's *Fiction*.

[22]Ibid., pp. 169-209.

[23]Perhaps we should state explicitly how we know that commentary provided by the implied author of Mark is "reliable." As Booth uses the term, reliability refers to consistent adherence to the norms implied in the work (*Fiction*, pp. 158-59). In other words, we know that the implied author of Mark provides reliable commentary because he consistently espouses the same fundamental set of norms throughout the gospel. He is no dissembler, advocating values and ideals that he will renounce later. As we noted in Chap. 2 above, one of the major ways in which the anonymous, omniscient narrator of the gospel (the spokesman for the implied author and virtually indistinguishable from him) is shown to be a reliable commentator is through the extravagant use of repetition in the gospel. We noted, for example, that in some cases the narrator informs the reader of a certain matter just before a character in the story states the same thing in the same language, thereby demonstrating the reliability of the omniscient narrator. As a further indication of the consistency with which the implied author carries through with the implied norms of his work, we may point to another kind of repetition, the fulfillment in one part of the narrative of a prediction (usually by Jesus) in an earlier part. Jesus, as the implied author's protagonist, is a major avenue through which reliable knowledge is channeled to the reader, and his ability to predict the future--prediction and fulfillment occur right in front of our eyes--reassures the reader of his reliability.

[24]Similarly, Norman Perrin has suggested that the "you" of 14:62 refers to the reader of the gospel and not the High Priest; "The High Priest's Question and Jesus' Answer," p. 92.

[25]Petersen, *Literary Criticism*, p. 70.

[26]". . . in 8,27ff. the disciples recognize Jesus as the Christ for the first time. The reader has known that he is the Christ since at least 1,1. The reader knows more about him--that

he is the Son of God (1,1.11)" (Quesnell, *Mind of Mark*, p. 132).

[27] Much of what we have said about the prospective function of the title and epigraph of the gospel is applicable to the whole introductory section of Mark (1:1-15). As Petersen states: "In 1:1-15 the reader is supplied with both information and expectations that give the reader a point of view--the narrator's--from which to construe what follows" (*Literary Criticism*, p. 54).

[28] See the lengthy discussion of "parenthetical clauses" in Mark by Pryke, *Redactional Style*, pp. 32-61.

[29] For example, the statement that "all the Jews do not eat unless they wash their hands" (7:3) sounds more like a Gentile caricature of Jewish custom than anything else.

[30] Boomershine, "Mark, the Storyteller," pp. 270-71.

[31] Quesnell, *Mind of Mark*, p. 65. See also Norman Perrin, "The Christology of Mark," in *L'Évangile selon Marc: Tradition et rédaction*, ed. M. Sabbe, BETL, no. 34 (Leuven: Leuven University Press, 1974), p. 477.

[32] Perrin, "The High Priest's Question and Jesus' Answer," p. 92.

[33] C. H. Bird, "Some γαρ clauses in St. Mark's Gospel," *JTS* 4 (1953): 171-87.

[34] See above, p. 207, n. 82.

[35] See our discussion of Mark 6:31 in Chap. 2 above.

[36] *Kingdom*, p. 100.

[37] *Aretalogy Used by Mark*, p. 10.

[38] Ibid., p. 10, n. 48.

[39] Pryke, too, recognizes that Mark often positions a γάρ clause "after the main statements," often "as an afterthought to clarify a previously obscure statement." Referring to the explanatory γάρ clauses in Mark, Pryke observes: "Thirty-three of the redactional examples are of this kind, needing no other explanation than that of a non-literary writer who delays important details until after the facts have tumbled out of his mind, sometimes reversing the logical order so that what we consider to be a logically prior statement comes second" (*Redactional Style*, pp. 45, 40, 127-28).

[40] Here we have used the list of Markan insertions provided by Donahue (*Trial Narrative*, pp. 241-43), to which we have added 6:35//35, 7:1-2//5, and 8:1//2. This list is far from exhaustive, but a full accounting of the recurrent use of this technique in Mark is not possible within the bounds of this study.

[41]Ibid., pp. 77-84.

[42]We have used the list provided by Neirynck (*Duality*, p. 133), who prefers the term "sandwich arrangement."

[43]On inside views see Booth, *Fiction*, pp. 17-18 (regarding inside views in the gospel of Mark!), 160-65; and Boomershine ("Mark, the Story-teller," pp. 273-75), who classifies inside views into "perceptions," "emotions," "inner knowledge/motivation," and "inner statements."

[44]*Self-Consuming Artifacts*, p. 60. For similar comments on the potency of the unanswered question, see Dibelius, *Tradition*, pp. 94-95; Kenneth R. R. Gros Louis, "The Gospel of Mark," in *Literary Interpretations of Biblical Narrative*, ed. Kenneth R. R. Gros Louis, with James S. Ackerman, and Thayer S. Warshaw (Nashville and New York: Abingdon, 1974), pp. 310-11.

[45]As Kee observes: "Using the device of a rhetorical question, or one that only the discerning reader is prepared to answer accurately, Mark poses the issue as to who could triumph over storm and waves. . . . The rhetorical questions place the responsibility on the reader to decide the identity of the one who performs such deeds (4:41)" (*Community*, pp. 121, 167).

[46]Again, Kee states: ". . . by his much-favoured interrogative device (. . . 6:2a) he puts the responsibility on the reader to provide the answer" (ibid., p. 117).

[47]Similar to the function of the unanswered question is that of gossip. We are thinking here especially of 6:14-16 and 8:28, parallel pieces of gossip about Jesus in which it is said that he is John the Baptist *redivivus*, Elijah, or another prophet. This certainly does not provide reliable commentary for the reader--it is only gossip, after all--but it is not to be taken lightly either. These possible identities twice proposed for Jesus encourage the reader to look for the similarities between Jesus and these figures that would make such speculation possible. Thus gossip guides the reader's thoughts in a manner similar to that of unanswered questions.

[48]"Disciples in Mark," p. 391.

[49]Ibid. We note, for example, that some of the inside views provided by the implied author are presented to the reader, not by means of the omniscient narrator, but as insights of Jesus into other characters in the story (2:5, 8, 3:5, 4:40, 8:16-21, 33, 10:38, 12:15, 24, 34, 14:18, 27, 30), thereby merging the perspective of the implied author with that of Jesus.

[50]"The Reading Process," p. 287.

[51]"The High Priest's Question and Jesus' Answer."

[52]This is often noted; see, for example, Perrin, *Introduction*, pp. 155-58.

[53]"Peter's Curse and Cursed Peter," p. 111.

[54]Although we have discussed these examples of prospective passages with a literary critical approach, concerning ourselves with the function of these passages in the gospel as a whole, we should note that the three examples we have discussed follow closely the familiar categories of form criticism. Mark 6:30-44 is narrative material ("Erzählungsstoff": Bultmann, *Geschichte*, pp. 231-32); 3:1-19 is mostly redactional in nature, containing "die redaktionellen Bildungen" of 3:7-12 and 3:13-19 (ibid., p. 366; also see Dibelius, *Tradition*, p. 224); 8:27-9:1 is largely discourse material, sayings of Jesus ("Herrenworte": Bultmann, *Geschichte*, pp. 86, 163). Clearly some material that, on form critical grounds, belongs to different categories may, on literary critical grounds, be seen to serve a similar function in the context of the gospel as a whole.

[55]Furthermore, only a literary critical method is able to demonstrate how an evangelist constructs ironies while at the same time equipping the reader to see through them.

CHAPTER V

NOTES

[1]He is also abandoned by his God, but 16:1-8 serves to
place the finality of that abandonment in doubt. Mark 16:7 may
also be intended to place the disciples' abandonment in doubt.

APPENDIX I

THE BOAT MOTIF IN MARK: THE BOAT TRIPS

	I		II		III	
	4:1-2, 35-36/ 5:1-2	5:18, 21/ 5:21	6:32-33/ 6:34-35	6:45-47/ 6:53-55	8:9-10/ 8:9-10	8:13-14/ 8:22
1. ἐμβαίνω	x	x		x	x	x
εἰς τὸ πλοῖον	x	x		x	x	x
2. ἐξέρχομαι	x		x	x		
ἐκ τοῦ πλοίου	x			x		
3. ὄχλος	3	x	x	x		
(πολλοί)			x			
πολύς		x	x			
(πλεῖστος)	x					
συνάγω	x	x				
(συντρέχω)			x			
(περιτρέχω)				x		
{ ἀπολύω				x	x	
{ ἀφίημι	x					x
4. Cognate of ἔρχομαι in Aorist	x		x	x	x	x
(διαπεράω)		x		x		
(διέρχομαι)	x					
ἐν τῷ πλοίῳ	x	x	x			x
5. εἰς τὸ πέραν	2	x		x		x
εἰς τὴν χώραν τῶν Γερασηνῶν	x					
εἰς ἔρημον τόπον			x			
εἰς βηθσαϊδάν						x
πρὸς βηθσαϊδάν				x		
εἰς Γεννησαρέτ				x		
εἰς τὰ μέρη Δαλμανουθά					x	
ἐπὶ τὴν γῆν				x		
6. { ὀψίας γενομένης	x			x		
{ ὥρας πολλῆς γενομένης			x			
7. διδάσκειν	2		x			
(διδαχή)	x					
ἄρχομαι auxiliary	x		x			
πολλά	x		x			
8. θάλασσα	4	x		x		
9. γῆ	x			2		
10. πάλιν	x	x				x
11. εὐθύς	x			2	x	

APPENDIX II

MARKAN INSERTIONS IN 6:31-32; 6:35; 8:1-2

κατ' ἰδίαν εἰς ἔρημον τόπον

οὐδὲ φαγεῖν εὐκαίρουν

εἰς ἔρημον τόπον κατ' ἰδίαν

                    μὴ ἐχόντων τί φάγωσιν

                    προσκαλεσάμενος τοὺς
                    μαθητὰς λέγει αὐτοῖς

    ἐσπλαγχνίσθη ἐπ' αὐτοὺς   σπλαγχνίζομαι ἐπὶ τὸν
                    ὄχλον

                    οὐκ ἔχουσιν τί φάγωσιν

καὶ ἤδη ὥρας πολλῆς γενομένης

    προσελθόντες αὐτῷ οἱ
    μαθηταὶ αὐτοῦ ἔλεγον

    ἔρημός ἐστιν ὁ τόπος

καὶ ἤδη ὥρα πολλή

ἀπόλυσον αὐτοὺς   ἐὰν ἀπολύσω αὐτοὺς

   (τί φάγωσιν)   (ἐπ' ἐρημίας)

APPENDIX III

A SYNOPSIS OF THE TWO FEEDING STORIES

6:30 Καὶ συνάγονται οἱ ἀπόστολοι
πρὸς τὸν Ἰησοῦν, καὶ ἀπήγγειλαν
αὐτῷ πάντα ὅσα ἐποίησαν καὶ ὅσα ἐδίδαξαν. 31 καὶ λέγει αὐτοῖς, Δεῦτε
ὑμεῖς αὐτοὶ κατ᾽ ἰδίαν εἰς ἔρημον
τόπον καὶ ἀναπαύσασθε ὀλίγον. ἦσαν
γὰρ οἱ ἐρχόμενοι καὶ οἱ ὑπάγοντες
πολλοί, καὶ οὐδὲ φαγεῖν εὐκαίρουν.
32 καὶ ἀπῆλθον ἐν τῷ πλοίῳ εἰς ἔρημον τόπον κατ᾽ ἰδίαν. 33 καὶ εἶδον
αὐτοὺς ὑπάγοντας καὶ ἐπέγνωσαν πολλοί, καὶ πεζῇ ἀπὸ πασῶν τῶν πόλεων
συνέδραμον ἐκεῖ καὶ προῆλθον αὐτούς.
34 καὶ ἐξελθὼν εἶδεν πολὺν ὄχλον,
καὶ ἐσπλαγχνίσθη ἐπ᾽ αὐτοὺς ὅτι ἦσαν
ὡς πρόβατα μὴ ἔχοντα ποιμένα, καὶ
ἤρξατο διδάσκειν αὐτοὺς πολλά.
35 Καὶ ἤδη ὥρας πολλῆς γενομένης
προσελθόντες αὐτῷ οἱ μαθηταὶ αὐτοῦ
ἔλεγον ὅτι Ἔρημός ἐστιν ὁ τόπος,
καὶ ἤδη ὥρα πολλή· 36 ἀπόλυσον αὐτούς, ἵνα ἀπελθόντες εἰς τοὺς κύκλῳ
ἀγροὺς καὶ κώμας ἀγοράσωσιν ἑαυτοῖς
τί φάγωσιν. 37 ὁ δὲ ἀποκριθεὶς
εἶπεν αὐτοῖς, Δότε αὐτοῖς ὑμεῖς
φαγεῖν. καὶ λέγουσιν αὐτῷ, Ἀπελθόντες ἀγοράσωμεν δηναρίων διακοσίων
ἄρτους καὶ δώσομεν αὐτοῖς φαγεῖν;
38 ὁ δὲ λέγει αὐτοῖς, Πόσους ἄρτους
ἔχετε; ὑπάγετε ἴδετε. καὶ γνόντες
λέγουσιν, Πέντε, καὶ δύο ἰχθύας.
39 καὶ ἐπέταξεν αὐτοῖς ἀνακλῖναι
πάντας συμπόσια συμπόσια ἐπὶ τῷ
χλωρῷ χόρτῳ. 40 καὶ ἀνέπεσαν πρασιαὶ πρασιαὶ κατὰ ἑκατὸν καὶ κατὰ
πεντήκοντα. 41 καὶ λαβὼν τοὺς
πέντε ἄρτους καὶ τοὺς δύο ἰχθύας
ἀναβλέψας εἰς τὸν οὐρανὸν εὐλόγησεν καὶ κατέκλασεν τοὺς ἄρτους καὶ
ἐδίδου τοῖς μαθηταῖς αὐτοῦ ἵνα
παρατιθῶσιν αὐτοῖς, καὶ τοὺς δύο
ἰχθύας ἐμέρισεν πᾶσιν. 42 καὶ
ἔφαγον πάντες καὶ ἐχορτάσθησαν·
43 καὶ ἦραν κλάσματα δώδεκα κοφί-
νων πληρώματα καὶ ἀπὸ τῶν ἰχθύων.
44 καὶ ἦσαν οἱ φαγόντες πεντακισχί-
λιοι ἄνδρες. 45 Καὶ εὐθὺς ἠνάγκα-
σεν τοὺς μαθητὰς αὐτοῦ ἐμβῆναι
εἰς τὸ πλοῖον καὶ προάγειν εἰς τὸ
πέραν πρὸς Βηθσαϊδάν, ἕως αὐτὸς
ἀπολύει τὸν ὄχλον. 46 καὶ ἀποτα-
ξάμενος αὐτοῖς ἀπῆλθεν εἰς τὸ ὄρος
προσεύξασθαι.

8:1 Ἐν ἐκείναις
ταῖς ἡμέραις πάλιν
πολλοῦ ὄχλου ὄντος
καὶ μὴ ἐχόντων τί
φάγωσιν, προσκαλε-
σάμενος τοὺς μαθη-
τὰς λέγει αὐτοῖς,
2 Σπλαγχνίζομαι
ἐπὶ τὸν ὄχλον ὅτι
ἤδη ἡμέραι τρεῖς
προσμένουσίν μοι
καὶ οὐκ ἔχουσιν τί
φάγωσιν· 3 καὶ ἐὰν
ἀπολύσω αὐτοὺς νή-
στεις εἰς οἶκον
αὐτῶν, ἐκλυθήσονται
ἐν τῇ ὁδῷ· καί τινες
αὐτῶν ἀπὸ μακρόθεν
ἥκασιν. 4 καὶ ἀπε-
κρίθησαν αὐτῷ οἱ
μαθηταὶ αὐτοῦ ὅτι
Πόθεν τούτους δυνή-
σεταί τις ὧδε χορ-
τάσαι ἄρτων ἐπ᾽ ἐρη-
μίας; 5 καὶ ἠρώτα
αὐτούς, Πόσους ἔχετε
ἄρτους; οἱ δὲ εἶ-
παν, Ἑπτά. 6 καὶ
παραγγέλλει τῷ ὄχλῳ
ἀναπεσεῖν ἐπὶ τῆς
γῆς· καὶ λαβὼν τοὺς
ἑπτὰ ἄρτους εὐχαρι-
στήσας ἔκλασεν καὶ
ἐδίδου τοῖς μαθηταῖς
αὐτοῦ ἵνα παρατιθῶ-
σιν καὶ παρέθηκαν
τῷ ὄχλῳ. 7 καὶ εἶ-
χον ἰχθύδια ὀλίγα·
καὶ εὐλογήσας αὐτὰ
εἶπεν καὶ ταῦτα
παρατιθέναι. 8 καὶ
ἔφαγον καὶ ἐχορτά-
σθησαν, καὶ ἦραν
περισσεύματα κλα-
σμάτων ἑπτὰ σπυρίδας.
9 ἦσαν δὲ ὡς τετρα-
κισχίλιοι. καὶ ἀπ-
έλυσεν αὐτούς.
10 Καὶ εὐθὺς ἐμβὰς
εἰς τὸ πλοῖον μετὰ
τῶν μαθητῶν αὐτοῦ
ἦλθεν εἰς τὰ μέρη
Δαλμανουθά.

SELECTED BIBLIOGRAPHY

Abrams, M. H. *The Mirror and the Lamp: Romantic Theory and the Critical Tradition*. London, Oxford and New York: Oxford University Press, 1953.

Achtemeier, Paul. "On the Historical-Critical Method in New Testament Studies: Apologia pro Vita Sua." *Perspective* 11 (1970): 289-304.

_____. "Toward the Isolation of Pre-Markan Miracle Catenae." *Journal of Biblical Literature* 89 (1970): 265-91.

_____. "The Origin and Function of the Pre-Marcan Miracle Catenae." *Journal of Biblical Literature* 91 (1972): 198-221.

_____. "Gospel Miracle Tradition and the Divine Man." *Interpretation* 26 (1972): 174-97.

_____. "Miracles and the Historical Jesus: A Study of Mark 9:14-29." *Catholic Biblical Quarterly* 37 (1975): 471-91.

Anderson, Bernard W. "The New Frontier of Rhetorical Criticism." In *Rhetorical Criticism: Essays in Honor of James Muilenburg*, pp. ix-xviii. Edited by Jared J. Jackson and Martin Kessler. Pittsburgh Theological Monograph Series, no. 1. Pittsburgh: Pickwick Press, 1974.

Annen, Franz. *Heil für die Heiden: Zur Bedeutung und Geschichte der Tradition vom besessenen Gerasener (Mk 5,1-20 parr.)*. Frankfurter theologischer Studien, no. 20. Frankfurt am Main: Josef Knecht, 1976.

Barthes, Roland. *S/Z*. Translated by Richard Miller. Preface by Richard Howard. New York: Hill and Wang, 1974.

Ben-Amos, Dan. "Themes, Forms, and Meanings: Critical Comments." *Semeia* 3 (1975): 128-32.

Berger, Peter L., and Luckmann, Thomas. *The Social Construction of Reality: A Treatise in the Sociology of Knowledge*. Garden City, N.Y.: Doubleday, 1966.

Best, Ernest. *The Temptation and the Passion: The Markan Soteriology*. Society for New Testament Studies Monograph Series, no. 2. Cambridge: Cambridge University Press, 1965.

_____. "Mark's Preservation of the Tradition." In *L'Evangile selon Marc: Tradition et rédaction*, pp. 21-34. Edited by M. Sabbe. Bibliotheca Ephemeridum Theologicarum Lovaniensium, no. 34. Leuven: Leuven University Press, 1974.

239

Best, Ernest. "The Role of the Disciples in Mark." *New Testament Studies* 23 (1977): 377-401.

Bird, C. H. "Some γαρ clauses in St. Mark's Gospel." *Journal of Theological Studies* 4 (1953): 171-87.

Boobyer, G. H. "The Eucharistic Interpretation of the Miracles of the Loaves in St. Mark's Gospel." *Journal of Theological Studies* 3 (1952): 161-71.

Boomershine, Thomas E. "Mark, the Storyteller: A Rhetorical-Critical Investigation of Mark's Passion and Resurrection Narrative." Ph.D. dissertation, Union Theological Seminary--New York, 1974.

Booth, Wayne C. *The Rhetoric of Fiction*. Chicago: University of Chicago Press, 1961.

_____. *A Rhetoric of Irony*. Chicago: University of Chicago Press, 1974.

Bornkamm, Günther; Barth, Gerhard; and Held, Heinz Joachim. *Tradition and Interpretation in Matthew*. Translated by Percy Scott. Philadelphia: Westminster Press, 1963.

Branscomb, B. Harvie. *The Gospel of Mark*. New York and London: Harper & Bros., n.d.

Brown, Raymond E. "Jesus and Elisha." *Perspective* 12 (1971): 85-104.

Bultmann, Rudolf. *The History of the Synoptic Tradition*. Translated by John Marsh. Rev. ed. New York: Harper & Row, 1968.

_____. *Die Geschichte der synoptischen Tradition*. 8th ed. Göttingen: Vandenhoeck & Ruprecht, 1970.

_____. *The Gospel of John*. Translated by G. R. Beasley-Murray, R. W. N. Hoare, and J. K. Riches. Philadelphia: Westminster Press, 1971.

Burkill, T. A. "Mark 3:7-12 and the Alleged Dualism in the Evangelist's Miracle Material." *Journal of Biblical Literature* 87 (1968): 409-17.

_____. *New Light on the Earliest Gospel: Seven Markan Studies*. Ithaca and London: Cornell University Press, 1972.

Buse, Ivor. "The Gospel Accounts of the Feeding of the Multitudes." *Expository Times* 74 (1963): 167-70.

Cadbury, Henry J. "Four Features of Lucan Style." In *Studies in Luke-Acts: Essays presented in honor of Paul Schubert, Buckingham Professor of New Testament Criticism and Interpretation at Yale University*, pp. 87-102. Edited by Leander E. Keck and J. Louis Martyn. London: SPCK, 1968.

Carpenter, Ronald H. "Stylistic Redundancy and Function in Discourse." *Language and Style* 3 (1970): 62-68.

Cerfaux, L. "La section des pains." In *Synoptische Studien: Festschrift für A. Wikenhauser*, pp. 64-77. Munich: K. Zink, 1953.

Clavier, Henri. "La méthode ironique dans l'enseignement de Jésus." *Études théologiques et religieuses* 4 (1929): 224-41, 323-44; 5 (1930): 58-99.

_____. "L'ironie dans l'enseignement de Jésus." *Novum Testamentum* 1 (1956): 3-20.

_____. "L'ironie dans le quatrième Évangile." *Studia Evangelica* I. *Texte und Untersuchungen* 73 (1959): 261-76.

_____. "La multiplication des pains dans le ministère de Jésus." *Studia Evangelica* I. *Texte und Untersuchungen* 73 (1959): 441-57.

Coote, Robert B. "The Application of Oral Theory to Biblical Hebrew Literature." *Semeia* 5 (1976): 51-64.

Crossan, John Dominic. *In Parables: The Challenge of the Historical Jesus*. New York: Harper & Row, 1973.

_____. "Mark and the Relatives of Jesus." *Novum Testamentum* 15 (1973): 81-113.

_____. "Waking the Bible: Biblical Hermeneutic and Literary Imagination." *Interpretation* 32 (1978): 269-85.

Culley, Robert C. "Structural Analysis: Is It Done with Mirrors?" *Interpretation* 28 (1974): 165-81.

_____. "Themes and Variations in Three Groups of Old Testament Narratives." *Semeia* 3 (1975): 3-13.

_____. "Oral Tradition and the Old Testament: Some Recent Discussion." *Semeia* 5 (1976): 1-33.

_____. *Studies in the Structure of Hebrew Narrative*. Semeia Supplements, no. 3. Missoula, Mont.: Scholars Press, 1976.

Cummings, D. W.; Herum, John; and Lybbert, E. K. "Semantic Recurrence and Rhetorical Form." *Language and Style* 4 (1971): 195-207.

Dahl, Nils Alstrup. *Jesus in the Memory of the Early Church*. Minneapolis: Augsburg, 1976.

Danker, Frederick W. "Mark 8:3." *Journal of Biblical Literature* 82 (1964): 215-16.

Deiss, Lucien. *Early Sources of the Liturgy*. Translated by Benet Weatherhead. Staten Island, N. Y.: Alba House, 1967.

De la Potterie, I. "Le sens primitif de la multiplication des pains." In *Jésus aux origines de la Christologie*, pp. 303-29. Bibliotheca Ephemeridum Theologicarum Lovaniensium, no. 40. Leuven: Leuven University Press, 1974.

Denis, A.-M. "Jesus' Walking on the Waters: A Contribution to the History of the Pericope in the Gospel Tradition." *Louvain Studies* 1 (1967): 284-97.

_____."La section des pains selon S. Marc (6,30-8,26), une théologie de l'Eucharistie." *Studia Evangelica* IV. *Texte und Untersuchungen* 102 (1968): 171-79.

Dewey, Joanna. "The Literary Structure of the Controversy Stories in Mark 2:1-3:6." *Journal of Biblical Literature* 92 (1973): 394-401.

Dewey, Kim. "Peter's Curse and Cursed Peter (Mark 14:53-54, 66-72)." In *The Passion in Mark: Studies on Mark 14-16*, pp. 96-114. Edited by Werner H. Kelber. Philadelphia: Fortress Press, 1976.

Dibelius, Martin. *From Tradition to Gospel*. Translated by Bertram Lee Woolf. New York: Charles Scribner's Sons, n.d.

Dix, G. *The Shape of the Liturgy*. Philadelphia: Westminster Press, 1945.

Dobschütz, Ernst von. "Zur Erzählerkunst des Markus." *Zeitschrift für die neutestamentliche Wissenschaft* 27 (1928): 193-98.

Donahue, John R. *Are You the Christ? The Trial Narrative in the Gospel of Mark*. Society of Biblical Literature Dissertation Series, no. 10. Missoula, Mont.: Scholars Press, 1973.

_____. "Temple, Trial, and Royal Christology (Mark 14:53-65)." In *The Passion in Mark: Studies on Mark 14-16*, pp. 61-79. Edited by Werner H. Kelber. Philadelphia: Fortress Press, 1976.

Doudna, John C. *The Greek of the Gospel of Mark*. Society of Biblical Literature Monograph Series, no. 12. Philadelphia: Society of Biblical Literature, 1961.

Egger, Wilhelm. "Die Verborgenheit Jesu in Mk 3,7-12." *Biblica* 50 (1969): 466-90.

_____. *Frohbotschaft und Lehre: Die Sammelberichte des Wirkens Jesu im Markusevangelium*. Frankfurter theologische Studien, no. 19. Frankfurt am Main: Josef Knecht, 1976.

Elliott, J. E. "The Synoptic Problem and the Laws of Tradition: A Cautionary Note." *Expository Times* 82 (1971): 148-52.

Enslin, M.S. "The Artistry of Mark." *Journal of Biblical Literature* 66 (1947): 385-99.

Farrer, Austin. *A Study in St. Mark.* London: Dacre Press, 1951.

_____. "Loaves and Thousands." *Journal of Theological Studies* 4 (1953): 1-14.

_____. *St. Matthew and St. Mark.* London: Dacre Press, 1954.

Fiebig, P. *Jüdische Wundergeschichten des neutestamentlichen Zeitalters.* Tübingen: J. C. B. Mohr (Paul Siebeck), 1911.

Fish, Stanley E. "Literature in the Reader: Affective Stylistics." *New Literary History* 2 (1970): 123-62.

_____. *Self-Consuming Artifacts: The Experience of Seventeenth-Century Literature.* Berkeley: University of California Press, 1972.

Fitzer, Gottfried. "Sakrament und Wunder im Neuen Testament: Eine Betrachtung zu E. Lohmeyers Deutung des Brotwunders." In *In Memoriam Ernst Lohmeyer*, pp. 169-88. Edited by Werner Schmauch. Stuttgart: Evangelisches Verlagswerk, 1951.

Fridrichsen, Anton. *The Problem of Miracle in Primitive Christianity.* Translated by Roy A. Harrisville and John S. Hanson. Minneapolis: Augsburg, 1972.

Friedrich, Gerhard. "Die beiden Erzählungen von der Speisung in Mark 6,31-44; 8,1-9." *Theologische Zeitschrift* 20 (1964): 10-22.

Frye, Roland M. "A Literary Perspective for the Criticism of the Gospels." In *Jesus and Man's Hope: Essays from the Pittsburgh Festival on the Gospels*, 2:193-221. Edited by D. G. Miller and D. Y. Hadidian. Pittsburgh: Pittsburgh Theological Seminary, 1971.

_____. "On the Historical Critical Method in New Testament Studies: A Reply to Professor Achtemeier." *Perspective* 14 (1973): 28-33.

Fuller, Reginald H. *Longer Mark: Forgery, Interpolation, or Old Tradition?* Protocol of the Colloquy of the Center for Hermeneutical Studies in Hellenistic and Modern Culture, no. 18. Berkeley: The Center for Hermeneutical Studies in Hellenistic and Modern Culture, 1976.

Funk, Robert W. *Language, Hermeneutic, and Word of God: The Problem of Language in the New Testament and Contemporary Theology.* New York: Harper & Row, 1966.

_____. *Jesus as Precursor.* Semeia Supplements, no. 2. Missoula, Mont.: Scholars Press, 1975.

Gager, John G. "The Gospels and Jesus: Some Doubts about Method." *Journal of Religion* 54 (1974): 244-72.

Gager, John G. *Kingdom and Community: The Social World of Early Christianity.* Englewood Cliffs: Prentice-Hall, 1975.

Gaston, Lloyd. *Horae Synopticae Electronicae: Word Statistics of the Synoptic Gospels.* Society of Biblical Literature Sources for Biblical Study, no. 3. Missoula, Mont.: Scholars Press, 1973.

Gavin, F. *The Jewish Antecedents of the Christian Sacraments.* London: SPCK, 1928; reprint ed., New York: Ktav Publishing House, 1969.

Georgi, Dieter. *The Records of Jesus in the Light of Ancient Accounts of Revered Men.* Protocol of the Colloquy of the Center for Hermeneutical Studies in Hellenistic and Modern Culture, no. 4. Berkeley: The Center for Hermeneutical Studies in Hellenistic and Modern Culture, 1975.

Glasswell, M. E. "The Use of Miracles in the Markan Gospel." In *Miracles*, pp. 149-62. Edited by C. F. D. Moule. London: Mowbray, 1965.

Good, Edwin M. *Irony in the Old Testament.* Philadelphia: Westminster Press, 1965.

Goodenough, Erwin R. *Jewish Symbols in the Graeco-Roman Period.* Vols. 5 and 6: *Fish, Bread, and Wine.* New York: Bollingen Foundation, 1956.

Gould, Erza P. *The Gospel According to St. Mark.* International Critical Commentary. New York: Charles Scribner's Sons, 1896.

Goulder, Michael D. *Midrash and Lection in Matthew: The Speaker's Lectures in Biblical Studies, 1969-71.* London: SPCK, 1974.

Grant, Frederick C., ed. *Hellenistic Religions: The Age of Syncretism.* Indianapolis and New York: Bobbs-Merrill, 1953.

Grant, Robert M. *Miracle and Natural Law in Graeco-Roman and Early Christian Thought.* Amsterdam: North-Holland Publishing Co., 1952.

Grassi, Joseph A. "The Five Loaves of the High Priest." *Novum Testamentum* 7 (1964): 119-22.

_____. "The Eucharist in the Gospel of Mark." *American Ecclesiastical Review* 168 (1974): 595-608.

Gros Louis, Kenneth R. R. "The Gospel of Mark." In *Literary Interpretations of Biblical Narratives*, pp. 296-329. Edited by Kenneth R. R. Gros Louis, with James S. Ackerman and Thayer S. Warshaw. Nashville and New York: Abingdon Press, 1974.

_____, ed; with Ackerman, James; and Warshaw, Thayer S. *Literary Interpretations of Biblical Narratives.* Nashville and New York: Abingdon Press, 1974.

Greenwood, David. "Rhetorical Criticism and Formgeschichte: Some Methodological Considerations." *Journal of Biblical Literature* 89 (1970): 418-26.

Güttgemanns, Erhardt. *Offene Fragen zur Formgeschichte des Evangeliums: Eine methodologische Skizze der Grundlagenproblematik der Form- und Redaktionsgeschichte.* Beiträge zur evangelischen Theologie, no. 54. Munich: Chr. Kaiser, 1970.

Gunn, David M. "On Oral Tradition: A Response to John Van Seters." *Semeia* 5 (1976): 155-63.

Hägg, Tomas. *Narrative Technique in Ancient Greek Romances: Studies of Chariton, Xenophon Ephesius, and Achiles Tatius.* Skrifter Utgivna av Svenska Institutet i Athen, Octavo Series, vol. 8. Stockholm: Svensak Institutet i Athen, 1971.

Haenchen, Ernst. *Der Weg Jesu: Eine Erklärung des Markus-Evangeliums und der kanonischen Parellelen.* 2d ed. Berlin: Walter de Gruyter, 1968.

Hahn, Ferdinand. *Christologische Hoheitstitel: Ihre Geschichte im frühen Christentum.* Forschungen zur Religion und Literatur des Alten und Neuen Testaments, no. 83. Göttingen: Vandenhoeck & Ruprecht, 1963.

_____. *The Titles of Jesus in Christology: Their History in Early Christianity.* Translated by Harold Knight and George Ogg. New York and Cleveland: World Publishing Co., 1969.

_____. *The Worship of the Early Church.* Translated by David E. Green. Edited, with an Introduction, by John Reumann. Philadelphia: Fortress Press, 1973.

Hammer, R. A. "Elijah and Jesus: A Quest for Identity." *Judaism* 19 (1970): 207-18.

Hartmann, Gerhard. *Der Aufbau des Markusevangeliums.* Neutestamentliche Abhandlungen, no. 17. Münster: Aschendorff-schen Verlagsbuchhandlung, 1936.

Hausman, Robert A. "The Function of Elijah as a Model in Luke-Acts." Ph.D. dissertation, University of Chicago, 1975.

Hawkins, John C. *Horae Synopticae: Contributions to the Study of the Synoptic Problem.* 2d ed. Oxford: Clarendon Press, 1909; reprint ed., Grand Rapids: Baker Book House, 1968.

Hayes, John E., ed. *Old Testament Form Criticism.* Trinity University Monograph Series in Religion, no. 2. San Antonio: Trinity University Press, 1974.

Hebert, A. G. "History in the Feeding of the Five Thousand." *Studia Evangelica* II. *Texte und Untersuchungen* 87 (1964): 65-72.

Heising, Alkuin. "Exegese und Theologie der alt- und neutestamentlichen Speisewunder." *Zeitschrift für katholische Theologie* 86 (1964): 80-96.

_____. *Die Botschaft der Brotvermehrung*. Stuttgarter Bibelstudien, no. 15. Stuttgart: Katholisches Bibelwerk, 1966.

_____. "Das Kerygma der wunderbaren Fischvermehrung (Mk 6, 34-44 parr.)." *Bibel und Leben* 10 (1969): 52-57.

Heirs, Richard H., and Kennedy, Charles A. "The Bread and Fish Eucharist in the Gospels and Early Christian Art." *Perspectives in Religious Studies* 3 (1976): 20-47.

Hirsch, E. D., Jr. *Validity in Interpretation*. New Haven: Yale University Press, 1967.

_____. *The Aims of Interpretation*. Chicago: University of Chicago Press, 1976.

Holladay, William L. *The Architecture of Jeremiah 1-20*. Lewisburg: Buchnell University Press, 1976; London: Associated University Presses, 1976.

Holland, Norman N. *The Dynamics of Literary Response*. New York: Oxford University Press, 1968.

_____. "Stanley Fish, Stanley Fish." *Genre* 10 (1977): 433-41.

Horn, R. C. "The Use of the Greek New Testament." *Lutheran Quarterly* 1 (1949): 301.

Horstmann, Maria. *Studien zur markinischen Christologie: Mk 8,27-9, 13 als Zugang zum Christusbild der zweiten Evangeliums*. Neutestamentliche Abhandlungen, Neue Folge, no. 6. Münster: Aschendorffschen Verlagsbuchhandlung, 1969.

Hort, F. J. A., with Murray, J. O. F. "A Note by the late Dr. Hort on the Words κόφινος, σπυρίς, σαργάνη." *Journal of Theological Studies* 10 (1909): 567-71.

Horton, Susan R. "The Experience of Stanley Fish's Prose or the Critic as Self-Creating, Self-Consuming Artificer." *Genre* 10 (1977): 443-53.

Hull, John M. *Hellenistic Magic and the Synoptic Tradition*. Studies in Biblical Theology, Second Series, no. 28. Naperville: Allenson, 1974.

Iser, Wolfgang. "The Reading Process: A Phenomenological Approach." *New Literary History* 3 (1972): 279-99.

_____. *The Implied Reader*. Baltimore: Johns Hopkins University Press, 1974.

Jenkins, Luke H. "A Markan Doublet: Mark 6:31-7:37 and 8:1-26."
     In *Studies in History and Religion: Presented to H. Wheeler
     Robinson,* pp. 87-111. Edited by Ernest A. Payne. London:
     Lutterworth, 1942.

Jeremias, Joachim. *The Eucharistic Words of Jesus.* Translated by
     Norman Perrin. London: SCM Press, 1966.

Johnston, Edwin D. "The Johannine Version of the Feeding of the
     Five Thousand--an Independent Tradition?" *New Testament
     Studies* 8 (1961-62): 151-54.

Jónsson, Jakob. *Humour and Irony in the New Testament:
     Illuminated by Parallels in Talmud and Midrash.* Reykjavík:
     Bókaútgáfa Menningarsjóds, 1965.

Juel, Donald. "The Function of the Trial of Jesus in Mark's
     Gospel." In *Society of Biblical Literature 1975 Seminar
     Papers,* Vol. 2, pp. 83-104. Edited by George MacRae.
     Missoula, Mont.: Scholars Press, 1975.

_____. *Messiah and Temple: The Trial of Jesus in the Gospel
     of Mark.* Society of Biblical Literature Dissertation Series,
     no. 31. Missoula, Mont.: Scholars Press, 1977.

Keck, Leander E. "Mark 3:7-12 and Mark's Christology." *Journal
     of Biblical Literature* 84 (1965): 341-58.

Kee, Howard Clark. "Mark as Redactor and Theologian: A Survey
     of Some Recent Markan Studies." *Journal of Biblical
     Literature* 90 (1971): 333-36.

_____. *Aretalogies, Hellenistic "Lives," and the Sources of
     Mark.* Protocol of the Colloquy of the Center for Hermeneuti-
     cal Studies in Hellenistic and Modern Culture, no. 12.
     Berkeley: The Center for Hermeneutical Studies in Hellenis-
     tic and Modern Culture, 1975.

_____. *Community of the New Age: Studies in Mark's Gospel.*
     Philadelphia: Westminster Press, 1977.

Kelber, Werner H. "Mark 14:32-42: Gethsemane." *Zeitschrift für
     die neutestamentliche Wissenschaft* 63 (1972): 166-87.

_____. *The Kingdom in Mark: A New Place and a New Time.*
     Philadelphia: Fortress Press, 1974.

_____, ed. *The Passion in Mark: Studies on Mark 14-16.*
     Philadelphia: Fortress Press, 1976.

Kertelge, Karl. *Die Wunder Jesu im Markusevangelium: Eine
     redaktionsgeschichtliche Untersuchung.* Studien zum Alten
     und Neuen Testament, no. 23. Munich: Kösel, 1970.

Kilpatrick, G. E. "Some Notes on Marcan Usage." *The Bible
     Translater* 7 (1956): 2-9, 51-56, 146.

Klostermann, Erich. *Das Markusevangelium*. Handbuch zum Neuen Testament, no. 3. 4th rev. ed. Tübingen: J. C. B. Mohr (Paul Siebeck), 1950.

Knackstedt, J. "Die beiden Brotvermehrungen im Evangelium." *New Testament Studies* 10 (1964): 309-35.

Koch, Klaus. *The Growth of the Biblical Tradition: The Form-Critical Method*. Translated by S. M. Cupitt. London: Black, 1969.

Kolenkow, Anitra Bingham. "Healing Controversy as a Tie Between Miracle and Passion Material for a Proto-Gospel." *Journal of Biblical Literature* 95 (1976): 623-38.

Konings, J. "The Pre-Markan Sequence in Jn. VI: A Critical Re-examination." In *L'Évangile selon Marc: Tradition et rédaction*, pp. 147-77. Edited by M. Sabbe. Bibliotheca Ephemeridum Theologicarum Lovaniensium, no. 34. Leuven: Leuven University Press, 1974.

Kuhn, Heinz-Wolfgang. *Ältere Sammlungen im Markusevangelium*. Studien zur Umwelt des Neuen Testaments, no. 8. Göttingen: Vandenhoeck & Ruprecht, 1971.

Lagrange, M.-J. *Évangile selon Saint Marc*. Études Bibliques. 3d ed. Paris: Librairie Victor Lecoffre, 1920.

Lambrecht, Jan. *Die Redaktion der Markus-Apokalypse: Literarische Analyse und Strukturuntersuchung*. Analecta Biblica, no. 28. Rome: Pontifical Biblical Institute, 1967.

_____. "La structure de Marc XIII." In *De Jésus aux Évangiles: Tradition et Rédaction dans les Évangiles synoptiques*, pp. 141-64. Edited by I. de la Potterie. Bibliotheca Ephemeridum Theologicarum Lovaniensium, no. 25. Gembloux and Paris: Duculot, 1967.

_____. "Redaction and Theology in Mk., IV." In *L'Évangile selon Marc: Tradition et rédaction*, pp. 269-307. Edited by M. Sabbe. Bibliotheca Ephemeridum Theologicarum Lovaniensium, no. 34. Leuven: Leuven University Press, 1974.

_____. "Jesus and the Law: An Investigation of Mk 7,1-23," *Ephemerides Theologicae Lovanienses* 53 (1977): 24-82.

LaVerdiere, Eugene A. "The Emmaus Journey Narrative (Lk 24:13-35): A Study in Lukan Redaction and Composition." Ph.D. dissertation, University of Chicago, 1977.

_____. "Feed My Sheep: Eucharistic Tradition in Mark 6:34-44." In *Bread From Heaven*, pp. 45-58. Edited by Paul Bernier. New York, Ramsey, and Toronto: Paulist Press, 1977.

Leitzmann, Hans. *Mass and Lord's Supper*. Translated by Dorothea H. G. Reeve. Introduction and Supplementary Essay by Robert D. Richardson. Leiden: E. J. Brill, 1953-

Lightfoot, Robert Henry. *History and Interpretation in the Gospels*. New York: Harper & Bros., 1934.

_____. *Locality and Doctrine in the Gospels*. New York: Harper & Bros., 1938.

_____. "A Consideration of Three Passages in St. Mark's Gospel." In *In Memoriam Ernst Lohmeyer*, pp. 110-15. Edited by Werner Schmauch. Stuttgart: Evangelisches Verlagswerk, 1951.

_____. *The Gospel Message of St. Mark*. London: Oxford University Press, 1962.

Lindars, Barnabas. "Elijah, Elisha and the Gospel Miracles." In *Miracles*, pp. 61-80. Edited by C. F. D. Moule. London: A. R. Mowbray, 1965.

Lohmeyer, Ernst. *Das Evangelium des Markus*. Kritisch-exegetischer Kommentar über das Neue Testament, no. 2. 17th ed. Göttingen: Vandenhoeck & Ruprecht, 1967.

Lohr, Charles. "Oral Techniques in the Gospel of Matthew." *Catholic Biblical Quarterly* 23 (1961): 403-35.

Loisy, Alfred. "Le Second Évangile." *Revue d'Histoire et de Littérature Religieuses* 8 (1903): 513-27.

_____. *Les Évangiles Synoptiques*. 2 vols. Ceffonds, Près Montier-en-Der (Haute-Marne): By the Author, 1907-8.

_____. *L'Évangile selon Marc*. Paris: Émile Nourry, 1912.

Long, Burke O. "Recent Field Studies in Oral Literature and the Question of *Sitz im Leben*." *Semeia* 5 (1976): 35-49.

Lord, Albert B. "Formula and Non-Narrative Theme in South Slavic Oral Epic and the Old Testament." *Semeia* 5 (1976): 93-105.

MacRae, George W. "Theology and Irony in the Fourth Gospel." In *The Word in the World: Essays in Honor of Frederick L. Moriarty*, pp. 83-96. Edited by George W. MacRae and Richard J. Clifford. Cambridge: Weston College Press, 1973.

Magne, J. "L'épisode évangélique de la multiplication des pains dans l'exégèse depuis D. F. Strauss." *Revue de l'Histoire des Religions* 175 (1969): 121-27.

Mailloux, Steven. "Reader-Response Criticism?" *Genre* 10 (1977): 413-31.

Marxsen, Willi. *Mark the Evangelist*. Translated by James Boyce et al. Nashville: Abingdon Press, 1969.

Meeks, Wayne A. *The Prophet-King: Moses Traditions and the Johannine Christology*. Novum Testamentum, Supplements, no. 14. Leiden: E. J. Brill, 1967.

_____. "The Man from Heaven in Johannine Sectarianism." *Journal of Biblical Literature* 91 (1972): 44-72.

Michiels, Josee. "La multiplication des pains dans la pensée chrétienne primitive." Doctoral dissertation, University of Leuven, 1952.

Minear, P. S. "Audience Criticism and Markan Ecclesiology." In *Neues Testament und Geschichte: Historisches Geschehen und Deutung im Neuen Testament. Oscar Cullmann zum 70. Geburtstag*, pp. 79-89. Edited by Heinrich Baltensweiler and Bo Reicke. Zürich: Theologischer Verlag, 1972; Tübingen: J. C. B. Mohr, 1972.

Morgenthaler, Robert. *Statistik des neutestamentlichen Wortschatzes*. Zürich and Frankfurt am Main: Gotthelf-Verlag, 1958.

Moule, C. F. D., ed. *Miracles*. London: A. R. Mowbray & Co., 1965.

Muecke, D. C. *The Compass of Irony*. London: Methuen & Co., 1969.

_____. *Irony*. Critical Idiom Series, no. 13. London: Methuen & Co., 1970.

Muilenburg, J. "A Study in Hebrew Rhetoric: Repetition and Style." *Vetus Testamentum, Supplements* 1 (1953): 97-111.

_____. "The Gains of Form Criticism in Old Testament Studies." *Expository Times* 71 (1959): 229-33.

_____. "Form Criticism and Beyond." *Journal of Biblical Literature* 88 (1969): 1-18.

Neirynck, Frans. "Hawkins's Additional Notes to his 'Horae Synopticae.'" *Ephemerides Theologicae Lovanienses* 46 (1970): 78-111.

_____. "Mark in Greek." *Ephemerides Theologicae Lovanienses* 47 (1971): 144-98.

_____. "Duality in Mark." *Ephemerides Theologicae Lovanienses* 47 (1971): 394-463.

_____. "Duplicate Expressions in the Gospel of Mark." *Ephemerides Theologicae Lovanienses* 48 (1972): 150-209.

_____. *Duality in Mark: Contributions to the Study of the Markan Redaction*. Bibliotheca Ephemeridum Theologicarum Lovaniensium, no. 31. Leuven: Leuven University Press, 1973.

Neirynck, Frans. "L'Évangile de Marc: À propos d'un nouveau commentaire." *Ephemerides Theologicae Lovanienses* 53 (1977): 153-81.

Neirynck, Frans, ed., in collaboration with Hansen, Theo, and Van Sebroeck, Frans. *The Minor Agreements of Matthew and Luke against Mark with a Consultative List.* Bibliotheca Ephemeridum Theologicarum Lovaniensium, no. 37. Leuven: Leuven University Press, 1974.

Neusner, Jacob. "The Rabbinic Traditions about the Pharisees before A.D. 70: The Problem of Oral Transmission." *Journal of Jewish Studies* 22 (1971): 1-18.

_____. *Early Rabbinic Judaism: Historical Studies in Religion, Literature and Art.* Studies in Judaism in Late Antiquity, no. 13. Leiden: E. J. Brill, 1975.

_____, ed. *Contemporary Judaic Fellowship in Theory and in Practice.* New York: KTAV, 1972.

Nineham, D. E. *Saint Mark.* Baltimore: Penguin, 1963.

Nock, Arthur Darby. *Arthur Darby Nock: Essays on Religion and the Ancient World.* Edited by Zeph Stewart. 2 vols. Oxford: Clarendon Press, 1972.

Notopoulos, J. A. "Parataxis in Homer: A New Approach to Homeric Literary Criticism." *Transactions of the American Philological Association* 80 (1949): 1-23.

_____. "Continuity and Interconnexion in Homeric Oral Composition." *Transactions of the American Philological Association* 82 (1951): 81-101.

Oesterley, W. O. E. *The Jewish Background of the Christian Liturgy.* Oxford: Clarendon Press, 1925.

Olrik, Axel. "Epic Laws of Folk Narrative." In *The Study of Folklore,* pp. 129-41. Edited by Alan Dundes. Englewood Cliffs: Prentice-Hall, 1965.

Ong, Walter J. "The Writer's Audience Is Always a Fiction." *Publications of the Modern Language Association of America* 90 (1975): 9-21.

Ortutay, Gyula. "Principles of Oral Transmission in Folk Culture." *Acta Ethnographica* 8 (1959): 175-221.

Perrin, Norman. *What is Redaction Criticism?* Philadelphia: Fortress Press, 1969.

_____. "The use of *(para)didonai* in Connection with the Passion of Jesus in the New Testament." In *Der Ruf Jesu und die Antwort der Gemeinde: Festschrift für Joachim Jeremias zum 70. Geburtstag,* pp. 204-12. Edited by Edward Lohse, Christoph Burchard, and Berndt Schaller. Göttingen: Vandenhoeck & Ruprecht, 1970.

Perrin, Norman. "Towards an Interpretation of the Gospel of Mark."
In *Christology and a Modern Pilgrimage: A Discussion with
Norman Perrin*, pp. 1-78. Edited by Hans Dieter Betz.
Claremont: The New Testament Colloquium, 1971.

_____. "The Evangelist as Author: Reflections on Method in
the Study and Interpretation of the Synoptic Gospels and
Acts." *Biblical Research* 17 (1972): 5-18.

_____. "Historical Criticism, Literary Criticism, and
Hermeneutics." *Journal of Religion* 52 (1972): 361-75.

_____. *The New Testament: An Introduction. Proclamation and
Parenesis, Myth and History*. New York: Harcourt Brace
Jovanovich, 1974.

_____. "Eschatology and Hermeneutics: Reflections on Method
in the Interpretation of the New Testament." *Journal of
Biblical Literature* 93 (1974): 3-14.

_____. "The Christology of Mark." In *L'Évangile selon Marc:
Tradition et rédaction*, pp. 471-85. Edited by M. Sabbe.
Bibliotheca Ephemeridum Theologicarum Lovaniensium, no. 34.
Leuven: Leuven University Press, 1974.

_____. *A Modern Pilgrimage in New Testament Christology*.
Philadelphia: Fortress Press, 1974.

_____. "The Interpretation of the Gospel of Mark." *Inter-
pretation* 30 (1976): 115-24.

_____. "The High Priest's Question and Jesus' Answer (Mark
14:61-62)." In *The Passion in Mark: Studies on Mark 14-16*,
pp. 80-95. Edited by Werner H. Kelber. Philadelphia:
Fortress Press, 1976.

Pesch, Rudolf. *Das Markusevangelium*. Herders theologischer
Kommentar zum Neuen Testament, no. 2. 2 vols. Freiburg,
Basel, and Vienna: Herder, 1976-77.

Petersen, Norman R. *Literary Criticism for New Testament Critics*.
Philadelphia: Fortress Press, 1978.

Peterson, K. "Zu den Speisungs- und Abendmahlsberichten."
Zeitschrift für die neutestamentliche Wissenschaft 32
(1933): 217-18.

Poulet, Georges. "Phenomenology of Reading." *New Literary History*
1 (1969-70): 53-68.

Prat, F. "Les doublets et la critique des évangiles." *Revue
Biblique* 7 (1898): 541-53.

Preisendanz, Karl, ed. and trans. *Papyri graecae magicae: die
griechischen Zauberpapyri*. 2 vols. Leipzig: B. G. Teubner,
1928-31.

Pryke, E. J. *Redactional Style in the Marcan Gospel*. Society for New Testament Studies Monograph Series, no. 33. Cambridge: Cambridge University Press, 1978.

Quesnell, Quentin. *The Mind of Mark: Interpretation and Method through the Exegesis of Mark 6,52*. Analecta Biblica, no. 38. Rome: Pontifical Biblical Institute, 1969.

Rawlinson, A. E. J. *St. Mark*. London: Methuen, 1925.

Reichert, John. *Making Sense of Literature*. Chicago and London: University of Chicago Press, 1977.

Richardson, Alan. "The Feeding of the Five Thousand." *Interpretation* 9 (1955): 144-49.

Ricoeur, Paul. *Interpretation Theory: Discourse and the Surplus of Meaning*. Fort Worth: Texas Christian University Press, 1976.

Rigaux, Béda. *The Testimony of St. Mark*. Translated by Malachy Carroll. Chicago: Franciscan Herald Press, 1966.

Robbins, Vernon K. "The Christology of Mark." Ph.D. dissertation, University of Chicago, 1969.

_____. "Last Meal: Preparation, Betrayal, and Absence (Mark 14:12-15)." In *The Passion in Mark: Studies on Mark 14-16*, pp. 21-40. Edited by Werner H. Kelber. Philadelphia: Fortress Press, 1976.

Robertson, David. *The Old Testament and the Literary Critic*. Philadelphia: Fortress Press, 1977.

Robinson, James M. "The Literary Composition of Mark." In *L'Évangile selon Marc: Tradition et rédaction*, pp. 11-19. Edited by M. Sabbe. Bibliotheca Ephemeridum Theologicarum Lovaniensium, no. 34. Leuven: Leuven University Press, 1974.

Robinson, James M., and Koester, Helmut. *Trajectories through Early Christianity*. Philadelphia: Fortress Press, 1971.

Rofé, Alexander. "The Classification of the Prophetical Stories." *Journal of Biblical Literature* 89 (1970): 427-40.

Rohde, Joachim. *Rediscovering the Teaching of the Evangelists*. Translated by Dorothea M. Barton. London: SCM, 1968; Philadelphia: Westminster Press, 1968.

Roloff, Jürgen. "Das Markusevangelium als Geschichtsdarstellung." *Evangelische Theologie* 29 (1969): 73-93.

Sabbe, M., ed. *L'Évangile selon Marc: Tradition et rédaction*. Bibliotheca Ephemeridum Theologicarum Lovaniensium, no. 34. Leuven: Leuven University Press, 1974.

Sanders, E. P. *The Tendencies of the Synoptic Tradition.*
    Society for New Testament Studies Monograph Series,
    no. 9. London: Cambridge University Press, 1969.

Sandmel, Samuel. "Prolegomena to a Commentary on Mark."
    Journal of Bible and Religion 31 (1963): 294-300.

_____. *The First Christian Century in Judaism and
    Christianity: Certainties and Uncertainties.* New York:
    Oxford University Press, 1969.

_____. *Judaism and Christian Beginnings.* New York: Oxford
    University Press, 1978.

Sandy, Gerald H. "Foreshadowing and Suspense in Apuleius'
    Metamorphoses." *The Classical Journal* 68 (1973): 232-35.

Schenke, Ludger. *Die Wundererzählungen des Markusevangeliums.*
    Stuttgarter biblische Beiträge. Stuttgart: Katholisches
    Bibelwerk, 1974.

Schmid, Josef. *Matthäus und Lukas: Eine Untersuchung des
    Verhältnisses ihrer Evangelien.* Biblische Studien, vol. 23,
    nos. 2-4. Freiburg im Breisgau: Herder, 1930.

Schmidt, Karl Ludwig. *Der Rahmen der Geschichte Jesu.* Berlin:
    Trowitzsch & Sohn, 1919; reprint ed., Darmstadt: Wissen-
    schaftliche Buchgesellschaft, 1969.

Schnackenburg, R. "Die Erwartung des 'Propheten' nach dem
    Neuen Testament und den Qumran-Texten." *Studia Evangelica
    I. Texte und Untersuchungen* 73 (1959): 622-39.

Scholes, R., and Kellog, R. *The Nature of Narrative.* New York:
    Oxford University Press, 1966.

Schweizer, Eduard. "Anmerkungen zur Theologie des Markus." In
    *Neotestamentica et Patristica: Eine Freundesgabe, Herrn
    Professor Dr. Oscar Cullmann zu seinem 60. Geburtstag
    überreicht,* pp. 35-46. Novum Testamentum, Supplements, no.
    6. Leiden: E. J. Brill, 1962.

_____. "Die theologische Leistung des Markus." *Evangelische
    Theologie* 24 (1964): 337-55.

_____. *The Good News According to Mark.* Translated by
    Donald H. Madvig. Atlanta: John Knox Press, 1970.

Shaw, Alan. "The Marcan Feeding Narratives." *Church Quarterly
    Review* 162 (1961): 268-78.

Slatoff, Walter J. *With Respect to Readers: Dimensions of Literary Response*. Ithaca, N.Y.: Cornell University Press, 1970.

Smith, Morton. *Tannaitic Parallels to the Gospels*. Society of Biblical Literature Monograph Series, no. 6. Philadelphia: Society of Biblical Literature, 1951.

_____. "A Comparison of Early Christian and Early Rabbinic Tradition." *Journal of Biblical Literature* 82 (1963): 169-76.

_____. *Clement of Alexandria and a Secret Gospel of Mark*. Cambridge: Harvard University Press, 1973.

_____. "On the Problem of Method in the Study of Rabbinic Literature." *Journal of Biblical Literature* 92 (1973): 112-13.

_____. *The Aretalogy Used by Mark*. Protocol of the Colloquy of the Center for Hermeneutical Studies in Hellenistic and Modern Culture, no. 6. Berkeley: The Center for Hermeneutical Studies in Hellenistic and Modern Culture, 1975.

_____. *Jesus the Magician*. San Francisco: Harper & Row, 1978.

Snoy, Thierry. "La rédaction marcienne de la marche sur les eaux (Mc., VI, 45-52)." *Ephemerides Theologicae Lovanienses* 44 (1968): 205-41, 433-81.

_____. "Les miracles dans l'évangile de Marc: Examen de quelques études récentes." *Revue Théologique de Louvain* 3 (1972): 449-66; 4 (1973): 58-101.

_____. "Marc 6,48: ' . . . et il voulait les dépasser.' Proposition pour la solution d'une énigme." In *L'Evangile selon Marc: Tradition et rédaction*, pp. 347-63. Edited by M. Sabbe. Bibliotheca Ephemeridum Theologicarum Lovaniensium, no. 34. Leuven: Leuven University Press, 1974.

Starobinski, Jean. "The Struggle with Legion: A Literary Analysis of Mark 5:1-20." *New Literary History* 4 (1973): 331-56.

Stauffer, Ethelbert. "Zum apokalyptischen Festmahl in Mc. 6:34ff." *Zeitschrift für die neutestamentliche Wissenschaft* 46 (1955): 264-66.

Stegner, W. R. "Lucan Priority in the Feeding of the Five Thousand." *Biblical Research* 21 (1976): 19-28.

Stein, Robert H. "The Proper Methodology for Ascertaining a Marcan Redaktionsgeschichte." Doctoral dissertation, Princeton Theological Seminary, 1968.

_____. "What is Redaktionsgeschichte?" *Journal of Biblical Literature* 88 (1969): 45-56.

_____. "The 'Redaktionsgeschichtlich' Investigation of a Markan Seam (Mc 1:21f.)." *Zeitschrift für die neutestamentliche Wissenschaft* 61 (1970): 70-94.

Stein, Robert H. "The Proper Methodology for Ascertaining a Markan Redaction History." *Novum Testamentum* 13 (1971): 181-98.

Stephenson, T. "Classification of Doublets in the Synoptic Gospels." *Journal of Theological Studies* 20 (1919): 1-8.

Strauss, David Friedrich. *The Life of Jesus Critically Examined.* Translated by George Eliot. Edited and with an Introduction by Peter C. Hodgson. Philadelphia: Fortress Press, 1972.

Swete, Henry Barclay. *The Gospel According to St. Mark.* 3d ed. London: Macmillan, 1909.

Tagawa, Kenzo. *Miracles et Évangile: La Pensée personelle de l'évangéliste Marc.* Études d'Histoire et de Philosophie Religieuses, no. 62. Paris: Presses Universitaires de France, 1966.

Talbert, Charles H. *Literary Patterns, Theological Themes and the Genre of Luke-Acts.* Society of Biblical Literature Monograph Series, no. 20. Missoula, Mont.: Scholars Press, 1974.

Tannehill, Robert C. *The Sword of His Mouth.* Semeia Supplements, no. 1. Missoula, Mont.: Scholars Press, 1975.

_____. "The Disciples in Mark: The Function of a Narrative Role." *Journal of Religion* 57 (1977): 386-405.

Taylor, Vincent. *The Gospel According to St. Mark.* 2d ed. London: Macmillan, 1966.

Teeple, Howard M. "The Oral Tradition That Never Existed." *Journal of Biblical Literature* 89 (1970): 56-68.

Theissen, Gerd. *Urchristliche Wundergeschichten: Ein Beitrag zur formgeschichtlichen Erforschung der synoptischen Evangelien.* Studien zum Neuen Testament, no. 8. Gütersloh: Gütersloher Verlagshaus, 1974.

_____. "Itinerant Radicalism: The Tradition of Jesus Sayings from the Perspective of the Sociology of Literature." *Radical Religion* 2 (1975): 84-93.

Thompson, William G. *Matthew's Advice to a Divided Community: Mt. 17,22-18,35.* Analecta Biblica, no. 44. Rome: Pontifical Biblical Institute, 1970.

Thomson, J. A. K. *Irony: An Historical Introduction.* Cambridge: Harvard University Press, 1927.

Tiede, David L. *The Charismatic Figure as Miracle Worker.* Society of Biblical Literature Dissertation Series, no. 1. Missoula, Mont.: Scholars Press, 1972.

Tolbert, Mary Ann. "The Parables: Form and Interpretation." Ph.D. dissertation, University of Chicago, 1977.

Turner, C. H. "Marcan Usage: Notes, Critical and Exegetical, on the Second Gospel." *Journal of Theological Studies* 25 (1924): 377-86; 26 (1925): 12-20, 145-56, 225-40, 337-46; 27 (1926): 58-62; 28 (1927): 9-30, 349-62; 29 (1928): 275-89, 346-61.

Van Cangh, J.-M. "Le thème des poissons dans les récits évangéliques de la multiplication des pains." *Revue Biblique* 78 (1971): 71-83.

_____. "Les sources de l'Évangile: les collections pré-marciennes de miracles." *Revue Théologique de Louvain* 3 (1972): 76-85.

_____. "La Multiplication des pains dans l'évangile de Marc: Essai d'exégèse globale." In *L'Évangile selon Marc: Tradition et rédaction*, pp. 309-46. Edited by M. Sabbe. Bibliotheca Ephemeridum Theologicarum Lovaniensium, no. 34. Leuven: Leuven University Press, 1974.

_____. *La Multiplication des pains et l'Eucharistie.* Lectio Divina, no. 86. Paris: Cerf, 1975.

Van der Loos, H. *The Miracles of Jesus.* Novum Testamentum, Supplements, no. 9. Leiden: E. J. Brill, 1968.

Van Iersel, B. "Die wunderbare Speisung und das Abendmahl in der synoptischen Tradition." *Novum Testamentum* 7 (1964): 167-94.

Van Seters, John. *Abraham in History and Tradition.* New Haven: Yale University Press, 1975.

_____. "Oral Patterns of Literary Conventions in Biblical Narrative." *Semeia* 5 (1976): 139-54.

Vansina, Jan. *Oral Tradition: A Study in Historical Methodology.* Translated by H. M. Wright. Chicago: Aldine Publishing Co., 1965.

Via, Dan Otto. *The Parables: Their Literary and Existential Dimension.* Philadelphia: Fortress Press, 1967.

_____. *Kerygma and Comedy in the New Testament.* Philadelphia: Fortress Press, 1975.

Wead, David W. "Johannine Irony as a Key to the Author-Audience Relationship in John's Gospel." In *Biblical Literature: 1974 Proceedings. Preprinted Papers for the Section on Biblical Literature, American Academy of Religion, Annual Meeting, 1974*, pp. 33-44. Compiled by Fred O. Francis. Tallahassee, Fla.: American Academy of Religion and Florida State University, 1974.

Weeden, Theodore J. "The Heresy that Necessitated Mark's Gospel." *Zeitschrift für die neutestamentliche Wissenschaft* 59 (1968): 145-58.

_____. *Mark--Traditions in Conflict*. Philadelphia: Fortress Press, 1971.

Wellek, R., and Warren, A. *Theory of Literature*. New York: Harcourt, Brace and World, 1956.

Wellhausen, Julius. *Das Evangelium Marci*. 2d ed. Berlin: Georg Reimer, 1909.

Wendling, Emil. *Ur-Marcus: Versuch einer Wiederherstellung der ältesten Mitteilungen über das Leben Jesu*. Tübingen: J. C. B. Mohr (Paul Siebeck), 1905.

_____. *Die Entstehung des Marcus-Evangeliums*. Tübingen: J. C. B. Mohr (Paul Siebeck), 1908.

Wheelwright, Philip. *Metaphor and Reality*. Bloomington: Indiana University Press, 1962.

Widengren, Geo. "Tradition and Literature in Early Judaism and the Early Church." *Numen* 10 (1963): 42-83.

Wilder, Amos N. *Early Christian Rhetoric: The Language of the Gospel*. Cambridge: Harvard University Press, 1971.

_____. *Theopoetic: Theology and the Religious Imagination*. Philadelphia: Fortress Press, 1976.

Wink, Walter. *John the Baptist in the Gospel Tradition*. Society for New Testament Studies Monograph Series, no. 7. Cambridge: Cambridge University Press, 1968.

Wittig, Susan. "Formulaic Style and the Problem of Redundancy." *Centrum* 1 (1973): 123-36.

_____. "Theories of Formulaic Narrative." *Semeia* 5 (1976):65-91.

Wrede, William. *Das Messiasgeheimnis in den Evangelien: Zugleich ein Beitrag zum Verständnis des Markusevangeliums*. 3d ed. Göttingen: Vandenhoeck & Ruprecht, 1963.

_____. *The Messianic Secret*. Translated by J. C. G. Greig. Cambridge and London: James Clarke & Co., 1971.

Yu, Anthony C., ed. *Parnassus Revisited: Modern Critical Essays on the Epic Tradition*. Chicago: American Library Association, 1973.

Zerwick, Max. *Untersuchungen zum Markus-Stil: Ein Beitrag zur stilistischen Durcharbeitung des Neuen Testaments*. Scripta Instituti Pontificii Biblici, no. 5. Rome: Pontifical Biblical Institute, 1937.

Ziener, G. "Das Brotwunder in Markusevangelium." *Biblische Zeitschrift* 4 (1960): 282-85.

DATE DUE